Sweating Saris

Priya Srinivasan

Sweating Saris

Indian Dance as Transnational Labor

TEMPLE UNIVERSITY PRESS
Philadelphia

TEMPLE UNIVERSITY PRESS
Philadelphia, Pennsylvania 19122
www.temple.edu/tempress

Library of Congress Cataloging-in-Publication Data

Srinivasan, Priya
   Sweating saris : Indian dance as transnational labor / Priya Srinivasan.
      p. cm.
   Includes bibliographical references and index.
   ISBN 978-1-4399-0429-9 (cloth : alk. paper) —
   ISBN 978-1-4399-0430-5 (pbk. : alk. paper) —
   ISBN 978-1-4399-0431-2 (e-book)
   1. Dance—Social aspects—India.   2. Dance—Social aspects—United States.   3. Women
dancers—India—Social conditions.   4. Women dancers—United States—Social conditions.
5. Bharata natyam—Social aspects—United States.   6. Foreign workers, East Indian—United
States—Social conditions.   7. East Indians—United States—Ethnic identity.   I. Title.
   GV1693.S75 2011
   793.3'1934—dc22

                                                                       2011016213

∞ The paper used in this publication meets the requirements of the American National
Standard for Information Sciences—Permanence of Paper for Printed Library Materials,
ANSI Z39.48-1992

Printed in the United States of America

2   4   6   8   9   7   5   3   1

For Ashok
and for Rishi and Anjan,
feminists in the making

May they always remember the past
while looking toward the future

Contents

Preface

We are in a garage. The floor is concrete, and the slapping of feet against it creates loud thwacking sounds. The open windows mercifully allow air and light to circulate in the space. The guru chants complex rhythmic syllables: *Tam tata kita naka jam, takun tari kita taka, tata kita taka naka jam, kukun tari kita taka. Taka jam taka nam, taka rum, taka dhim.* The dancers move their arms and shift quickly between several different mudra formations (symbolic hand gestures) while their feet slap out intricate rhythms. Their bodies jump, twist, and turn depending on the step they are performing. *Tam taka kita.* Suddenly, the guru stops her chanting. "Girls, you do not look graceful," she admonishes them. "Your *anga suddha* is nonexistent, and your rhythm is completely off. And not only that—look at the way you are all dressed. Your saris are just spilling out because you have not tied the cloth correctly. Any minute either you will trip over yourself or the saris are going to fall off you." She says this in a very calm voice, but it implies a great deal of frustration. The five students are indeed unkempt and disheveled, sweating profusely, and panting. The garage is becoming hotter with the presence of many bodies. I try to sit unobtrusively in a corner, having met the guru only recently and been invited to visit her classes as an observer.

The girls smile sheepishly, looking at each other and at me from time to time. One student lets out what sounds like a fart in nervousness, or perhaps it is her sari ripping as she steps on it one too many times. This student has tied her sari too loosely, and the pleats are falling out in front. It is very difficult to keep a straight face, but I perform too. Another girl has tied her sari too long, and it looks like she could trip over the material at any moment. A larger student has tied hers too short, and the sari looks like a miniskirt over the pants she wears underneath. She cannot open her legs wide enough to sit in *araimandi*, the half-seated position. A chic-looking student has not given the *pallu* enough room, and so the top part keeps falling off to reveal her blouse and her pierced navel. She frequently adjusts the cloth in the middle of her dancing. These are young teenagers, clearly not used to wearing saris often. A girl with long hair braided down to her hips has managed to tie the sari on in the ideal way, but she is sweating profusely over her entire body; wet traces and patches mark her sari blouse. The telltale circles of her underarms are imprinted on the cotton cloth. They begin dancing again. *Tam tata kita takita dikita tat dit ta*. As the dancing steps become more vigorous, the sweat pours onto their saris, and the material begins to weigh them down. They make many mistakes, and their sweat continues to flow out.

I have to agree with the guru; their *anga suddha* is nonexistent. I can't maintain my placid countenance. I do feel bad for the girls and the guru for a variety of reasons. I am caught in between. Part of my dilemma stems from the fact that as I was growing up in Australia, I was trained in Bharata Natyam, along with three other girls (Kavitha, Anu, and Priya), by a perfectionist guru. Dr. Chandrabhanu was a formidable and powerful force in our youth whose disciplinary training in the classroom helped shape our bodies, minds, and aesthetics in ways that later made me want to both defy all gurus I met and submit to them at the same time. This contradiction manifests in my own understanding of *anga suddha*. I heard similar critiques from my guru over the years about clear lines, clean appearance, gracefulness, perfect sari length, and the like, and so I know what it takes to get the female Indian dancing body to look that way.

To create *anga suddha*, or body purity, a clarity and crispness of limbs and their lines, formations, rhythms, and gestures is required. In the aural sense, *anga suddha* is understood in performance to mean the precise, rhythmic beating of feet on the ground. Visually, it can represent an articulateness of transitions of mudras between rhythm, lyrics, and song. The way a dancer appears visually, dressed neatly in her sari with her hair tied back while her face and body belie the labor of the dance, is also a key contributor to *anga suddha*. When everything appears just right both in the classroom and onstage, a dancer can feel ecstatic. There is real pleasure in knowing that your body is in perfect synergy—its arms, legs, feet, fingers, eyes, head, neck, eyebrows, cheeks, and lips all in harmony with the music. But what interrupts this ideal body performance are the bodily fluids that betray us despite our efforts to cover them up.

Sweat and tears, we know as dancers, emerge from all kinds of crevices, sometimes oozing slowly and other times rushing as fast as a river current. Our muscles tire out from the arduous labor of movement. Deposits of lactic acid residue will hurt us even more the next day, but there's no time to ponder that as we gasp for air and pretend we are not out of breath for fear of our guru's wrath. But neither our saris nor our bodies can lie for very long, even when our faces still wear a synthetic smile. Performing a simple *adavu* step in three different speeds exhausts us from sheer repetition. The body oozes our inside juices onto the cotton or silk fabric of the sari, and the sky blue, leafy green, or sunset orange colors with *ikat* borders darken with our fluids. Only a deep red *kohlapuri* or black *dharmavaram* sari could perhaps conceal our lie for a bit longer than the lighter colors. The illusion that the dance is effortlessness is undone through the bodily juices seeping and creeping onto the sari, and the sari becomes a part of the Indian dancing body. The fluids even leak onto the dance floor when we have a hard taskmaster who pushes our bodies to perfection in the attempt to achieve *anga suddha*. But *anga suddha*, also associated with ideal Indian womanhood, is an impossibility— idealized perfection is belied by sweating bodies, patches on a wet blouse, and slipping sari fabric.

The sari has another material and political reality. Khadi cotton fabric was a nationalist totem used by Mahatma Gandhi to combat British colonialism in India. The nationalist practice of weaving and wearing one's own cloth became extremely important in Indian struggles for independence. Subsequently, the culture-bearing agendas of the nation were embedded into Indian women, who were expected to display their culture continuously by wearing cultural symbols such as the sari, even while men wore Western clothes. This notion permeates from the nation to diaspora and especially in Indian dance classrooms.

Saris worn in specific ways construct the dancing body. Saris sweat in classrooms, in everyday life, and onstage. The sweating sari is a metonym for the dancing body as labor, and it is the main thread that weaves its way through this book. Exploring multiple diasporas and history over a century, *Sweating Saris: Indian Dance as Transnational Labor* argues that the Indian dancing girl's sweaty, sari-laden body represents an unrecognized form of labor. Her sweat-stained garment—at times disheveled, untucked, slipping, and out of place—becomes, in this book, the symbol for the contradictory relationships among the sari, the female body, and labor. Examining the Indian dancer as laborer, and her multiple failures and mistakes in the dance practice, makes possible alternative readings of immigration and citizenship.

Acknowledgments

This book was conceptualized during my dissertation project at Northwestern University but did not reach its current form until several years after I earned my Ph.D. and had my first son, Rishi. The labor of his birth triggered key insights that shaped the foundation of this book. My studies at Northwestern were invaluable, and the contributions of my committee members, including Margaret Thompson Drewal, the late Dwight Conquergood, Susan Manning, and Ji-Yeon Yuh, were key. In addition, my interactions with my colleagues and Ph.D. students at the University of California–Riverside Dance Department enabled me to rethink this project in integral ways. For this, I am indebted to Anthea Kraut, Susan Rose, Wendy Rogers, Marta Savigliano, Jacqueline Shea Murphy, Anna Scott, Linda Tomko, and Derek Burrill, who have collectively and individually enhanced my work and pushed me to forge new paths.

I have been fortunate to secure travel and research grants from the University of California Office of the Senate to help me continue my research. I thank the Center for Ideas at the University of California–Riverside (UCR) for a research quarter spent with Rickerby Hinds, Toby Miller, and Piya Chatterjee. Their useful feedback, especially that of Emory Elliott, who gave sage advice and timely guidance, is greatly appreciated. The Feminist South Asia gathering at the University of California–Irvine proved to be a wonderful space to share my work and I am thankful to the attendees for their critical feedback and encouragement. In particular, Gayatri Gopinath's support has been an inspiration in so many ways. I very much enjoyed the yearly gatherings of dance scholars at UCLA convened by Susan Foster in the production of an anthology titled *Worlding Dance*. This small group, which included Marta Savigliano, Anna Scott, Anthea Kraut, Jacqueline Shea Murphy, Lina Hammergren, Yutian Wong, and Ananya Chatterjea, met over a period of several years, and their feedback pushed and propelled me in astounding ways. I am grateful to the Association for Asian American Studies, the Society of Dance History Scholars, the Association for Theatre in Higher Education, and the American Studies Association for giving me the opportunity to present my work and gain crucial feedback. I am deeply indebted to the Asian American performance studies working group, including Josephine Lee, Karen Shimakawa, Lucy Burns, San San Kwan, Sean Metzger, Dan Bacalzo, Yutian Wong, and Esther Kim Lee, who have not only given valuable feedback but also been extremely supportive over the years.

Portions of Chapter 3 originally appeared in *Discourses in Dance* 4, no. 1 (2007): 7–48. Sections of Chapter 2 originally appeared in *Women and Performance: A Journal of Feminist Theory* 19, no. 1 (March 2009): 3–22. Susan Foster was instrumental in giving me insightful editorial advice and feedback in the publication of my essay for *Discourses in Dance*. Parts of Chapter 6 originally appeared as "A Material-ist Reading of the Bharata Natyam Dancing Body," in *Rethinking World Dance Histories*, ed. Susan Foster, 53–75 (New York: Palgrave, 2009). These are reproduced with permission of Palgrave Macmillan.

I thank the staff of the New York Public Library's dance collection. I greatly benefited from the research I conducted there. The archives at the Theosophical Society in Adyar, Chennai, proved difficult to access, but once I was there, Gnanambal Laxman was extremely kind and considerate of my needs in searching for obscure holdings. I also thank the librarians at the Kalakshetra Center in Adyar, Chennai. In addition, the University of Chicago Library holdings provided key books and research data for this project.

Several Ph.D. students have served as my research assistants over the years, providing invaluable help with research, collating, and feedback. In particular, I am grateful to Anusha Kedhar, Maral Yessayan, Jennifer Buscher, Ahalya Satkunaratnam, Melissa Templeton, and Hannah Schwadron for their support and belief in my work.

When I first arrived at UCR, Piya Chatterjee, Tracy Fisher, and I formed a working group on campus. Similarly, off campus, Lucy Burns, San San Kwan, and I formed another group, which met regularly. As women of color, in both groups, we shared not only research but also struggles in academic life. Their friendship and critical feedback has had a profound impact on this book. Cindy Garcia, Yutian Wong, Adria Imada, and Rickerby Hinds have given me timely and crucial feedback on chapters in this book. Sujatha Fernandes has been my long-distance writing partner and role model over the years. I also thank my fellow dance conspirator and copyeditor, Parijat Desai, for her enthusiasm, passion, and excitement for my work. Anthea Kraut has been not only a friend but also the wisest and most caring colleague one could hope for, bringing joy to my time at UCR; my research has greatly benefited from her unwavering support and critical and insightful feedback through these years. This book would not have come about without the constant and unwavering support of Lucy Burns, a colleague and friend whose vital feedback helped form the foundations of this book.

Avanthi Meduri turned the light on for me when I first met her at UCLA as she was completing her dissertation. I was a captivated student in her classes as I first encountered *devadasis* and Indian dancing girls from a critical perspective, and for this I am deeply grateful. David Gere, Moe Meyer, and Esha Niyogi De all were important guides at UCLA who helped me bring together issues in dance studies with those in performance studies and women's studies early on in my work. Marta Savigliano has been a constant mentor who has generously given both critical feedback and gentle guidance on chapters in this book and enabled me to think and write in contradiction. Susan Rose continues to be my co-conspirator, guide, and mentor, always reminding me to think critically from an artistic perspective.

Of course, this project put me in close touch with many performers, including gurus and students. While I cannot name all of them, I do thank them collectively for their important influence on this project by showing me new ways of seeing Bharata Natyam and conceptualizing dance. Although I learned from each of them for only short periods, my first dance guru, S. Rajalakshmi (Kolkata, India), and later gurus Padma Bhushan Kalanidhi Narayanan (Chennai, India) and Ramya Harishankar (Los Angeles, California) have influenced my dancing tremendously. I admire their patience and strength as role models and strong female gurus. In Melbourne, Australia, I gained the bulk of my dance training under Dr. Chandrabhanu, who, together with his partner, the late Geoffrey Goldie, helped shape my artistic life in critical and essential ways. Dr. Chandrabhanu's life as a dancer, choreographer, and intellectual who lived in the margins and who continues to push the boundaries of race, gender, sexuality, and class has had a profound impact on my artistic work and in the writing of this book.

I am grateful to Temple's reviewers for supporting this book and pushing me to higher levels. I am also thankful to Janet Francendese, my editor; Amanda Steele, her assistant; Charles Ault at Temple University Press; and Rebecca Logan at Newgen North America, who saw this book through its various stages of publication.

I am also thankful for the camaraderie and support provided by family, friends, and well-wishers over the years, who have cheered me on and provided food, shelter, prayer, and moral support when needed through phone calls, e-mails, and Skype messages from far-flung cities such as Melbourne, Chennai, Los Angeles, and Shanghai. They include Shyam Srinivasan, Swetha Rajagopalan, Arnaliss Urquhart-O'Connell, Kalyani Sridhar, Dr. T. Sridhar, Tara Rajkumar, Dr. Raj Rajkumar, Prasanna Srinivasan, the late B. T. Sampath, Professor G. Narasimhan, Kavitha McGinty, Priya Saratchandran, Anu Vats, Dr. Sunil Kothari, Dr. Anita Ratnam, Hema Srinivasan, Geetha Nath, Ramya Harishankar, Harish K. Murthy, the late Lakshmi Krishnamurthy, Chandrika Kedhar, Dr. Rajasree Seshadri, Anita Desai, Rekha Rohila, Amisha Gupta, Sunil Shivaram, Kala Ganapathy, Mina and Sam Chamberlain, Anita Moorthy, Dr. Ketu Katrak, Ginley Regencia, Shikha Jamwal, Aranga Lokuge, Shikha Kela, and Xiao Wen.

My family encouraged my thirst for knowledge, my love for and appreciation of the arts, and especially my desire to question. My parents, Indira and C. S. Srinivasan, and grandmother, C. S. Rangam, have shared the burdens and successes of my academic life, albeit from thousands of miles away. Their unwavering support and faith has enabled me to arrive at this juncture. My father, an engineer by profession (and a closet intellectual), has read everything I have written since the age of five and continues to this day to correct my grammar and provide helpful feedback, even on this book. My mother has helped take care of my children in all corners of the globe and rushed to my aid whenever needed so I could write, publish, and teach. They have taught me to follow my dreams no matter what, and for this I am extremely grateful.

This book could not have come about without my partner, Ashok, and our two boys, Rishi and Anjan. It is Ashok's patience and enthusiasm for my work that enable me to pursue dance as an artist, scholar, and teacher in various parts of the world.

Nachwalis, 1880. "Nautch Dancers," *New York Clipper*, January 22, 1881, 345.

A HUMAN GOBBLER.

What a Girl in a Indiana Madhouse Developed—A Monstrosity With Singular Habits.

(Subject of Illustration.)

About twelve miles north of Lawrenceburg, Ind., in Manchester township, on a dreary road which is rarely good by anyone but hunters, and which, it is, leads anywhere, might lead to the mythical mother of Hades, flows deeply known as the "Mud son," is located a bit of dilapidated, broken-down, ramshackle buildings, which, taken together, constitutes the County lunacy. In the rear of the forsaken spot stands an old stone pile, unused save to avoid, under which exists a being which resembles masculine humanity, but which exhibits all the traits and characteristics of a turkey gobbler...

"A HOLY KISS."
ANOTHER PASTOR-CHURCH SCANDAL AT ROXBURY, N. Y.

WAKING A NAUTCH GIRL.
DEATH WATCH BY ONE OF THE GIRLS OF THE QUEER TROUPE PERFORMING IN NEW YORK.

"WHAT IS IT?"
A HUMAN GOBBLER IN AN INDIANA MADHOUSE.

A PASTOR'S IMPRUDENCE.

It Wins Holy Kiss That a Pastor gave a Parishioner's Pretty Wife.

(Subject of Illustration.)

The Rev. B. C. Miller, the Reformed Church pastor at Roxbury, Delaware county, who, as stated in the Police Gazette last week, threw that little village into a whirl of excitement by kissing the wife of David Williams, with whom he boarded, in the church parsonage, and submitting to publicity, has since resigned his pastoral charge there...

A NAUTCH GIRL'S WAKE.

Death Watch of the Dark-Skinned Survivors of the Troupe of Hindoo Customs in New York.

(Subject of Illustration.)

It was a touching scene that was witnessed at No. 970 Broadway, where, on Sunday evening, alia Sunday, one of the troupe of Nautch dancing, jugglers and musicians, brought to this country from India by Augustin Daly, for the play of "Zanina," now being performed at his theatre...

Ruth St. Denis as Radha. "Ruth St. Denis in *Radha*," Denishawn Collection, c. 1906.

St. Denis and Indian men. "Ruth St. Denis with Native Hindus in *Radha*," Denishawn Collection, 1906.

St. Denis and students. "Ruth St. Denis and Denishawn Pupils in a Nautch Evening at the Denishawn Tent Theatre at Westlake Park," Denishawn Collection, 1918.

Kapaleeswarar Temple, Chennai, India.

Introduction

N
ew York was cold in December 1880 when the *nachwali*[1] Sahebjan, who had traveled from India[2] with other company members to perform in Augustin Daly's theater production *Zanina*, went into labor and gave birth to her baby boy. To many New Yorkers' amazement, Sahebjan was back on her feet within days, performing with her troupe. She stomped her feet on the hard, cold stage floors, turning softly so that the cloth she wore spun out from her body as she gestured to a carefully selected love song. Her troupe was featured during the intermission between acts of the main show, and they had only thirty minutes to make their mark. It was difficult to know what would please the audience. Initially they received excited applause, but within a week, the audience had dwindled. The baby, too, did not thrive. He became sick, and when February came and the weather grew colder, he died. The doctors said he had had typhomalarial fever. Sahebjan's son had been a citizen of the United States, if only for a brief time. Sahebjan, on the other hand, was merely a visitor. She had come to the United States a contract laborer and was forced to leave after the show's failure.

I encountered Sahebjan in 2000 in warm, sunny Southern California, while studying in the library archives of the University of California–Irvine. A few years earlier, in 1996, my friend, dancer and guru Ramya Harishankar (a naturalized U.S. citizen), had given birth to a healthy son, an American citizen, who is now fifteen years old. Ramya went back to dancing within a few weeks of giving birth, performing an Indian classical dance called

Bharata Natyam with her students (collectively known as the Arpana Dance Company) at the William Bristol Civic Auditorium in Bellflower, California. She earns a living through teaching and performing Indian dance.

The parallels and striking differences between these two Indian dancers in the United States—separated by time, class, immigration, citizenship, dance forms, and even their experiences of birth and death—moved me to write *Sweating Saris*. The labor of these dancers giving birth to American citizens propelled me to investigate their labor as dancers. Indian dancers have labored as contract workers and as independent artists in the United States, negotiating the terms of U.S. citizenship in different ways. Considering this complexity, I realized that neither a linear historical narration of their experiences nor an ethnography of my experience of encountering them would suffice. To reveal the complex, intertwining histories of immigration, labor, and the dancing body, I needed to do both.

Drawing on archival records between 1880 and 1907, and ethnographic field research of contemporary Indian dance in Southern California, Australia, and India, this project seeks to understand Indian women dancers as transnational laborers on the global stage. This is not conducted through a linear history because there is no continuous diasporic history, set of bodies, or single dance form to trace. Rather, a genealogical inquiry offers a way of reading an alternative archive, to think through the fragmentation of history and diasporic practices from an embodied perspective and from the vantage point of bodily practices (Foucault 1984).[3] Such a genealogical inquiry does not search for origins and instead demonstrates multiple and contradictory pasts that reveal the effect that power has had on truth. Thus, this reading of Indian dance is a reading of fragments and distortions through movement.

In *Sweating Saris* I look for the "work" of Indian dance, even though the dancers strive to hide their toil by smiling and making their movements seem effortless, belying the effort that goes into performing. But their labor can still be seen through their sweat, blood, tears, slipping or stained saris, callused feet, missteps, or familiar gestures, such as giving the finger. Indian dancers' labor can also become visible through acts such as suing or marrying, even if these acts fail, because they intersect with the law and enter mainstream archives. Dance labor includes the work that goes into costuming the dancer: the making of the sari, bells, ornaments, and flowers that adorn the Indian dancing body.

I cannot sit still as I note the hidden labor of dance, the migration patterns of dancers, and the connection between their successes or failures and immigration laws. In one respect, my body is involved in the research through the act of practicing the dance and through my kinesthetic responses to the information gathered. In another respect, I am restless as I find it imperative to unpack multiple points of view to reveal Indian dance within a broader political economy. For these reasons, throughout the book, I participate as the "unruly spectator." This unruly spectator offers a feminist perspective on spectatorship and takes an active role in uncovering the ways that power can be negotiated by examining dance mistakes such as a slipping sari, a bleeding foot, or sweaty sari blouses. I become an active spectator in conducting my ethnography of the Indian dance archive and through bodily interaction with dancers at contemporary sites. I also write this book in a manner that requires the reader/spectator to be active. This book is choreographed to follow a circuitous narrative rather than a linear one. Chapters, therefore, must be read as performances and as partial glimpses into the narratives of dancers' lives.

I encountered many dancing bodies in the archives. Some are people who traveled to and lived in the United States, whom I can name. Dancers such as Oomdah, Bhooribai, and Sahebjan danced from the microfilm in front of my eyes. Then there was Ala Bundi, who contracted typhomalaria and died just weeks after Sahebjan's baby died of the same disease. Others remain nameless because the archive has not yet revealed their names to me. Many important but nameless dancers came to Coney Island in 1904 to perform for the show *Durbar of Delhi*. These dancers were historically important because Ruth St. Denis, one of the "mothers" of American modern dance, viewed and was very influenced by their performance. After this bodily encounter with them, St. Denis went on to establish her career as a soloist and choreographer, thereby launching what we know today as American modern dance. Mohammed Ismail, Mogul Khan, and Inayat Khan, as well as several unnamed Indian men, performed with St. Denis on and off for several years as she toured.

These men and women eventually faded from the annals of modern dance. By the late 1920s, there were few Indians left in the United States, and it was not until 1965 that large numbers of Indians began to enter again. Ramya, the dancer who gave birth to a son in Southern California in 1996, was one of the new wave of Indian immigrant dancers who arrived in 1981. Unlike her predecessors, such as Sahebjan, Bhooribai, and Mohammed Ismail, Ramya was granted U.S. citizenship in due course and maintains her residence in the United States. Her student Ahila Gulasekaram (who graces the front cover of this book) is of Sri Lankan descent and was born and brought up in the United States. Glimpses into these dancers' lives suggests that dance is a form of labor that offers not only economic but also cultural capital, albeit in a limited fashion, to its practitioners (Bourdieu 1985).[4] But the circumstances of Indian dancers in the United States vary widely, depending on their class background, and their stories change over time. I use a critical lens to explore forgotten examples or "subjugated knowledges" of Indian dance that do not yet have a place within the larger narrative of Indian or American dance history (Foucault 1980).[5] Taking up Michel Foucault's call to critical action in examining subjugated knowledges, I ask what would happen if we unmasked these marginally appearing dancing bodies as laborers and what such knowledges would bring.

Considering these dancers as laboring bodies in movement helped shape the key ideas in this book. Attention to movement, a key element in dance, not only destabilizes any fixed notion of identity or claims of cultural purity but also challenges monolithic understandings of citizenship: in other words, transnational, migrant artists can inhabit multiple positions in the spectrum of citizenship—from contract laborer, to F-1 student visa or H-1 work visa holder, to green card holder, to citizen. The various citizenship positions inhabited by Indian dancers can be understood through an examination of the oscillation between their absence and presence in historical archives. These fluctuations are not just about a swing back and forth between fixed positions of visibility and invisibility.

Building on subaltern theorist Gayatri Spivak's (1985, 1988, 1999) and ethnographer Kamala Visweswaran's (1994) arguments, I show how the dancers' experiences illustrate how subalterns can move elusively through modes of representation and occupy different subject positions within a spectrum, embodying various roles. Such a process of mapping subaltern movements is important in understanding the very construction of the archives. I am interested in noting which acts and bodily movements appear in the archives and whether they are centralized as major events, are sidelined as nonevents, or function as historical negatives (Stoler 2010). In the process, I construct my own archive, much as Anjali Arondekar (2009) does. As Jacques Derrida (1998) argues, speech, film, thought, and writing—and I would add dance— are architracings. These traces left behind by individuals—what he also calls the "twinkling of presence"—are not stable or fixed. Yet this twinkling leaves remnants of a human body's movement in the historical record.

Sweating Saris: Indian Dance as Transnational Labor is a meditation on dance as labor and the female Indian dancing body as a laboring body. This book challenges dominant approaches to histories of Indian diaspora in the United States as well as to modern dance history. The research on Indian labor in the United States has thus far focused predominantly on male laborers, most likely because, historically, there were greater numbers of Indian men than women traveling to the United States. In addition, the emphasis has been on male laborers who worked on roads and rail systems, on farms, or more recently, in the IT industry. Often, these studies foster stereotypical understandings of the immigrant experience by focusing on men and representing them as victims of racist immigration laws, or as wealthy middle-class professionals who have achieved the American dream. Meanwhile, studies of Indian dancers are relegated to the aesthetic realm and deemed to have no sociopolitical relevance.[6] I challenge the binary framing of the Indian immigrant experience as one of either manual labor and poverty or white-collar success to prompt a deeper and more complex understanding of immigration policy.

I learned repeatedly in this investigation how the terms of immigration and citizenship in the United States—that is, what it means to "belong" here—are constantly moving and how dancers negotiate these terms. Attending to the labor of transnational dancing bodies, I make visible the notion that citizenship is always "in process." I have observed in writing this book that just as many bodies create the solo dancer (as in the case of Ruth St. Denis in the early twentieth century), so too have collective bodies who move in and out of the spectrum of visibility created the "ideal citizen," such as the model minority Bharata Natyam dancer of the late twentieth century. To make this evident, I move the many marginal figures of Indian female dancers to center stage, where these artists and laborers in Indian American history can tell their untold stories.

Examining Indian dancing women as transnational laborers allows us to reimagine Indian diaspora in the United States as differentially classed, contested, and negotiated. By placing these dancing women and feminized men at center stage, this book turns the spotlight on Indian dance as a form of embodied, gendered labor that transforms our understanding of the politics of Asian American racialization, citizenship, and migration since the late nineteenth century.

Dance as Labor

Although the dancing body is often viewed only in aesthetic terms, it is also a laboring body and works in multiple ways to create art. The dancer labors in training her hands to form mudras.[7] She labors in learning to slap her feet on the ground. She labors to turn and travel effortlessly. Her labor is revealed in sweat and even blood spilled onstage. The sculpted bodily form moving in space is her labor made visible.

Marxist theories posit that labor is separate from the means of production. But in *Culture and Materialism*, Raymond Williams argues that the conditions of production in the work of art-making have been overlooked (1980, 46). In dance, even more than in other disciplines, the labor of dancing cannot be separated from its means of production, the dancing body. Dance is also unique in that labor is equivalent to the product in dance: the dancing body's very "liveness" and the display of its labor in performance produces a dance product. Therefore, the dancing body as a laboring body disrupts traditional Marxist understandings of the act of labor, the means of production, and the product.

In the aesthetic realm, audiences are trained not to see the labor of dance, but they are still consumers of that effort. In *Sweating Saris*, I contend that it is important to recognize the productive labor of the dancer. If the dancing body's labor is accounted for in politico-economic terms, we begin to see her work within the larger structure of production, labor, and migration.

I examine the conditions of producing dance by focusing on the body's materiality. Raymond Williams suggests (1980, 117) that Marxists have embraced the idea of a physical body differently from psychoanalysts and poststructuralists, who read the body only as signaling subjecthood and/or as a sign. According to Williams, Marxists examine the body as more than a sign and as having material impacts through sweat and labor. Dance and performance scholars, on the other hand, push analysis of the body still further: they posit that the body not only creates physical or material effects but also produces its own forms of discourse.

Dance scholars who have made visible how the body is discursive include Susan Foster (1988), who looks at the body as it writes itself; Marta Savigliano (1995), who examines the politico-historical body; Ann Cooper Albright looks at feminist and material readings of the body (1997); and Jane Desmond (1991), who investigates the cultural body, for example. Others, such as Mark Franko (2002) and Ellen Graff (1997), have built on this work to explore dance and labor. In particular, Franko and Graff have studied performances created for the labor movement, as well as ways that the labor movement inspired modern dancers in the 1930s and 1940s. Going beyond how the labor movement manifested in performance, I examine the intersection between danced labor and race. Considering the experiences of Asian American dance laborers sheds light on how their bodies have been racialized by the performance-going public as well as by the state, and how racialized bodies have migrated to and labored in the United States.

To inspect the intersections between labor, race, and gender in the stories of Indian dancers in the United States, *Sweating Saris* brings together scholarship in Asian American studies on immigration, citizenship, and labor, and particularly women's labor histories.[8]

Dancers as Transnational Labor and Wage Earners

I also raise concerns of third world feminists, transnational feminists,[9] and postcolonial feminists regarding gender and the laboring body. *Sweating Saris* asks that the contentious term *transnational laborer* be reconsidered to include Indian women dancers and several male performers from the nineteenth and twentieth centuries. I duly note the call of sociologists such as Saskia Sassen (1990); globalization theorists such as Inderpal Grewal and Caren Kaplan (1994; 2005); and third world feminist scholars such as Chandra Mohanty, Anne Russo, and Lourdes Torres (1991), who problematize third world women's transnational labor within the twentieth-century politico-historical realities of capital flow and migration. Saskia Sassen's argument in considering transnational labor as a late-twentieth-century phenomenon particular to women is of signficance to this argument. Sassen believes that the reason immigrant labor from the global periphery to the industrialized world is attractive—and the reason spaces such as export processing zones (EPZs) are created—is to employ young women who were previously unwaged workers because they are the most docile form of labor (1990). I am not suggesting that the flow of Indian dancers follows this trajectory in the nineteenth and twentieth centuries. The specifics I discuss are different, but I refer to Indian women dancers as *transnational laborers* because the term allows me to consider dancers who move from peripheral to central spaces of industrialization and capital formation as wage earners (T. Davis 1991)[10] in the formal and informal economy. For instance, Sahebjan and her troupe of *nachwalis* were primarily operating in an informal economy in the 1880s on the streets of Delhi and Kolkata but became wage earners in the formal economy with formal contracts and payment for their performances when they traveled to New York. Ruth St. Denis also operated in the formal economy, emerging as an independent female artist in the early twentieth century by making money through her performances of Indian dances (among other Asian forms). Mohammed Ismail and other Indian men were not formally paid for their services precisely because they were racially emasculated and feminized by St. Denis's body onstage. It is in this murky in-between space that the labor of Mohammed Ismail (who attempted to sue St. Denis) in helping create St. Denis's dances is contested. And although some Indian dance teachers have operated in the informal economy since 1965, most have firmly settled into the formal economy after establishing large schools and dance companies in the United States. This unique phenomenon of independent Indian women as wage-earning dance gurus is in significant ways a diasporic manifestation (Yessayan 2010). The sheer number of women in this position of power is something that was unlikely in India, as male gurus dominated the market until recently.[11]

But wage-earning women and feminized men still need to be subjected to the rigors of a transnational feminist analysis, and power differentials between women must be accounted for. I have learned about unpacking power through the work of Chandra Mohanty and colleagues (1991), Margo Okazawa-Rey and Kirk (2004), and Piya Chatterjee (2001), who argue that there can be no feminist analysis without a critique of capital.[12] Mohanty (1991) argues for a materialist analysis that simultaneously addresses issues of identity, agency, and community and calls for an examination of women's bodies that considers their materiality and not just Woman as trope, in order to fully understand how power operates.[13] A feminist and materialist analysis of American dance history must focus on the labor of poor and young women of color (here, women dancers and their practices from India, as well as feminized men) traveling in the late nineteenth and twentieth centuries. Paying attention to the specific material concerns of women such as Sahebjan, Ruth St. Denis, and Ramya and the power differentials between them in race, class, and time allows me to consider how different dancers negotiated their movement between the informal and formal economy.

I locate colored dancing women and their stories within specific historical political economies and ask what kinds of performances, performance histories, and discourses of citizenship are produced when the analysis begins with questions of gendered labor, knowledge, power, and access. The focus on particular sociopolitical economies and material realities of Indian dancers also allows an examination of how each dancer negotiates the terms of her citizenship.

Dance and Citizenship

I inspect the intersections between labor, race, and gender in the stories of Indian dancers in the United States. Before 1965, citizenship had been elusive for most Indians. Since the nineteenth century, Indians' entrances into and exits from the United States have been controlled by fluctuating U.S. policies on immigration and citizenship. For example, many male laborers who became farmers and landowners were U.S. citizens until they were denaturalized in 1923. Indian dancers, like other Indian and Asian laborers, have toiled and sweated (in the cultural sphere), but their experiences as workers and as immigrants have not been accounted for in Asian American or American labor history.

In *Sweating Saris*, I turn to dance as an unrecognized form of labor to critique the discourses through which citizenship has been constructed. Paying attention to Indian dancers' movements to and from the United States highlights how the rules for entry into the United States are defined and redefined. Because of changing immigration laws, Indian dancers have worked in the United States under varying auspices: as aliens, temporary contract workers, H1-B workers, permanent residents, naturalized citizens, or denaturalized citizens. In examining the shifts in policies and the ensuing impacts on dancers' lives, this book suggests that citizenship is in process and is made visible by dance labor.

Certain immigration policies enacted between 1868 and 1965 were particularly relevant to Asian American labor,[14] and the dancers I encountered
in the archive were shaped by these policies. I begin with the 1868 passage
of the Fourteenth Amendment, which granted citizenship to all persons born
or naturalized in the United States. This law enabled African Americans to
obtain full citizenship and opened the door to citizenship for immigrants,
including Indians and other Asians. The 1882 Chinese Exclusion Act, which
restricted Chinese laborers from entering the United States, led to the
recruitment of Indian laborers as substitutes or competition for the Chinese
laborers already in the country. Like other Indian laborers, Indian dancers
benefited from this law and began entering the United States in greater
numbers.

Until 1923, Indians were allowed to become citizens, but the decision
in *United States v. Bhagat Singh Thind* that year denaturalized all Asian U.S.
citizens (Chan 1991, 93–94; Takaki, 1990, 299). This law culminated a
long debate on the question of race and citizenship for Asians in America.[15]
In 1965, the National Origins Immigration Act altered the immigration
landscape for Indians again. The act gave preference to seven categories of
immigrants, including laborers and those with advanced degrees. Many Asian
professionals were thus able to enter the United States for the first time and
apply for citizenship, and they did so in great numbers. This influx included
Indian male professionals who came for work or further studies, and some
came with wives who had trained as dancers in India. For *Sweating Saris*, I
studied the experiences of specific artists who migrated and worked during
each of these policy phases.

Historically, the research on Indian dance focuses on its contributions
to cultural diversity in the United States and assumes that dance is devoid
of politics. However, as Aihwa Ong (1999), Lisa Lowe (1996), May Joseph
(1999), and Lok Siu (2001) argue, cultural practices can offer understandings of citizenship in both intimate and public ways, and accordingly, culture
and cultural practices can intervene in political framings of citizenship. Ong
and Lowe develop the notions of flexible citizenship and cultural citizenship
to study the everyday practices of Asian bodies in the United States and in
the diaspora.[16] Siu defines cultural citizenship as those behaviors and practices that allow an understanding of citizenship as a lived experience within
uneven power structures. Although these terms describing citizenship were
introduced in the late twentieth and early twenty-first centuries, I find them
useful in considering the practices of transnational Indian dancers who
were negotiating unfair and discriminatory terms of labor and citizenship
from as early as 1880 until the present. The lived behavior of dancers, and
particularly the Indian dancing body, reveals how their movements, practices,

and toil can change our understanding of the discourses of cultural and political citizenship.

For instance, although in 1881 the *nachwali* Sahebjan could not become a citizen with her contract-visa status, in performing on a New York stage, her brown body symbolically heightened white fears that citizenship could become a possibility. Her baby son, born on U.S. soil, was in fact a citizen for a short time until he died. Mogul Khan, one of Ruth St. Denis's stage performers, thought he could cement his citizenship by marrying a white American woman (St. Denis's maid), but laws preventing miscegenation rendered his marriage—and newly obtained citizenship—null and void. However, he held his citizenship for a few years at least. Indians arriving in the United States after 1965 have fared differently from those who preceded them; Indians and other Asians began to acquire a "model minority" status. In other words, they began to be—and still are—viewed as an ideal minority group that moves up economically, taking advantage of the so-called American dream. They gain green cards, become permanent residents, eventually obtain citizenship, and become cosmopolitans inhabiting multiple spaces with flexible citizenship possibilities. Indian dancers attain this ideal minority citizenship through their teaching of dance to young Indian girls (and the occasional non-Indian girl or woman), staging performances at cultural events, and working with communities during Indian festivals. They live their negotiations of "cultural citizenship" through performance as minority subjects.

On Ethnography

Sweating Saris intervenes in studies of labor, immigration, and citizenship in two ways. First, as noted, this book examines dance as unrecognized labor. Second, it offers the methodology of the unruly spectator; this spectator sees dance as labor and seeks signs and traces of the laboring dancing body. She looks for telltale signs of the body's work from the position of an ethnographer. This unruly spectator is a feminist ethnographer who simultaneously conducts an interactive auto-ethnography, an ethnography of the archive, and an ethnography of living bodies.

The methodology I use in *Sweating Saris* arose from my frustration with the ethnography I conducted in California dance classrooms in the 1990s. I increasingly questioned the social, political, and often ahistorical framework that encircled Indian dance in the United States. My love of and frustration with Indian dance drove me to find a way to write about it that made sense to me. So, the unruly spectator, a viewer who offers a nonpassive feminist perspective, was born.

This dance ethnographer as unruly spectator could not write a "traditional" ethnography. That is, I was not writing about an encounter with an alien subject in an alien country. Yet I was not content to write a narrative solely on my encounter with dancers in my known world. My frustration with the current practice of Indian dance led me to study its past, which then allowed me to return to contemporary and familiar spaces with a greater understanding of their politico-historical contexts.

As unruly spectator, I focus on bodily encounters with my subjects, those living and those in the archive, using dance and choreography as not only a method but also an object of study. Part of the challenge of this book is the method engendered by the unruly spectator, who conducts an ethnography of the archive of bodies past and present. As the unruly spectator, I am interested in Indian dance forms that have become emblematic of particular cultural, political, and labor formations at key moments in Asian immigration in the United States. It is important to note that there are many Indian classical dance forms present in the United States post-1965, including Odissi, Kathak, and Kuchipudi, to mention a few. Although I am not tracing the history of any one form of Indian dance in the United States, I frame the book from the embodied study (as a dancer and practitioner of the form) of the contemporary practice of Bharata Natyam (a South Indian classical dance form problematically labeled as "traditional"). In the process, I am not conflating the form to stand in for all Indian dance. Rather, I use it to imagine and understand U.S. Indian dance practices historically, from an embodied experiential perspective of a more dominant diasporic form in the contemporary moment.

The dance performance ethnographer is interested in engaging with what I call the "bodily archive."[17] This archive leaves its traces in live bodily interactions, whose history remains captured in muscle memory and through bodily labor and kinesthetic contact. The traces can then be uncovered by searching for movement in the written record and in the live encounter between bodies. The historical archive is, after all, a place to find and exhume unmoving dead bodies, not living, moving ones.[18] Yet what I am interested in are dead bodies that once moved. As Carolyn Steedman (2002), Ann Laura Stoler (2010), and Antoinette Burton (2006) argue, archives are often composed of selected documents from the past and an assorted jumble of fragments that no one intended to preserve. Layered on this source material is the reality of the body that moves and sorts through this archive (Burton 2006). In *Sweating Saris*, I narrate the physical and messy experience of searching the archive and juxtapose that search with the complex encounters with living beings, much as Amitav Ghosh does when he brings together the archival and the ethnographic in his search for Bomma the slave (1992).

Marta Savigliano (2003) persuasively argues that a postcolonial, transnational feminist ethnography must be both an ethnography and a critique of the ethnographic predicament. But how does the unruly spectator achieve this? Savigliano suggests that a critique is made more effective when the line between fiction and ethnography is blurred. In the process, we begin to see how much of what is presented depends on the point of view of the ethnographer. It is because of the failures of ethnographic research that I, too, choose to blur reality and fiction. Savigliano also asks, "How [do we] deliver an ethnographic account that retains the tension of the ethnographic encounter, the romance and the fallings-out, the fascination and the disgust, the wealth and the poverty of ethnographic knowledge—and the differences for its participating subjects and objects?" (141). I pursue these real-life tensions by narrating experiences from the dancer's point of view—a perspective that changes dramatically from era to era.

At the center of my research and writing is the interdisciplinary approach of performance ethnography. Despite the epistemological and philosophical critiques of its anthropological methods, performance ethnography is used as a methodology because of its engagement with material bodies and bodily experience. As a researcher, I put my body on the line while training with and otherwise engaging other dancers. Dwight Conquergood (1991) argues that performance ethnography allows a dialogic engagement between performance and research and encourages performer-researchers who share experiences with their subjects to enter the field. Although we invariably stabilize events when we record field experience, I locate my research in performance methodology, which attempts to destabilize the writing itself. I weave my experiences into the representational process of the writing, because they reveal the multiple perspectives and incongruities in any observed event.

I draw from the bodily archive and its repertoire while also drawing attention to the ethnographic predicament. I use a performative auto-ethnography to demonstrate how different kinds of social spaces are produced by different bodily experiences and to frame questions of research from my own body. Auto-ethnography has been critiqued as a "navel-gazing" reductionist approach, but it developed primarily because of critiques over the impossibility of objectivist research methods. Feminist ethnographers, such as Judith Stacey (1999), note the difficulty of conducting feminist ethnography without inserting the self into the project. Postcolonial and third world feminist ethnographers, such as Kamala Visweswaran (1994), Lila Abu-Lughod (1998), Ruth Behar (2003), Gloria Anzaldua and Ana Louise Keating (2002), and Marta Savigliano (1995, 2003), add that the notion of inserting the self into ethnography emerged as third world women and women of color first began writing for themselves; that is, the "natives" began "writing back."

Politically, auto-ethnography is more than navel-gazing and, in effect, challenges anthropological writing that views "natives" as objects of study rather than as co-performers in the field (Conquergood 1991). I argue, however, that "natives writing back" need to contextualize the "auto" in the "ethnography" within larger political historical frameworks.

Through dialogic and auto-ethnography, in which as ethnographer I not only fail my informants but also betray my dancing self, I demonstrate how dance writes itself on the body and examine the meanings it produces in different social settings: in my own training locations, Australia and India, and in training locations in Southern California. I frame the auto-ethnography within larger questions of race, gender, class, and politics and show how the laboring young female body is simultaneously empowered, disciplined, and punished through the training process.

The researcher's role in the "field" is murky. It would appear that in conducting my research in Bharata Natyam classrooms in the United States, and in the archival records, I was an "insider" in my "home," and yet, as my research reveals, my presence disrupts the dichotomy of "field site" and "home site," destabilizing notions of "insider" or "outsider." As a young girl born in South India, a fluent speaker of Tamil and English learning Bharata Natyam in Kolkata, an Indian-Australian and later a U.S. citizen, and a researcher masquerading as a dance student in South Asian American "ethnic" enclaves, I have been many selves. I have held insider and outsider status simultaneously, and each research site has been both "home" and "field" for me, the only constant being the practice of dance.

The gurus I have worked with were all first-generation immigrants, usually fifteen to thirty years older than I am. It would appear that we shared some similarities—being born in India, migrating as first-generation immigrants, speaking Tamil and English—but there were also many generational and cultural differences. The dance students I interviewed and studied with were two to twenty years younger than I. Our commonalities included growing up and learning to dance in a Western country, speaking English, and belonging to the same generation. There were several differences as well, including that my upbringing in Australia had been structured within a different kind of racism from theirs. What perhaps united us in the end were our class similarities, because, after all, we were variously situated middle-class dancers living in the "first world." This encounter was substantially different from my encounters with the Indian dancing women in the archives of late nineteenth and early twentieth centuries, whose class, language, and migrant labor background differed from my own and that of the gurus and students in the late twentieth century. Therefore, I ask here what is the "field site" and what is the "home site"? Rather than claim either status and choose between "insider" and "outsider," I consider how these positions are being performed, by whom, and for what purpose. For example, in my research in U.S. dance classrooms, the insider/outsider question is related to the notion of the "authentic" Indian subject and dancer. The dichotomy feeds into debates over authenticity that plague diaspora and diasporic subjects. This issue yields a different set of questions from those usually asked by "first world" ethnographers who insert themselves into traditionally "third world" field sites. In other words, I am mobilized by the questions that a "first world" field site raises for variously placed "first-third" world subjects and researchers.

I aim to be transparent as I determine what experiences to represent and what to leave out. I highlight certain aspects of the form either to demon-strate an argument or because those aspects hold certain meanings for me as a performer and researcher. At times I focus more on learning particular dances than on learning basic steps because the former are far more mean-ingful to me. However, basic steps are equally important in a dancer's life because they are the building blocks of the dances. I have no qualms about admitting that in Chapter 1, I focus on the dramatic components of the repertoire far more than the rhythmic components. This is because I love to perform *abhinaya* pieces, the narrative dances that require role-playing, far more than the abstract, rhythm-based pieces such as the *jathiswaram* or *thillana*. This has been the case from my earliest days of dance training, and I stay true to my interests and strengths. Someone else focusing on rhythmic aspects of the repertoire might therefore uncover very different material and insights.

In writing about the dance spaces that my body haunted, I take the posi-tion of a participant-observer; but I understand this position in a triangulated framework rather than in terms of self-other dualities. Within the Bharata Natyam form, there exist three main "characters": the *nayika* (heroine), the *nayaka* (hero), and the *sakhi* (female friend). The dancer usually sustains the position of the *nayika* throughout a lyrical text-based piece and, in inter-preting the text, will briefly assume the position of the *nayaka* or *sakhi*. The *nayaka* is often absent and is frequently referred to by the heroine, while the *sakhi* is a constant but often silent presence. The dancer speaks her inner-most feelings to the *sakhi*, and if the *sakhi* is loyal, she faithfully interprets the *nayika's* feelings to the *nayaka*. The *sakhi* is the translator, a mediary, who may or may not be faithful to the *nayika*. She makes no promises to the *nayika* while watching and listening to her and is therefore not always trust-worthy. The *sakhi* might have designs on the hero herself and may therefore purposely misinterpret the *nayika's* message, or she might not deliver the message at all. This triangle between the heroine, her friend, and the hero, stages the possibility for homosocial/homoerotic desire within the structure of the dance. In the case of Bollywood films, Gayatri Gopinath has persua-sively argued that a queer triangulated reading of the hero/heroine/friend of heteronormative bodies is possible from a transnational diasporic perspective. "A queer reading might allow for the possibility of a triangulated desire that does not solidify into 'lesbian' or 'heterosexual' but rather opens up a third space where both hetero- and homoerotic relations coexist simultaneously" (2005, 105). The relationship between the *nayika* and the *sakhi* opens up a homosocial space for queer desire even as it operates within the framework of heterosexual desire. These spaces of desire, however, are not safe.

I liken my position as dance performance ethnographer to the *sakhi* in the sense that ethnographers are not to be trusted. They do not necessarily relay the truth of any experience but only offer partial perspectives (Clifford 1994). The *sakhi* is elusive, just like the ethnographer, who, although she comes and goes as she pleases, still must be summoned by the *nayika*. Hearing the mes-sage of the *nayika* through the *sakhi* is always a mediated experience, as is the narration of the "field message" by the ethnographer. There is no guarantee that the *sakhi*/ethnographer will not betray, misinform, lie, or fail the *nayika*/informants. This is the crisis of doing ethnographic work, and these are issues I deal with throughout this book. But there is a twist to this scenario. I am not always the *sakhi*.

I take on the role of the *nayika*, too, because of my own bodily experi-ences and training in the Bharata Natyam form. The embodied perspective comes from the experience of being a Bharata Natyam student and then a professionally trained dancer and choreographer. I become my own infor-mant. True to the structure of the Bharata Natyam form, I allow myself to morph back and forth between *sakhi* and *nayika*, just as I might do in perfor-mance. I also become an audience member, a *rasika*, the aficionado. But I am not always an ideal spectator, as the *rasika* is expected to be, and therefore I foreground the tensions around this spectatorial position.

Several feminist scholars articulate models of spectatorship and alternate ways of viewing cinema.[19] Janet Staiger's (2000) work on perverse spectators is an important model that allows for tension in viewing not only cinema but also the live female performing body. Perversity, as she describes it, could indicate a willful turning away from what is expected of the female spectator or an inability to do otherwise. Queer readings of the female body in perfor-mance also offer unruly ways of seeing. These include the idea of adopting a transgender gaze of female masculinity (Halberstam 2001), or a feminist lesbian gaze (Dolan 1991), or most intriguing, the triangulated desire of a diasporic queer gaze (Gopinath 2005). Countless dance scholars, too, have argued for alternate, feminist spectatorial positions.[20] What these dance scholars offer to theories of spectatorship is the kinesthetic identification between audiences and performers that occur in the live encounter between bodies. These messy bodily relationships in concert dance settings enable spectators to move away from viewing the dancing female body solely as the object of white heterosexual male desire and instead allow a female gaze and desire to coexist.

The unruly spectator adopts a female, feminist, and at times homosocial gaze and desires to find men's and women's bodies in the bodily archive both past and present. When she finds these hidden bodies, she makes them visible through her desire. This desire is, of course, partial, personal, and very subjective, just as all ethnography is, even if it does not purport to be so. Just as the *nayika* takes on "emotional states" in performance, the unruly spectator reads the past and present from emotional states. For instance, when the unruly spectator finds Sahebjan's photo in an 1880 issue of the *New York Clipper*, she is stunned and cries in astonishment and from an overwhelming sense of justice that a black-and-white microfilm image of this dancer attests to her existence. The unruly spectator is angry when she reads of the injustice in the 1923 immigration policies against Indians (among other minorities) but focuses on how these policies affect Indian dancing bodies. She is dismayed when she sees contemporary Bharata Natyam being practiced and taught devoid of historical and political context and seeks to address this imbalance by examining power differentials in class changes with changing immigration waves.

Each chapter in the book combines the focus of the unruly spectator, who recognizes dance as labor and citizenship as a process that is constantly changing for Indians. Chapter 1 offers a glimpse of the laborious, rigorous training in learning the repertoire that young female bodies undergo in Bharata Natyam dance classrooms in the United States and Australia. Despite bringing together my own experiences in learning the form and how it culturally empowers young girls to become minority citizens, I disclose some of the problems in the pedagogical process. I suggest that the discourse of the model minority myth contextualizes why Bharata Natyam is taught in an ahistorical manner, and I alert readers to the fact that my ethnographic narrative of the classroom thus far has been purposefully ahistorical. Chapter 1 is the launchpad for the argument that a genealogical context is requisite to better understanding Indian dance as labor in the United States and its changing relationship to citizenship.

Chapter 2 tells the untold stories of Indian dancers who traveled from India to the United States between 1880 and 1907. Their physical presence on the stages of New York disrupts North American imaginings of the "Oriental dancing girl." I analyze how the moving material body of the performing Indian dancer was framed within the discourses of U.S. orientalism and reflected the changing racial and class tensions surrounding the Indian laborer. I focus on the birth and death of the dancer Sahebjan's baby to discuss what possibilities temporary U.S. citizenship offered Indians at the time.

Chapter 3 focuses on Ruth St. Denis, one of the foremothers of American modern dance, who was influenced by Indian women dancers in Coney Island in 1904. Her dancing body evinces the labor of her material and racialized interactions with Indian dancing women. I suggest that the spiral turns and whirls in St Denis's choreography are evidence of kinesthetic traces left through bodily interaction between dancing women of different races. By highlighting the labor of the Indian artists who worked with and inspired St. Denis's grand debut *Radha*, I argue that the inception of modern dance in America was a collective endeavor. This chapter recalls these nearly forgotten Indian female figures and shows that U.S. citizenship was made available to white women who became economically independent wage earners by using Indian and Asian dance practices.

In Chapter 4 I address the Indian men who also enabled St. Denis to launch and sustain her career as an Oriental dancer. I explore how U.S. citizenship is contested, albeit temporarily, by transnational Indian male performers in ways that Indian women dancers were unable to do. That Ruth St. Denis employed Indian male dancers as part of her entourage during her early performances (1906) and subsequently when she toured her Oriental dances (1909–1911) is well known. While the research on St. Denis addresses orientalism and imperialism, no one has paid attention to the actual Indian bodies performing onstage with St. Denis. Through three key acts, these male performers—including one who sued St. Denis, another who married her maid, and a third who tried to escape her company while on tour—made themselves visible in the archives and demonstrated how they negotiated citizenship.

Chapter 5 addresses two mid-twentieth-century changes to citizenship—one cultural and the other political—that are central to the story of Indian dancers in the United States. American modern dance severed its ties to Indian dance in the 1940s as part of a larger effort to establish ethnic dance as a distinct aesthetic project. This fabricated division between modern and ethnic dance paved the way for Indian dance to emerge as an ethnic minority form shortly before provisions in the 1965 immigration act encouraged educated and professional workers to immigrate from India (and other countries). Indian female dancers, many the wives of white-collar workers, were now able to enter and set up dance schools, thereby becoming economically independent wage-earning gurus. These dancers, unlike their predecessors, were able to obtain permanent residency status through green cards and then become U.S. citizens, albeit as minorities.

In Chapter 6, I use feminist dance and performance ethnography to examine the labor of middle-class female Indian dance gurus and their students in California studios after 1995 in order to expose the contradictions of minority citizenship. I examine the bodily encounters that occur in garages, basements, and home spaces where Bharata Natyam dance is taught. I place this dance practice in dialogue with Asian American discourses on cultural nationalism and the rhetoric of the model minority. By examining bodily labor through the sweat that emerges from the dancers' pores as they dance, I present new possibilities for understanding the labor of dance and how citizenship is inhabited differently by Indians after 1965.

In Chapter 7, I frame the performance of a young Indian American dancer in California in 2002 as a global commodity from the perspective of an unruly spectator. I argue that even as the young Indian American dancer attempts to efface her own labor in performing her solo concert recital (*arangetram*), her sweat, costumes, and paraphernalia betray her efforts. I trace one important performance of the young Indian American dancer as she prepares for the culmination of her many years of training in the form—that is, her *arangetram*. This chapter examines the "performative" to expose the multiple economies and bodies at work that sustain the performance of the "ideal" minority citizen on the U.S. stage. I argue that the young Indian dancing girl in performance both masks and makes visible the transnational economies of labor required to maintain ethnic difference and cultural citizenship for mainstream and minority communities in a U.S. context.

This book is an interdisciplinary project at its core. Using a variety of discourses that centralize the moving, dancing body, *Sweating Saris* places on center stage minority bodies of transnational Indian women who have traveled between India and the United States and shaped U.S. culture but have been overlooked in both Indian and U.S. dance scholarship. *Sweating Saris* examines Indian women dancers as laborers in cultural formation and explores how U.S. citizenship is a moving discourse that can be contested, defined, and refined.

1

An Invocation for Ethnohistories

Tei ha tei hee, tei ha tei. Tei ha tei hee, tei ha tei.
1, 2, 3, 4, tei ha tei. Tei ha tei hee, 5, 6, 7, 8.
Good work girls! *tei ha tei. Tei ha tei hee*, keep it up.
Sit lower, Kavitha, *tei ha tei.* Lift your heads, *tei ha tei.*
Tei ha tei hee, straighten up, *tei. Tei ha* shoulders back, *tei ha tei.*
Turn those knees out, Lakshmi, *tei ha tei.* Next speed—

The students, the guru, and I are in a rehearsal room. The wooden dance floor is sprung and can absorb the impact of the dancers' footwork. A large bronze statue of the god Siva as the Lord of Dance or Nataraja stands in the back of the room. The bodies present are many and their histories varied. The guru, in her late thirties, wearing a cotton sari, sits in the front of the room chanting rhythmic syllables, such as *tei ha tei hi tei ha tei*, while beating a stick against a wooden block. These are syllables that have no specific meaning; they merely reflect the sounds the drum makes to guide the dancers in their footwork. Dressed in a *salwar*, I sit next to the guru, tapping the *tala* with my hand. There are six girls aged between six and eight, also dressed in *salwars*, each with a cloth *dupatta* tied around her waist and a *bindi* on her forehead. Their mothers, between thirty and forty years old, wear saris, pants, sweaters, or *salwars* and sit on the side watching the class.

We are watching a beginner's class in Bharata Natyam, a traditional Indian classical dance style, being taught in Orange County, California, in mid-September 1995. Ramya Harishankar is the guru. I am new to Los Angeles and have asked Ramya if I can come and talk with her about her guru, Kalanidhi Narayanan, who will be visiting from India to conduct workshops in Ramya's Orange County studio. I had explained my interest in learning from Kalanidhi, an esteemed artist trained in *padams*, a unique aspect of the Bharata Natyam repertoire. Ramya had cordially invited me to her home to discuss aspects of the workshop on a Thursday afternoon at 3:00 P.M. She explained that she would be teaching classes immediately after our meeting. In anticipation of the interview, I left my home at 2:00 P.M., presuming the sixty-mile drive would take an hour. I presumed wrong. After sitting in traffic for a two and a half hours, I finally pulled up at 4:30 P.M. behind an array of cars parked bumper to bumper on an otherwise empty, quiet, tree-lined, middle-class, suburban street.

I rang the doorbell, and a sweet, smiling elderly woman with bright eyes and silver hair answered the door. I felt an instant rapport with her because she reminded me of my grandmother in Melbourne. She was Lakshmi Krishnamoorthy, Ramya's mother-in-law, manager, and singer, I later learned. She directed me toward the back of the house where the classes were taking place. As I took off my shoes, I could hear the sound of the stick beating the rhythm and *chollu kattu* being chanted. *Tei ha tei hee, tei ha tei. tei ha tei hee, tei ha tei.* My heart began beating wildly. Was it the rhythmic pulse that was beckoning or fear of meeting the dance guru? I stopped for a moment and smiled as I realized which dance step they were practicing. When I had first begun learning my steps, I had hated this *adavu* because it required incredible thigh strength and overall stamina. Standing with the knees bent and turned out, one had to jump onto the balls of the feet and then drop the heels down sharply—up, down, up, down—working with gravity and not against it. The pull downward was fine for the first three or four repetitions, but by the eighth or ninth time, the muscle spasms would begin. I wondered whether her students hated it as much as I had.

Once past the living and dining rooms, I reached an opening leading into the dance studio, which probably had once been the family room. Ramya, with her large kohl-lined eyes, welcomed me with a warm smile, and waving away my apology for being late, she beckoned me to sit next to her. I was surprised by Ramya's relaxed attitude. Most gurus would have been irked by my tardiness, but she didn't seem to mind. I started to relax a little and smiled at the parents sitting over to the side, and they in turn nodded their heads at me, some smiling. The children looked nervously at me and did not smile. What was Ramya like as a guru? I wondered.

This was the first of many classes I observed over the next twelve years, in various classrooms in Southern California and Chicago. My project, like all ethnographic projects, is not impartial and is based on intimate relationships between women (Kedhar 2011). It is embedded in social relations and affected by my own emotions, desires, and choices. I was often drawn back to Ramya's classes, perhaps because I got along well with her. We became good friends over the years and even started collaborating on artistic work. On a still deeper level, through a research project, the ethnographer imagines herself living another life. It made sense that I had oriented aspects of my project around Ramya, because through her I imagined another life path for myself. Although I never wanted to become a guru myself, it was pleasurable to imagine where such a choice might have led: to have the ability to train young girls, to perform continuously, to be a pillar within local communities, and to feel that I was a part of a community of dancers with many shared experiences.

My research involved observation of classes, but I also participated at times. I felt good about myself when I danced. I felt strong, beautiful, and powerful. I could become anything I wanted for a few hours in class. Of course, the characters I could take on were always within the realm of Hindu mythology, and I respected the limits of the form. I could not for example become Jay-Z the rapper, a taxicab driver, a worker in a garment factory, an engineer, or an academic. But I could become Kali, the powerful black goddess with a large red tongue, who is the embodiment of life, death, and time itself, or Durga, the tiger-riding, demon-killing goddess with her long hair waving in the wind. I could take on the role of a male god such as Siva the destroyer or Vishnu the preserver, or narrate the trials of Prince Rama as told in the epic Ramayana. I could even detail the amorous exploits of the young god Krishna—both from his perspective and from the point of view of his maiden-lovers. Or I could focus on a mortal woman's experience of life, longing, and erotic love. That the dance form enabled me to perform all of these powerful selves was what captivated me for so many years.

These theatrical representations of gods, goddesses, and other characters were a vindication of sorts, especially for a young, brown-eyed, brown-skinned girl growing up outside of India in a harsh diasporic environment, where images of blue-eyed blondes saturated the media. Young, brown bodies dancing as beautiful, powerful goddesses offered alternate representations of female beauty, which I knew were important not only for me but also for other young girls. These performances onstage and in the classrooms offered catharsis and empowering alternate visions of oneself when one returned to the schoolyard.

Obtaining the bodily mastery to harness these other selves, however, did not come without a price, not to mention that these other selves were not always powerful. For example, some of the female characters required the performance of the "ideal" Indian woman's behavior. These characters did not question patriarchal authority and were subdued, muted sexual beings. I learned the self-effacement involved in portraying these characters in classrooms over the years. As a young girl, I had to subject myself to my guru for many years—literally to place myself at his feet—to gain the technical skill to dance and, more importantly, to gain his approval. Initially, I did not question this deference, but in later years I tried to grasp the complexity and contradictions of a young girl supplicating herself in dance classrooms to perform ideal images of Indianness and Indian womanhood. Young girls must let go of their egos and bow mentally, physically, and emotionally to a guru (male or female) to master the form. Letting go of one's ego is requisite, as Hindu texts extol the virtues of the student, who must supplicate himself or herself to the guru to gain physical and spiritual mastery.

This supplication makes sense when considering the philosophical texts that influenced the development of Bharata Natyam in the twentieth century. Advaita Vedanta is one branch of Indian philosophy that has come to inform a great deal of the reconstructed post-independence nationalist classical forms of Indian dance and its treatment of subjectivity and the body. When parsed in meaning, *Vedanta* is defined as the ultimate goal in knowledge, both spiritual and intellectual. As Adi Shankara, the foremost philosopher and exponent of Advaita Vedanta, taught in the eighth century C.E., this goal encourages the questioning of subjecthood and a human being's search for meaning in relation to the divine.[1] The body in Vedanta is seen as an illusory vehicle; it is incorporeal—something that houses the subject temporarily and that can be shed upon death before the subject (minus his or her memory of that particular life) moves on to another body for the next life. If there is no singular self and the body can only be perceived as a result of the senses and as a semiotic sign, then the body in itself cannot exist. Therefore, there is no "real" body to speak of; it is a simulacrum, or maya, in both the Beaudrillardian and Vedantic senses.[2] Even though the unruly spectator would disagree with this notion, such an understanding works well with post-independence nationalist and orientalist reconfigurations of the classical Indian dancing body that require the young girl to "empty" her own subjectivity and fill herself up with characters from Indian mythology.

The complexity arises in diasporic spaces when young girls are subjected to patriarchal Indian national visions of ideal womanhood as they simultaneously live in mainstream spaces that contradict such visions. The young girl must then learn to balance the subjection of the ego, the supplication of her body, and the gains and losses this creates.

What follows is an account of the training process I witnessed as a researcher in a Southern California dance classroom, as well as of my own training in Australia. It describes how young female bodies are disciplined through learning basic *adavu* steps, hand/body positions, and, eventually, complex repertoires. My account toggles between that of young dancers in Southern California and my own learning process in Australia and in Southern California. My stories illuminate the ritual labor that goes into disciplining the young female body in classrooms to create ideal Indian women and how power is enacted in the pursuit of Indian femininity.

At the same time, however, I purposely neglect to offer explanations of the larger sociocultural context for these teaching spaces. I choose to write descriptions of these classroom practices without providing historical context in order to reveal an ongoing failure in dance pedagogy: dance practitioners teach Indian classical dance as if it has no political-historical significance. A second and equally significant failure occurs in the research on Indian dance. Ethnographies of Indian dance typically observe practices as if they exist in a vacuum rather than in dialogue with historical, economic, and political discourses.

In this chapter, I mimic this ahistorical pedagogical process and ethnographic accounting of Indian dance to expose problems that arise from this incomplete perspective. I am moved by the work of historical anthropologists, such as John and Jean Comaroff (1992), and ethnohistorians, such as Nicholas Dirks (2008), to consider the possibilities of the reconstruction of a minority discourse on the past. My call to note failure in ethnography is also influenced by third world feminist ethnographers who examine miscommunications, silences, and other failures in the ethnographic process to reveal gendered and racial power differentials (Visweswaran 1994; Abu-Lughod 1998; Behar 2003; Anzaldua and Keating 2002). My hope is that these narratives reveal not only the embodied experience of dance training but also what is lacking when we do not historicize dance in our teaching and research. The account that follows in this chapter sets the stage of *Sweating Saris* by clarifying the relationship of ethnography to historicity and power.

The Training Process

Ramya turned out to be a kind teacher. Or at least that was how she seemed compared to my guru. He had been an excellent and loving teacher but also a strict disciplinarian who expected perfection and often screamed in anger to force our bodies into shape. He certainly got results! Ramya, on the other hand, seemed to enforce discipline through incessant repetition rather than anger. I marveled at her teaching approach. Her calmness, patience, and gentleness were new to me in the classroom. I expected an outburst of anger at any moment, but it did not happen, even in the most trying situations. Perhaps she was performing for me. But many of her students also attested to her patience and compassion even during difficult training sessions. When I talked to parents in Ramya's classes, I found that many of them had brought their daughters to learn from Ramya from the age of six. The parents said Ramya had been a good teacher and that she had begun their daughters' training gently, not wanting to frighten the children, although they did disclose that she had sometimes spoken with a harsh tone to the older students.[3]

I saw her teach young beginners in another class one day. Starting with simple eye, hand, and leg coordination exercises and then moving into *tattadavus* (the first series of steps), she progressed slowly while attempting to maintain the students' interest. She straightened their backs and helped them use their feet in the proper way by teaching them to lift the heel high enough to kick the buttock and then to slap the foot on the ground.

I remember when I first started learning dance with my guru Dr. Chandrabhanu in Australia.[4] Although I had been training in the form for several years in India with S. Rajalakshmi (who was from the Vazhavoor tradition), when my family migrated to Melbourne, I had to be retrained in the style that my new guru had learned from his guru, Adyar K. Lakshman. Lakshman was a disciple of Rukmini Devi from Kalakshetra. Passing on the impeccable training he received from this prestigious institute, Lakshman had imparted a strict disciplinary method of training to my guru, who in turn followed suit. I remember how difficult this initial training process was. My guru sat in front of the classroom facing all the students, who stood in several rows. Like Ramya, he hit a stick on a rectangular wooden block to keep the rhythm. First, he taught us how to maintain *araimandi*. To build strength in the legs and to enforce discipline, he asked us to maintain this position for two or three minutes at a time regardless of how painful it might be. In the early stages of my training, I remember having to sit in *araimandi* for fifteen minutes at one stretch, because I had not practiced a step he was testing us on in the class. I wondered whether this was punishment for having been trained by another guru in a different technique, but I had little time to ponder this, as the shooting pain in my legs and lower back soon became my main concern. *Adavus* were very hard to do sometimes, especially with the vigor and repetition my guru demanded. I was regularly disciplined in class for not holding my hands in mudra positions correctly. In trying to remember the precise dance steps, and in coordinating my eyes with my hands, feet, and torso, I would forget to pay attention to the muscles at the tips of my fingers. The mental and physical rigor—being challenged to remember minute aspects of various steps—would become overwhelming, and I would lapse frequently. My guru would send me to the back of the classroom, make me face the wall, and hold the hand gesture for a long time, so I would remember what it feels like. Although I hated being singled out in class, sometimes I enjoyed this punishment, because it gave me a respite from the torture of learning the movement. I would, as an unruly student, gaze out the window and daydream.

Ramya's Vazhavoor style is far less vigorous than my own training. It is much more fluid and elastic. In classes with older children, the gracefulness becomes evident, although at the beginning of my study I thought their movements were not fully finished or as rigorous as those of my tradition. I even thought the students were lazy and that the form was sloppy. I was not being patient. The unruly spectator did not want to sit on the sidelines waiting. I wanted to stand up and correct their arm and body positions. It took every ounce of power I had to stop myself from interrupting Ramya's class. Perhaps it was the guru in me straining to come out. Eventually, I mastered the art of quietly watching and listening like a good ethnographer should, or at least I tried to master it. It took time to unlearn my biases about vigor and rigor before I could appreciate the Vazhavoor tradition, which, ironically, was the first form I had been trained in. Training in any of the traditions takes an equally long time. Gaining mastery in the Bharata Natyam form can take anywhere from seven to twelve years. Under the auspices of a guru, a young girl can demonstrate her mastery of the form by performing an *arangetram*, the solo debut recital, which involves performing a *margam*—a full repertoire containing between seven and ten kinds of dances. The dances include a range of elements from the purely rhythmic, known as *nritta*, to the dramatic, or *nritya*. Dancers move from learning simple hand, eye, and leg coordination, to complex gestural formation and role-playing.

In Bharata Natyam, the young dancer's body develops muscle in odd places like the hands, fingers, toes, soles, pelvis, eyes, eyebrows, cheeks, mouth, and neck. Good dancers develop the ability to keep precise rhythm and become attuned to the classical Carnatic music structure. Experienced and committed dancers also learn to translate lyrics written in various Indian languages and interpret those texts through intricate gestural and facial expression. The dancer's understandings of her body change, and she becomes able to portray both femininity and masculinity fluidly. The stylized role-playing she has learned allows her to negotiate herself in the world in unique ways. Despite the rigid structure of the dance practice, interviews and discussions with dancers over the years reveal that a building of confidence and self-esteem is a direct result of the training process. But one could ask: Why is this structure accepted by the students and their parents, and enforced by the guru? Why did I sit silently watching the training unfold in this way both as an ethnographer and when I myself was a young student? What is invested in such rigidity and discipline? As a child I did not know the answer, yet I sometimes gained pleasure from this rigor and routine. I knew that learning the steps with discipline meant that I would learn whole dances soon. As an ethnographer I was invested in watching this discipline from the perspective of an adult who once experienced it myself. I felt a perverse pleasure in watching other bodies being subjected to the pain and torture that my aching sciatica and knees still remember. But I also felt bodily, aural, and kinesthetic pleasure. Hearing the rhythms being beaten out with the stick, pulsating like heartbeats, made my toes dance secretly underneath the shawl that was covering my feet. My fingers, though clasped around my knees, would form the mudras surreptitiously. The rhythm would carry me, even while seated, into being a dancer again.

Ramya and most gurus teach young girls components of *nritta* first. Teachers typically take two to four years to impart basic *adavu* steps, at which point students are taught how the *adavus* come together to form dances. Among the first items gurus teach is *jathiswaram*, a rhythmic piece that strings together a series of *adavus* to form *jathis* and *corveis* (several *adavus* strung together to form complex dance sentences). It takes another three to four years for young girls to learn rhythmic dances such as *alarippus* and *thillanas*, as well as more *jathiswarams*. These *nritta* pieces build rhythm into the young dancer's body. The dancer learns chains of *adavus* that form sequences called *jathis*. Through practice, she builds muscle memory of various such sequences, becoming adept at anticipating quick rhythmic shifts and crisp changes in body position.

During the next stage in a dancer's life, she learns the *nritya* or *abhinaya* pieces that have a dramatic or expressive component. Initially, the guru might teach a *sabdam* or *keertana* that involves simple dramatic elements, such as the myths and legends of the primarily Hindu gods, although some teachers do teach Christian-, Islamic-, or Buddhist-themed pieces. In these works, the dancer translates a sung poem into mime, often playing the role of the narrator, describing the deities, and occasionally portraying the gods themselves. The poems selected for Bharata Natyam dances are anywhere from one to eight hundred years old; they could be written in any Indian language, usually Sanskrit, Tamil, Kannada, Telugu, or Malayalam but occasionally Hindi. Nowadays, more contemporary musical compositions are used as well. The structure of these works plays out in multiple locations in Bharata Natyam dance classrooms across the globe. Watching young women's renderings of stylized classical heroines, I see evidence of national codices imprinted on women's bodies through this dance form.

The day I learned the *Sabdam Sarasijakshulu* was the day I began to love dance. Until then, often I went to dance class unwillingly, mostly to please my parents and to hang out with my friends. I was in a small class with three other Indian girls—Kavitha, Anu, and the other Priya—and we had become great friends (together we were called the four musketeers). We would also see each other outside of dance class despite living great distances from one another. Attending each other's slumber parties, dance practice parties, and birthday parties became a regular part of our lives. We imagined ourselves as sisters, and dance helped us form familial bonds, especially since we became united in our struggle to be disciplined by our guru and to gain mastery over the form. Until *Sarasijakshulu*, however, I had always felt I was the weakest dancer in the class. The other three were far ahead of me because they had trained with my guru longer. In addition, I was a lazy dancer and did not practice often unless the fear of the next class and the impending wrath of my guru forced me to hastily go through the steps I needed to learn. But that was the problem: the dance involved no more than steps, until now. *Sarasijakshulu* was a short, sweet piece about the god Krishna. The piece was set to multiple ragas but fixed to one *tala: misra chapu*, a staccato-like seven-beat cycle played in a "three-plus-four" structure. The dance had both narrative and abstract components, but the emphasis was on depicting a heroine who mocked Krishna for all his wrongdoings. I liked this heroine! Of course, my guru reminded us about the spiritual aspect of the story. The relationship between the maidens and Krishna served as an extended metaphor for the relationship between many souls and the divine. An existential crisis arises when a soul feels that God has abandoned them or left them bereft, without even clothes! I was fourteen; that parable went above my head.

From the first time we started this piece in class, I found my body transformed. I was able to maintain and portray the *nayika* easily. I felt what she was feeling, and I could communicate that to an audience. In the audience in class that day were (as was typical) my guru, my mother, and the mothers of my friends. I found my body suddenly fitting into this heroine's imagined body. With my back straightened and my arms to the side, hands hanging down, I felt elegant and graceful. The heroine begins in the third person narrator position. I found myself describing the lotus eyes of the maidens, who are taking a bath in the river when Krishna comes along and sneakily steals their clothes. He quickly climbs up a tree and hides their clothes and waits. The maidens, after their leisurely bath, realize their dilemma and beg Krishna to return their clothes. He continues to sit in the tree laughing at their plight. I am angry with Krishna and ask him, "Is this right of you, Krishna, you who are supposed to be a god?" I am even embarrassed for the maidens. Sick of this boy, who is such a pest, I switch to the first person perspective; instead of pleading with Krishna, I shout at him to return my clothes. "But he is sweet sometimes," I tell myself. "Do not get too angry with him. You have to trick him." So I change my tune and coyly ask Krishna to return my clothes. In return, I promise him something. He does not return anything and continues to sit in the tree and laugh. I have had it with him. I am really angry and then embarrassed. "What will I do now? How will I get home?" I again take on the narrator's role and wonder how long these poor maidens will continue to shiver in the cold water? Who will help them? This Krishna had gone too far.

Shifting between characters and convincing my guru, mother, and friends was the most pleasurable experience I had ever had in that classroom. For the first time in a very long time, my guru smiled and showed his happiness.

He asked me to repeat this section for the other dancers in the class, over and over. He asked them to look at my eyes and face and how convincingly I portrayed the characters. I left class skipping with joy down the alleyway to my parents' car that day!

There was a young girl in Ramya's class who had previously had problems with her walking but one day began to walk gracefully. For weeks, she had forgotten how to walk and was swinging her right arm forward awkwardly as her right foot moved ahead. It was truly sad to watch her unable to get the opposite hand and foot to work together. But that week her body learned to walk with grace, and she began to use her mudras in nuanced ways. Like other dancers who reach this stage, she realized the open-handed mudra, the *alapadma*, can be an elegant lotus flower one minute and the next it can be the bright sun, the roundness of a face, a beautiful body, the ripples on a river; it can describe birth, express ecstasy, and even show enlightenment. But the mudra means nothing without the emotions on the face and the bodily gestures to give it texture and context. The dancer thus learns to communicate inner emotions through externalizing them. Her eyebrows, her eyes, her chin, her lips, her neck, and her head become exquisitely sensitive as she begins feeling her nerve endings at the sensory points. She learns to manipulate the eyebrows to convey sorrow but knows she must feel the emotion within so that it does not appear as caricature. But it takes time.

I never did see Ramya teach a *sabdam*. She said she preferred to go straight to the *varnam* because she felt the *sabdam* was not meaty enough and did not let you explore the *nayika* in depth. The *varnam* is the most grueling aspect of the repertoire and involves both rhythmic and dramatic components. One *varnam* can last from thirty minutes to one-and-a-half hours when compared to the *sabdam*, which is often no more than five to seven minutes. The *varnam* conditions the body and strengthens it in unique ways. Like other aspects of the dance training, the young dancer's legs become muscular and the arms become toned. The dancer also learns to perform an extended piece that can last twenty-five to forty-five minutes or even an hour. She learns to pace herself between the fast and lactic-acid-building rhythmic *jathis* and the more leisurely pace of the *abhinaya* sections in between. It is also in the *varnam* that a dancer learns to take on roles of heroes and heroines, *nayakas* and *nayikas*, and moves beyond the narrator position. The dancer is taught to embody a character, following the shifting feelings as well as the overarching mood of a particular *nayika*, over the course of a piece. She cannot use rote memory alone to perform the *varnam*, because it requires an in-depth engagement with the textual and emotional material and a focus on maintaining the *nayika* character throughout. It can take a teacher between six months to one year to teach one *varnam*. My guru taught my class the

Rupa Mu Juchi varnam, a classic of sorts, in seven months. The *varnam* is dedicated to the god Siva and describes the *nayika's* longing for her union with him. She extols his virtues and waits for him, but when he doesn't come, she becomes frustrated and laments his absence. Of course, I could not master the *jathis* quickly enough, but I was enjoying the dramatic aspects of *abhinaya.* By now I had created a reputation for myself as a dancer who was particularly adept at *abhinaya.*

In my training in Australia, I found role-playing to be one of the most exciting parts of learning the form. While the music and coordinating rhythm offered high levels of adrenaline, for me, the analysis and interrogation of female heroines and character portrayals were the most charged aspects of training and performance. Although the heroines were often ahistoric, mythical, archetypal figures of ideal Hindu Indian womanhood, I reveled in the portrayal of them. I was always aware that role-playing was just that, but dance classes also forced particular views of Indian womanhood on my body. The hand had to be held a certain way. The walk of a young maiden was also prescribed, as was the movement of a demon or demoness.

But the true test of a dancer's ability to maintain the *nayika* role is a piece such as the *padam,* a love poem sung by the musician and interpreted by the dancer in numerous different ways. It is also one of the final aspects of the repertoire that dancers learn. Here, the performer mostly maintains the protagonist role (rather than shifting between characters) and describes other characters as needed. There are no rhythmic interludes, and the poetry is unbroken. Usually it takes on the emotional perspective of the woman, the *nayika* (historically the *devadasi,* the foremother of Indian dance, whose lifestyle became outlawed during the Indian independence movement).[5] The maintenance of the *nayika* role then becomes a challenge. What kind of *nayika* is she? Is she angry, is she sad, is she young, or is she old? Ultimately, there are conventions that determine how this *nayika* can be portrayed. What is acceptable and unacceptable movement for this character is again curtailed by an idealized Hindu Indian femininity. Nowhere was this imagined construct clearer than in my own training.

Most of what I know about Indian female role-playing I learned from my queer male guru. I was frequently awestruck watching my guru take on these characters as he taught us how to perform the roles. My guru often told us that his guru never got up to demonstrate female roles; instead, he had to figure them out for himself. I knew that as an anthropology student, my guru had conducted different kinds of research that informed how he constructed his *nayikas.* He had studied how women in Chennai walked, talked, spoke, and carried themselves. Temple sculptures, books, and treatises on Indian women also informed his performance. Yet I suspended this knowledge when

I watched him train me or perform on the stage. The role of the god Rama looked easy enough for him to portray, but it was more delightful to watch him play the role of the goddess Sita, Rama's beleaguered wife. My guru brought this Indian goddess/woman alive in front of my eyes. He demonstrated Sita with the sidelong glance, the demure lowering of eyelashes, the elegant sway- ing of arms, and the dainty steps. The highlight of a demonstration would be how Sita prepared herself by decorating and adorning her body before a mirror. Dressed in a masculine *kurta* and long white *veshti*, my guru would sit on the floor with one leg folded underneath his body while he placed the other delicately in front. He would pick up an imaginary mirror with his left hand and use his right to indicate putting kohl underneath his eye. He would dot a finger with imaginary *kumkum* and place it on his forehead as if making the female ritual mark of the *bindi*; turning to a make-believe chest, he would mimic taking out jewelry, such as bracelets, rings, necklaces, and earrings. He would then look at them as he imagined Sita would, decide which pieces to wear for the occasion, and slip them onto his body. In that moment, he made Sita the most elegant, beautiful, and desirable figure. In sum, I learned how to perform an ideal Indian Hindu goddess/woman by watching her per- formed by a Malaysian Muslim man (who converted to Hinduism). Despite the contradictions, it was powerful to watch him perform. He was an amaz- ing dancer who had the capacity to transform himself into various heroines before your very eyes.

In demonstrating the ideal ways for a woman to move, he was also show- ing what was not acceptable. The *dola* hand gesture, for example, is a hand with the forefingers held together, the wrist bent, and the thumb placed slightly behind. If the hand is not held with the right degree of finger pressure and at a 150-degree angle from the side of the body, and if it moves out of place even a little, the dancer destroys the elegance of the image. Similarly, if the dancer takes too large a step forward, lifts her feet above her waist, stands with her feet and legs apart (except in the prescribed positions), she is also deemed unwomanly. Essentially, such moves are seen as masculine or demonlike and inappropriate for a woman. These ideals, depicted in temple sculptures and described in literary texts, have obviously been constructed, but this is not always apparent to the student training in the form.

My training was unusual because gurus in India and in the diaspora today are typically Indian women. Students watch their female gurus performing idealized notions of Indian femininity. The disjuncture between the per- former and the construction of ideal Indian women is not as obvious when an Indian woman guru such as Ramya performs because she appears to be per- forming her natural self. Reflecting on my guru's demonstrations, I realize now that he revealed to me that Indian womanhood is a construction that he had mastered and then taught us. Nonetheless, the desire to emulate these model figures and conceive of them as real possibilities was overpowering. Why was that? What was it about this space created in the dance classroom that allowed me to find such resonance as I was growing up? Why did it affect me so much? Why did it stay with me over the years?

I accepted the disciplinary training enforced in the classroom as my guru beat my hand with the dance stick to correct my arm position, to indicate how my wrist should fall, to direct the focus of my eyes, and to amend how I should hold my back. I wanted to become an ideal Indian woman in the classroom and onstage. I bought in to the possibility of the authentic Indian woman, in part because it provided an alternative to the media bombardment of images of Anglo-Australian femininity and hypersexual, blonde-haired, blue-eyed women. I knew I could never find a place in the construction of whiteness, but I held on to the possibility that I could learn to perform ideal Indian womanhood instead. Although I was evoking an "ancient" ahistorical idea of womanhood, it made me feel attractive. I must have known I was playing a construct each time I performed, and yet I loved the feeling of power it gave me when I believed in the authenticity of the characters I portrayed. In later years, when my guru established the Bharatam Dance Company and we performed exotic and ideal Indian women on stages in concert halls and premier art institutions, I felt even more empowered. That is, by rendering myself exotic through the performance of authentic Indian womanhood for a primarily white Australian mainstream audience, I felt empowered, desired, and desirable.[6]

Thus far I have laid out a model of the dance practice with little historical context. I have done this to demonstrate how the form is taught. In other words, the pedagogy of the form is ahistorical, although it does have a unique set of politics. The stories and myths of Hindu gods and goddesses are taught without any significant information about the original dancers who performed the dance style in India or in the United States. Thus, the dance appears to exist in an orientalist immigrant nostalgic vacuum. This unruly spectator has produced an ethnography that is a failure but one that demonstrates the problems of the pedagogical process and ethnographic accounts that only describe the practice without truly interrogating it. Such an ethnography would have us understand Indian dance as a purely middle-class practice in the United States with a specific relationship to the terms of U.S. minority citizenship. But a deeper analysis of the history of Indian women's travel to the United States in the nineteenth century reveals a more complex relationship to class, labor, and the changing rules of U.S. citizenship. As Kamala Visweswaran (1994) suggests, one possibility of a third world feminist ethnography would be to foreground relationships between women in order to understand hierarchies of difference. A comparison between different groups of Indian dancers who have traveled to the United States in the last 130 years reveals significant power differentials based on class, region, and caste.

Failures, Some Conclusions, and Beginnings

After the 1965 immigration act, many Asian male professionals entered the United States primarily on H-1 work visas, and many wives soon followed. Between 1966 and 1977, 83 percent of Indian immigrants entered under the category of professional and technical workers; these were composed of about 20,000 scientists with Ph.D.s, 40,000 engineers, and 25,000 doctors (Rangaswamy 2000). Most were young males, although this opening allowed some women professionals to enter as well. What is not evident in these immigration statistics are the sexualized, gendered trends. There is an apparent heterosexual economy at work in which the male partner in the relationship is the primary breadwinner and professional, while the female is the "homemaker" who might have a university degree but arrives in the United States as a dependent (Rangaswamy 2000). For example, when Asian male professionals came to the United States on H-1 work visas, their wives entered on H-4 dependent visas that did not allow them to work in the United States.

There were some South Asian women who came as professionals in their own right, but the ratio of male professionals to female housewives was greater. It was this gendered situation that enabled South Asian wives to set up Bharata Natyam dance schools in several U.S. cities. Particularly in Northern and Southern California, Indian men had come for jobs as engineers and doctors and later, in the 1980s, as computer professionals. Thus, although major cities, such as New York, Chicago, Denver, and Houston, saw the establishment of numerous Bharata Natyam schools, the number of such schools in California remains the highest (Ratnam 1992).

Several Asian American scholars argue that this selective immigration policy formed a problematic middle-class community dubbed a "model minority." Members of this community rarely understand the irony of this label or recognize its racist implications (Chan 1991, 167–169; Lowe 1996, 6; R. Lee 1999, 149; Prashad 2000, 167). Although the label "model" seems a compliment, it asserts that the community will remain a minority and never join mainstream culture, a fact that escapes Indian communities that pride themselves on their "model" status. The myth also displaces the multiple histories of Asians of other classes and of those coming to America from various parts of the world (Chan 1996; Lowe 1996; R. Lee 1999; Palumbo-Liu 1999; Prashad 2000).

With the welcome offered to Asians in the form of model minority citizenship status, a contradiction arises between assimilation and the multicultural policies of the United States. Beginning in the 1980s, the United States supported a multicultural policy aimed at a celebration of cultural diversity. In this scenario, Asian Americans are valued and encouraged for the exotic, traditional, and ancient practices they bring to American culture, but are still relegated to the margins and thought of as aliens, not American citizens. As Karen Shimakawa (2002) critically and persuasively argues, Asian American bodies are effectively "abject" bodies, always at the margins, repudiated by the center. Several other Asian American scholars detail the historical processes that have rendered Asian Americans alien and not citizens (Chan 1996; Lowe 1996; R. Lee 1999; Tchen 2001).

The biases inherent in the terms of citizenship for Asian immigrants are not always immediately clear. On the one hand, the state encourages the assimilation of immigrant cultures into its historically white mainstream ethic. Eric Kramer (2003, 5) suggests that model minority compliance includes assimilation into American mainstream values, or the minority community's belief that they will be accepted as citizens if they so assimilate. However, unlike Jewish, Italian, Irish, German, or other European immigrants, Asians have been unable to assimilate and become "white."[7] The incarceration of Japanese Americans in internment camps on American soil during World War II and the persecution of Chinese during the Red Scare, Koreans during the Korean War, and Vietnamese during the Vietnam War are examples of how American nationalism has relentlessly defined Asians as alien. Tensions between the United States and certain Asian governments have been used as an excuse for the United States to render Asians perpetual aliens despite their multigenerational presence in America (Lowe 1996). Furthermore, although distinct groups of Asians have lived in the United States for more than 140 years, white America still lumps new waves of immigrants into one category. From the unfair and unlawful incarceration of Wen Ho Lee because of his perceived ties to the Chinese government (despite his valuable work as an American scientist) to the labeling of U.S. Olympic ice skater Michelle Kwon as non-American because her racial features were not Caucasian, there have been countless incidents in which Asians in America, despite their long-term presence, have been rendered alien. The ethnically motivated attacks after 9/11 on numerous South Asian American men and women who are American citizens, not to mention the unfair detainment of several hundred Muslim men purely because of their ancestry, reinforces this systemic violence and lays bare the continued status of Asians as foreigners in the United States.

Compliant citizenship is indeed heavily loaded for Asian American communities. Asian Americans are only beginning to recognize the problems inherent in model minority status. Although they are labeled "model," they remain a minority group that cannot break easily through the proverbial glass ceiling (R. Lee 1999). To cope with racist marginalization, differentiate themselves from more recent immigrants, and gain mainstream acceptance, many in second-, third-, and fourth-generation Asian American communities have strategically accepted the tenets of American assimilation. This has included a turn away from Asian communities toward white American cultural practices and involves exogamy as well. It is precisely this kind of assimilation that post-1965 first-generation Indian parents attempt to avoid in sending their daughters to Indian dance classes. Unlike many other Asian American communities whose cultural embodied practices are not necessarily so closely linked to the agendas of the nation state—for example, Chinese and Korean children learning to play the piano—these Indian parents hope that training in Indian dance, with its link to the nation and ideal Indian womanhood, will offer their children alternatives to exogamic practices and turn them toward endogamous practices.[8]

Because Bharata Natyam is a national dance form (like Kathak, Odissi, and Kuchipudi) that appropriately encodes Indian myth, history, language, art, and social behavior, it maintains links to Indian culture, especially for women, and has become a vital pedagogical tool in immigrant communities. Immigrant anxieties about cultural miscegenation and the loss of "pure" culture can be laid to rest when the community's women, who symbolize the Indian nation, perform and stage immigrant "nostalgia" on their own bodies. Bharata Natyam pedagogy, then, becomes an attempt to instill model Indian culture on ethnic Indian women. This model separates itself from mainstream American culture, and its audience prides itself on an uninterrupted two-thousand-year-old tradition that has absolutely no link to U.S. culture. In other words, the community places itself somewhere between its own orientalist imagination of itself and the struggle for cultural citizenship in the United States (Kwan 2011).

In attempting to maintain the ongoing performance of distinct cultural practices that are ancient, spiritual, and traditional, Indian diasporic communities contribute to and maintain the split between modern and traditional dance in America. In doing so, they help sustain the divisions between mainstream and minority communities and the myth of Americanness, including the view that American dance is white while Indianness and Indian dance is culturally pure.

In presuming the "model minority" thesis, it would appear that Indian dancers in the United States have always been model middle-class practitioners living in their ethnic enclaves and performing and laboring for their own communities. The ethnography I conducted would support such an argument, but this proves to be a synecdochic fallacy. Contemporary middle-class gurus and their students cannot stand in for the whole of Indian dance discourse in the United States since its history in America spans more than 120 years. An ethnohistorical interrogation and genealogical inquiry reveals the complex relationships that Indian dancers traveling to the United States in the late nineteenth and early twentieth centuries have with mainstream U.S. dance and culture. Such an inquiry reveals the fallacy of pure cultures and pure dance products. In the following chapters, I therefore conduct an ethnohistorical inquiry into the relationships between groups of Indian dancing women who have traveled to the United States at significant moments, who have been shaped by U.S. immigration law, and who have shaped citizenship processes.

2

Death, Citizenship, Law, and the Haunting of the Oriental Dancing Girl

On July 9, 1868, the 14th Amendment, which granted citizenship, due process and equal protection to "all persons born or naturalized in the United States," was ratified by South Carolina and Louisiana, allowing it to become part of the U.S. Constitution. (Berger 1989)

When Indian dancers known as "nautch" were first[1] mentioned in New York newspapers in 1880, they engendered deep curiosity, interest, and even admiration.[2] An Indian dance troupe had been contracted by Augustin Daly, the famed theater impresario, to perform interludes during his expensive, high-art opera production *Zanina*. Nautch women were a curiosity and an exotic commodity on the American landscape in 1880, especially considering that few women of color were performing on theater or opera stages at this time. The women in the troupe were prioritized in the newspaper reports and reviews that followed, often to the exclusion of the men. Soon after the troupe's first performance in January 1881, however, the show received poor reviews, and the failure of the production was attributed to the Indian dancers ("A Week of Novelties and Disappointments," *New York Mirror*, January 22, 1881). In the next few decades, more dancers from India arrived and performed on the street, in the circus with P. T. Barnum, in the dime museums, and in sideshows but not on the opera or theater stage. By 1907, nautch dancers had disappeared from the U.S. stage.

The material laboring bodies of the Indian women dancers on the New York stage left audiences disillusioned; they were not the imagined "Oriental dancing girls" of their dreams. The events surrounding the arrival and performances of the nautch women of 1880–1881 that led to their disappearance from the stage are examined in this chapter.

First, my focus on Indian women as artists and laborers uses third world feminist questions, posed by Chandra Mohanty and Kumari Jeyawardana, for example, with which to understand early Indian immigration and consider the violence that U.S. orientalism wrought on brown women's bodies. Using the work of French feminist Julia Kristeva and Asian American performance theorist Karen Shimakawa, I also situate the dancers within the discourse of materiality by examining audiences' "disappointment" after their arrival and point out that this disappointment is racialized through the material manifestation of dancing bodies.

Some of the questions I consider in examining these material dancing bodies include the following: Were the dark, sweating laboring bodies onstage mingled with slapping feet, turning wrists, and swirling skirts at issue? Was the smell of their bodies rubbing against their saris and wafting through the New York theater at issue? Were their saris not revealing enough? Was the lift of an eyebrow or the eager eyes insufficiently suggestive? Did their hips gyrate too slowly? I suggest it was all these things combined. But these questions can be understood only within an interrogation of U.S. orientalist discourse.

The discourse of U.S. orientalism in relation to female dancing bodies is key to understanding the racialization of Indians after the 1881 performances. Like John Tchen (2001), Lisa Lowe (1996), Robert Lee (1999), and other Asian American scholars, I suggest that U.S. orientalism is fundamentally connected to U.S. immigration and labor laws and that dance, immigration, and U.S. orientalism need to be considered relationally.[3] The violence of U.S. orientalism is evident when examining late-nineteenth-century performance practices in relation to racist immigration laws of the early twentieth century—that is, when the "material" bodies of people from the "Orient" are accounted for and not considered in the abstract of the aesthetic.[4] Therefore, I track reports of the Indian dancing bodies and the stages they were relegated to after the perceived economic and artistic failure of the 1881 performances.

Second, I frame the nautch dancers within the context of the anti-Asian sentiment and immigration law that had built up since the early 1900s and culminated in 1923, primarily against Indian male laborers (although Indian women were prevented from entering the United States by the late 1900s).[5] In 1923, following a long and protracted battle over Asian immigration rights, the U.S. Supreme Court ruled that Indians were just like other Asians, meaning that although they were Caucasian, they were not white. They would therefore be stripped of the rights of citizenship. Indian laborers, students, and activists (mostly male) did not understand how this ruling could have come about (Gould 2006). After all, racially they were

Caucasian, and according to the U.S. legislature, they should therefore have the same rights as "white" Caucasians. But the court insisted that the Caucasian right to citizenship was limited to "white" Caucasians. Asian American historians focus on 1923 as one of the most significant moments in the racialization of Indians in U.S. history and as something unexpected for the Indian male laborers who did not view themselves like "other" Asians living and working in the United States at the time (Chan 1991; Espiritu 1996; Gould 2006; Kantha Das 1923; Jensen 1988; Leonard 1992; Prashad 2000; Takaki 1990).

This focus on 1923 comes from a gendered bias. The interest in male laborers from India occludes possibilities of understanding the racialization of Indians that happened much earlier. By examining Indian women dancers from 1880–1881, I suggest that alternate readings of racialization, citizenship, and denaturalization are possible, particularly from an embodied performance perspective. Performance reviews and what happens onstage are linked to the political discourse of anti-Asian sentiment effected through anti-Asian law. In tracking the choreography of the Indian dancers on- and offstage, I am interested in how these dancers' movements relate to Asian bodies being moved on and off U.S. soil.

In this chapter I use the crucial performances and experiences of the 1881 Indian nautch dancers to argue that the 1923 U.S. legal court case was not a surprise. These dancing bodies offered insights into racial discrimination, anti-Asian sentiment, and exclusion laws long before 1923. Studying performances and female Indian dancing bodies creates an opportunity to view how the American public negotiated the racial ambiguity of Indian bodies and reconciled questions of race and gender pertaining to Indians preceding the federal ruling of 1923. Performance also allows a window into understanding how Indian bodies performed race, gender, and citizenship, and how these changed in a very short period of time.[6]

My turn to the nautch women of 1880–1881 seeks to open up sites of inquiry for changing Indian gendered racial formation. What is gained from examining the dancing Indian body as a laboring body on and off the stage in the late nineteenth century? Considering Lucy Burns's (forthcoming) argument about the migrant cultural laborer, how does the temporary work of women performers (as migrant cultural laborers) transform our notions of labor and social relations? How can these laboring bodies offer insights into questions of citizenship for Indians as this citizenship changed over time? The interaction between the ethnographer and unruly spectator's body and the bodies of the nautch women haunting the archive is brought to the forefront because it is an intersubjective encounter. The unruly spectator functions in this chapter to mine the ethnohistory of the dominant archive, to look for "ambivalence" (Bhabha 1994) in searching for a minority discourse and locate the bodies of Indian dancing women who have not been accounted for in either dance or immigration discourses.

Tracing a Nautch Woman's Journey

The unruly spectator enters the library feeling tired and full of body aches and pains. The thought of sitting at the cramped desk, watching reel after reel of unproductive, seemingly useless microfilm for the ninth consecutive day makes my stomach churn and my sciatic pain return. I have been at this desk searching for information about the elusive nautch dancers performing in New York in 1881. I steel myself to complete my search for them in the six remaining volumes of *New York Times* microfilm. I know they are in there somewhere. Even just a few more lines of information would be sufficient reward. I smile politely at the special collections librarian and climb upstairs to the microfilm room. The librarian recognizes me now and automatically hands me a reel I haven't yet seen. "So how is it going today?" he asks politely. I smile and shrug my shoulders. He smiles and motions for me to take a desk. I shuffle slowly and painfully, taking my time to settle at the desk. I see an older woman struggling to hook her film on the reel, and feeling compassionate (because I had been in that situation when I started my research), I go to help her. I then hook my reel up and get settled in. I switch the lights on and rewind the reel. I adjust the magnitude to reflect about half a page at a time and turn the toggle so that I am viewing the newspaper material at the correct angle. My wrist and hands hurt as my carpel tunnel flares up yet again. I pop an ibuprofen and secretly drink from the bottle of water I have hidden in my backpack. I get back to work.

I start moving the microfilm inch by inch, page by page, my eyes flitting from top to bottom and side to side over advertisements for various shows, cigarettes, help wanted, rooms for board, and more. Nothing catches my eye. The word "orientale" here turns out to be describing an exotic animal from the Orient. After about two hours I find my eyes closing. The unruly spectator as historian and archivist is tired and wants to rest. The material before me is blurred now. I rest my head on my hands for a few minutes, but the whirring sound of the microfilm does not permit any rest. I sneak a sip of water, checking to see if the librarian is watching, in the hopes of refreshing my dulled mind, shake my head a few times, slap my cheeks a bit, and do some eye exercises (thanks to my Indian dance training) to make my eyes more alert. This works for about three and a half minutes until I find myself being lulled into a daze once again. I am only at November 1880—still many more weeks', months', and years' worth of examination left.

My hands ache now and I can no longer control the toggle button on the side, and so I involuntarily push the forward button too far, and the film moves rapidly to the end of the reel. Hooray! I think I am done. But then I castigate myself. This will never do. The unruly ethnographer cannot accept that this is the end. I force myself to go back to November 1 and look at each week's edition. My fingers again accidentally slip, and I am taken ahead to November 21. I am tired again, but a small paragraph at the bottom left-hand corner of page 2 captures my attention:

> The dress of the women is peculiar, and in this country would be looked upon as somewhat immodest; but its wearers are said to be very modest and refined, according to the code of modesty and refinement in India. Each wears a satin vest, tied behind, which covers the bosom entirely, but leaves the waist, which is not cramped by the corsets of civilization, uncovered. A pair of satin breeches, extending from the hips to the ankles, completes the toilet proper. Over all is worn a light gauze shawl, or scarf, wound around the body in numerous coils, which lends a light and airy appearance which is very attractive, especially when the wearer is circling around in the graceful "Nautch dance." The ankles and feet are bare, and the toes and fingers are fairly covered with solid silver rings and pearls. The women wear anklets of solid silver and nose rings, their noses being pierced on each side and in the middle, precisely as American ladies pierce their ears. The Indian women wear ear-rings too, and one of them has so many glistening pearls affixed to the ears that those organs are totally hidden.
>
> Two of the women are of the party which performed the "Nautch" dance before Gen. Grant. They are of a soft olive complexion, and one of them is a Cashmere girl. All the women are considered in Bombay to be very beautiful, but the American standard of beauty is essentially different from that of India, and it is not for their beauty that they are brought to this country. Three of them are married to members of the party of jugglers who accompany them. Sahebhjan, the principal dancer and singer, is 18 years old, and the darkest colored of the women. She is one of the best "nautch" dancers in India, and is looked upon there as a great beauty. Bhooribai, another of the most prominent of Indian dancers, is 26 years old. The other three women are named respectively Vagoirbai, 15 years of age; Ala Bundi, 14 years of age; and Oondabai, the latter being a mere child of 12 years. Of the men, Abdoolally Esmailjee is the manager of a theatre in Bombay, and comes with the company to supervise their

performances. Goolamhoosan is a juggler and snake-charmer, as is also Oomerkhan. (*New York Times*, November 21, 1880, 2)

I am stunned. This is by far the most comprehensive evidence I have found of the presence of nautch women in the United States. According to this little scrap of information, five female dancers, along with male jugglers, musicians, and snake charmers, arrived in New York from India. What does all this mean? In what event did these nautch women perform for General Grant? I immediately put my card into the slot and photocopy the page several times to make sure I get this material. I take my time going through the rest of the reel, until the end of December; now I am fully awake and excited. But I find nothing more than some descriptions of a slow December season for the theater and the follies of some artists I am uninterested in.

I go back to September and October 1880, poring over every inch of the material. It takes another three hours. There is nothing more about the nautch dancers. I decide to take a break. I leave my seat, shutting the microfilm machine off. The whirring sound stops. I return the microfilm to the librarian and leave the room for a few minutes to go over the material I just photocopied. There is so much to think about here. That there is finally some detailed written evidence that these women were here on American soil amazes me. I walk out of the library and into the fresh air. I do some yoga stretches on the garden near the library, munch something hastily, drink some hot tea from my secret flask hidden in my backpack, and return to my seat.

I ask the librarian for the next volume, beginning January 1881. I am filled with hope and excitement about what I might find. In January 1881, the *New York Times* provides snippets of description, reviews, and tidbits of gossip about the nautch women brought by Daly to adorn his production of *Zanina*. But I find no more substantial information. I am a little disheartened but remind myself that this is more information than I had hoped to find. I decide to look at the *New York Clipper* next. I want to go straight to 1881, but of course, it is not available at the library, and the librarian informs me that it will take several days to order. I order it impatiently and leave the library thinking about the little bits and pieces of information I have found today.

I do not sleep for several nights thinking about the dancers. I know their names: Saheb, Oomdah, Bhoori, Ala Bundi, and Vagoir.[7] But are these really their names? What did they look like? How did they feel arriving in New York in November? It must have been quite cold. How did they cope with the strangeness of the city, the people, and the performances they were asked to do? As I sit at my computer typing my notes, I realize I need to take a break. This torture will never do. I sit in bed with several pillows to prop me up and a soft cotton blanket to cover me as I read some theoretical material to take my mind off the waiting. "Archive Fever" by Derrida and Prenowitz is good distraction; "Archiving represents both attempting to preserve something to be remembered and leaving out something to be forgotten" (1995). I wonder if this is why the dancers are so elusive. Maybe searching for the dancer's presence in the traces they have left will not provide anything more than shadows. I sleep, dreaming of shadows of dancers walking down the streets of New York in 1880.

Finally, two weeks later, getting my hands on the 1881 *New York Clipper* is a relief. I do not feel any pain this time at the microfilm machine. I am just nervous. The first few weeks of January reveal nothing extraordinary. Then suddenly I come to the front page for the week of January 22, 1881, and I see a sari. My hands shake a little from excitement and tension, and I lose the page. I force myself to steady my hand and return to the page. I feel tears welling up in my eyes. I do not know why I am so moved. I see Saheb, Bhoori, and Oomdah leaning on each other, tightly gripping one another. A photograph of three brown women dressed in saris. Their eyes look at me, and I look back at them. They are black and white, yet there is such clarity and depth to this photograph. It speaks volumes. I think I sit for many minutes just staring at this picture. I emerge from my reverie in fear of losing it or afraid that I merely imagined them. I quickly insert my card and take as many copies as I possibly can. I have the paper in my hand. The dancers are supposed to be remembered, not forgotten. I decide now that these women are meant to be preserved, and in the printing of these pages in the library from microfilm to paper, I am effectively preserving them in an archive I will create for them (see Derrida and Prenowitz 1995). Others who follow may decide that I have left out something else, and they must create their own archives. But in that moment, I felt what many historians have felt—a tremendous emotion, excitement, fear, and trembling at "finding" archival traces that others have passed over or not even felt worth searching for. Although I remember that it took my brown body to seek their black and white and plastic microfilmed bodies in the archive, they let themselves be found. They want their stories told in whatever partial truths remain. The image is even closer to me now. I see the forlorn look in their eyes, the staged positions of their bodies, the protective ways their saris envelop them, the short tight blouses, the numerous bracelets and rings on their arms and fingers, and their bare feet. Maybe Oomdah is not sad, perhaps she smiles a little. What amused her in that photography studio? Did the photographer say something? Did she understand what he said to her? How did they get to New York? On what ships? How difficult their journey must have been. They would not have been able to communicate well with anyone. I am tormented by thoughts of how these women came here. What made them leave their homes in Bombay and take the ship from Calcutta? My eyes close again. I cannot bear to look anymore because of the pleasure and pain these thoughts bring.

I am rocking back and forth in my library chair. The librarian is staring at me strangely. I do not care anymore. Bhoori had traveled onboard a ship bound from Calcutta to New York. Did Bhoori and her companions pass through Singapore and make their way to the West Coast first or straight to the shores of New York? How did she feel leaving Indian shores for the first time in her young life? Did she even know what would happen when she left? Did she know not all of them would return to their homeland?

Perhaps when Daly commissioned her troupe, with its dancing partners, snake charmers, and jugglers, they were excited by the money they would make on their journey. Were they scared of the adventure? Going to an unknown land is often hard, but in 1880 when journeys took so long by ship, it must have felt very difficult. When President Ulysses S. Grant visited them in Bombay, perhaps they were overwhelmed by his presence. Hearing that he had requested their presence in New York, perhaps they thought they must go and honor this man, who had honored them by visiting them and seeing their performances. They knew their room and board would be paid for and, of course, meals as well. What about their fee? It was arguably a hefty sum for a small entertainment troupe in 1881. Did Bhoori get to see much of that money? But how did Bhoori and her troupe handle the long journey of many months on the ship unable to speak to others on land? What happened after they arrived? How did they handle the cold weather and the strange people, places, and events that unfolded around them? Did the initial excitement surrounding the dancers' arrival in New York last for a long time? Were they welcomed with open arms? How were they treated?

I did not have time for a lunch break; I had to find out more. There had to be more. What happened to them? An obituary appeared in February 1881. One of the dancers, Saheb, had given birth to a baby on January 3, 1881.[8] The baby had lived for a few short days and died. Yet another obituary appeared a month later. I found a lithograph in the *National Police Gazette* with the caption "A Nautch Girl's Wake" (February 19, 1881). This time, one of the dancers had become sick and died of typhomalarial fever. I could see the wrapped-up body of the dead dancer as per Muslim custom. Who was it? The lithograph title did not say. I was tormented. Was it Oomdah, Bhoori, Saheb, or Ala Bundi? It took a few more days of research to learn which dancer it was. There were indeed spectators in New York eager and willing to consume any and all information about the Indian dancers, and they were not above making a spectacle of the death of one of them. Some writers were even joyful that the dancer had died since it allowed Augustin Daly to replace *Zanina* with another, more popular production.

By the time Ala Bundi died on February 2, 1881, the Indian dancers were no longer a stage sensation. Audiences were not only bored but also dismayed and wanted the dancers off the stage. Critics and reviewers were particularly punishing in their newspaper articles and were especially joyful when the Indian dancers were taken off the Daly show (Locke 1870–1920).

As I discovered increasingly more material, what I found particularly interesting was the rapid timing of the events and the change in the audience's temper toward the Indian performers.[9] While initial newspaper reports were excited about the dancers' arrival in November 1880, within a week of their performance in late January 1881, audiences and reviewers alike were eager to be rid of them. What had caused this abrupt shift in audience and reviewers' perceptions? I realized it was the conundrum of the Oriental dancing girl.

The Oriental Dancing Girl

Until the critique launched by Asian American and postcolonial scholars thirty years ago, U.S. orientalism (as opposed to the European and colonial orientalism outlined by Edward Said) had been regarded as a benign discourse, particularly in dance and performance studies. The contradictory audience response to Indian dancers in 1881—desiring Asian performance practices and philosophies and then rejecting them—did not occur in a depoliticized aesthetic realm. The gendered racialization of these Indian dancers was indicative of their reception. I consider the presence of material bodies from the Indian Orient on U.S. soil in the late nineteenth century in order to understand how these bodies negotiated different aspects of U.S. orientalism.

Orientalism in the U.S. context has a long, complex, and changing connection with Asians in America. Several Asian American scholars have considered U.S. orientalism to contain various branches (Tchen 2001, xx; Yoshihara 2003, 6–7). John Tchen defines three different strands of orientalism pertinent to American-Chinese relations: *patrician orientalism, commercial orientalism,* and *political orientalism* (2001, xx–xxiii). He suggests that these strands of orientalism have coexisted and are correlated.[10] For example, *commercial orientalism* popularized the desire and consumption of Chinese and other Asian goods, as well as cultural spectacle and even theater. Commercial orientalism was seemingly at odds with *political orientalism*— a strand that resulted in racist anti-Chinese immigration laws as early as 1882.[11] According to Tchen, although not always identified as racialized or even violent, commercial and political orientalism are equally problematic and racist. This indicates that the aesthetics of orientalist discourse were

always in dialogue with the political. The concept of commercial orientalism highlights the objectification of race, making palatable who and what is racialized as an idea, a form, or an object. Political orientalism is then necessary to control and restrain the racialized bodies that demystify the Oriental object, philosophy, or body.

These strands of orientalism are useful to further understand Indians in the American context and can be extended to include what Vijay Prashad calls *textual orientalism* (2000, 68). Prashad suggests that textual orientalism includes the notion of "Indian" in American thought, exemplified in the works of Henry David Thoreau and Ralph Waldo Emerson, as well as translations into English of esoteric, philosophical, and spiritual texts from Asia. Indian orientalist texts such as the Bhagavad Gita had been circulating in the United States since the early part of the nineteenth century and influenced those who have been recognized as quintessential early American writers of the transcendentalist movement. Such books as the Bhagavad Gita captured the imagination of the educated classes (Prashad 2000, 68; Gould 2006, 50). Trade between the United States and India had been ongoing since the eighteenth century, and an imagined exoticism of Indian goods and bodies was pervasive, not only among elites but also among some middle- and working-class people (Prashad 2000, 68; Gould 2006, 50–59).[12] In addition, newspaper reports and material gathered by American traders about dancing girls from India were in circulation (Gould 2006). For example, newspapers such as the *Gazette of the United States* (January 25, 1796, 2) cited articles from the *Asiatic Mirror Calcutta* (November 16, 1794) even in the late eighteenth century, and the *New-York Daily Advertiser* cited an article from the *Calcutta Star* ("Ram Gopal Mullick's Nautch," July 10, 1819, 2).

As dance critic and writer Deborah Jowitt (1989) argues, the Orient has harmlessly figured in the American dance imagination for at least two centuries, either as a sylph or bayadere (Oriental dancing girl), in the ballets of Taglioni in the early nineteenth century. The Oriental dancing girl is a fantastical, exotic image that has played in the minds of North American audiences ever since. Taglioni's ballet *La Dieu et la Bayadere*, also known as *The Maid of Cashmere*, was first performed at the Paris Opera on October 13, 1830, and featured dancing girls from India as its central characters (Jowitt 1989). In 1838, actual *devadasis* (temple dancers from South India) arrived to perform in Paris and London and were called "bayaderes."[13] Newspaper evidence in the London *Times* (September 5, 1838) and the London *Examiner* (vol. 1601, 1838) also records the presence of specific *devadasi* women in London and Paris during this time.[14] The idea of the bayadere, or Oriental dancing girl, quickly found its way from Europe to the United States. This iconic image was the discourse within which the nautch dancers took shape.

Subsequently, newspapers such as the *New York Mirror* ("From Our London Correspondent B," vol. 16, 1838, 175) and *New York Monthly Magazine* (vol. 14, 1839) in the United States also published information about these Indian dancing women. On July 14, 1858, at the Paris Opera, Lucien Petipa premiered the pantomimic ballet *Sacountala*, based on famous Indian poet Kalidasa's play *Sakuntala*. This ballet also featured characters who were dancing girls from India. Lucien Petipa's ballet prompted Marius Petipa (his brother) to choreograph the now-famous ballet *La Bayadere* (*Baiaderka*) at the Mariinsky Theatre in St. Petersburg, Russia, on February 4, 1877, which featured an Indian dancing girl (performed by a Russian ballerina) in the title role.[15] Reviews of these ballets also circulated in the United States. The added mystique of actual Indian dancers was enhanced by reports that U.S. President Ulysses Grant had watched the exotic Indian dancers' performance during his 1879 tour of India (Locke 1920, 38). It was also reported that Augustin Daly, the theater impresario who contracted the dancers from India, used the same manager who had introduced the dancers to President Grant a few years earlier (Locke 1920, 38).

Though the Indian dancing girl had been circulating as an orientalist fantasy in the form of popular ballets, actual dancers from India did not arrive in the United States until 1880 and held their first performance in 1881. The contradictory responses by audiences and reviewers to Indian women dancers reveal the disjuncture between the circulating discourse about the Oriental dancing girl and the actual women dancing on U.S. stages. Indian women's dancing bodies in the early 1880s became the nexus for commercial, textual, and political orientalism.

Most importantly, in 1881, there was little or no language to deal with Indian bodies as racialized subjects in a U.S. context. Unlike Chinese immigrants and laborers who had been brought to the United States since 1810 as indentured laborers and subsequently faced racism and prejudice,[16] Indians were not present in great numbers until the first decade of the twentieth century, and those who were in America were primarily male farm laborers and university students.[17] Therefore, much current research on early Indian immigration focuses on the contribution of Punjabi Sikh, Hindu, and Muslim male laborers, and there is a dearth of material on Indian women.[18] Even research on Indians who were not laborers but activists and students only cursorily mentions women (see, e.g., Basu 1975; Bhoi 1996; Gould 2006; Kantha Das 1923). Indians were peculiarly affected by immigration acts that successfully prevented women from entering in great numbers, in comparison to other Asians, such as Chinese and Japanese, who, despite racist exclusionary laws, were still able to bring their wives at a price. Sukhdeep Bhoi (1996), Harold Gould (2006), and Karen Leonard (1992) note that although Japanese and Chinese men were able to bring their wives with them for a price of $500, Indian men were not. A variety of reasons were provided by the U.S. and Canadian governments, including the threat of unassimilability. But primarily, excluding Indian women would be the only way to prevent the Indian male labor force from increasing in number and creating ethnic minority communities. Additionally, unlike China and Japan, which were still "free" nations, India was under the colonial rule of the British Raj and therefore subject to the laws of Britain. This prevented Indians from being able to have treaties with the United States that served their own interests. Single Indian women were also banned from entering the United States in significant numbers until after 1965.

It is necessary to focus on women as cultural laborers, even though their numbers were few, as this research enables us to better understand the complexity and contradictions of U.S. orientalism, immigration, and citizenship.

Materiality of the Corporeal Dancer

Various newspaper reports described with anticipation the vision of the Oriental dancing girl that had been circulating in newspapers and books, often conflating *devadasis* from South India and *maharis* from Orissa with the nautch women who had arrived from Bombay and Calcutta.[19] The following text reveals how various dancers from India were rolled into one:

> There are many to whom the Nautch girl is the Alpha and Omega of Hindoo [sic] civilization, and who regard all Indian history as revolving on her toes. They have seen her in fantastic illustrations, dancing on the marble terrace of the Taj, at Agra, with moonlight gleaming on the palm-trees, and the sacred river rolling its waters at her feet. They are curious to know whether she will realize this ecstatic vision at Daly's Theatre. (*The Critic*, January 15, 1881)

The *New York Clipper* even devoted a front-page article and photograph to three nautch women: Oomdah, Bhoori, and Saheb, who were to be featured in Daly's *Zanina* the following week (*New York Clipper* January 3, 1881, 334; see also January 24 1881, 358). *Zanina* was a comedic opera in three acts featuring an "Indian dancing girl" as the heroine. The main characters in the play, including the "Indian" dancing girl, were performed by white actresses and actors covered in brown paint.[20] The actual Indian performers would be featured in the "Incidentals" after the second act. As the program explains, "East Indian Divertisement will be given in which will participate the Tribe of Hindoo Natives expressly imported to the country for this play" (Locke 1920, *Playbill*). Since they had not yet performed, there was great curiosity and an imagined exoticism, reflected in the *New York Clipper* feature, about what the Indian women and their dancing would be like:

> It has been written of the "Nautch Maidens" that their dances do not resemble what we are accustomed to call dancing, but consist of light and graceful whirling, most marvelous in its quickness and some-times frenzy, and also in mystic weaving, and of subtle, pantomimic contortions, explained by their songs, and in time and theme with the spirit of their music. They have a warm, olive skin, and many of them are even almost fair. Many of them have a figure of great beauty and natural elegance of movement, which their drapery and rich clothing well become. . . . They are divided into two great classes—one called the Devadasi, or "Slaves of the Gods," and graded according to the ranks of the families from which they come and the dignity of the temples and the idols before which, distinctively, they are supposed to dance and sing. ("The Nautch Dancers," *New York Clipper*, January 22, 1881, 345)

Audiences' anticipation was raised to a fever pitch. Dancers were described as "almost fair" despite the photograph that revealed that the dancers were dark skinned. The dancers' racialization began soon afterward, intimately connecting gender, skin color, bodies, costuming, and dance.

Augustin Daly himself spoke highly of the dancers even before they arrived. He cautioned audiences, however, to open their minds and expect the unexpected. He explained that the dancers' performances would be neither titillating nor "exotic." He also attempted to tell newspaper reporters that the Indian dancers' form was aesthetically different from that of bawdy showgirls and other erotic performers (Locke 1920). In other words, he was asking audiences to consider a dance style alien to them as not simply enter-tainment but as serious performances that happened to be from another land. He requested that they try to understand the structure of the dance form they were about to witness. His warning remained unheeded.

Although the performances initially elicited interest, after the dancers' first few performances, the critical and public response changed dramatical-ly. The reviews reflected audiences' disorientation and disappointment and revealed the incongruity between what they had hoped for, the orientalized Indian dancing body, and the material body performing live in the theater. Audiences and reviewers were disappointed in numerous ways. Since articles preceding the dancers had described them as having "olive" or "fair" skin, audiences were shocked by the dark color of the dancers' skin. They were also disappointed with the dancers' costumes, jewelry, and lack of eroticism. For example, one reviewer noted their skin color first and then their dance: "The copper colored females came on the stage during the musical burlesque. It was an exceedingly grotesque dance in which they indulged, and is said to be the national dance of their country" (*Philadelphia Times*, February 1, 1881, cited in *Brooklyn Daily Eagle*, February 13, 1881, 1). Several writers remarked that the dancers "are not pretty, and their faces were disfigured by ugly ornaments" (*New York Mirror*, January 22, 1881, 7). The dancers wore numerous, large nose rings, which many audiences and reviewers found strange and ugly.

Whether or not they had absorbed what Daly had said, audiences' primary interest was not in aesthetic form but in deciding how to categorize the dancers. Initially, the dancers' racial status was ambiguous, but reviewers soon started creating racial comparisons and began fitting them within U.S. racial frameworks.[21] As noted, previews had described the dancers as "olive" and "fair" skinned; later reviewers described them as "copper," "chocolate," or "dark." One reviewer noted, "The women remind me somewhat of those one sees in Northern Mexico. They are all very dark, and the order of intellectual development to which they belong is apparently not high" (*Denver Tribune*, January 21, 1881). Another regarded them as of mixed race and ridiculed their performance:

> The house was crowded, public curiosity about the Nautch girls and the jugglers having been excited to fever heat; but as soon as the audience discovered that the tricks of the jugglers were stale, even as a side show to a circus, and that the famous Nautch dancers were four little mulatto girls, who twisted their big ugly hands in the air with the grace of a cow and the animation of a China mandarin, the public fled the theatre with words of scorn and smiles of derision. (Locke 1920, 31)

It must be remembered that this review preceded the 1882 Chinese Exclusion Act. Therefore, it is important to understand how Indian women found themselves located racially somewhere between African Americans, Mexicans, and Chinese. There was never a possibility in 1881 that these women (unlike the Indian men who followed later) might be mistaken as white.

Another aspect of the media's racialization of the dancers was reviewers' inability to understand Indian dance or appreciate the dancers' mastery of an art form. For most U.S. audiences at the time, the performance was probably incomprehensible and quite monotonous. The dancers, in turn, were perceived as having no technique:

> The Hindoo [sic] dancers appeared. They came upon the stage to weird music played by an Indian band. Sitting upon a long mat, they commenced a very unique song, which soon grew monotonous. At last they sprang to their feet and commenced the famous Nautch, which turned out to be even more monotonous than the singing. It consists of a very slow, half striding step, during which the girls sway their bodies gradually from side to side, and swing their arms. (*Brooklyn Daily Eagle*, January 23, 1881, 3)

Another reviewer suggested that the dancers showed

> no exhibition of agility, and no pretence of figure about it. To the monotonous thrumming and twanging of the native musicians went on the unvarying shuffle, shuffle, shuffle of the bare feet, the graceful swaying of the body, and waving of the jeweled arms. (Daly 1917, 340)

The dancing, just like the dancers, did not live up to audiences' expectations. To audiences, the music and dance aesthetics were displeasing. The reviewers refused, or were unable, to enter into the dance framework. In their descriptions of the "weird" songs, the slow "half striding" and "shuffle" of dance steps, the "swinging" arms, and the lack of agility, the reviewers distanced themselves from the dancers and suggested that the dancers and their bodies were too alien. But more than anything else, reviewers were disappointed that the dance technique was not more erotic or titillating. Perhaps, had the dancers been more erotic, wrote one reviewer, white audiences might have embraced the nautch women:

> I think the Nautch girls were a disappointment to most people. I don't know exactly what most people expected of them, but I am sure they did not come up to the general anticipation. I fancy that some of the audience whose ideas of the orient may have been a trifle hazy, had rather looked for some kind of indecorous eastern ballet, something a little different from, and a good deal more indiscreet than occidental Paris is prone to provide us. (*Courier des Etats-Unis* February 7, 1881)

Another reviewer complained that the dancers did not show enough of their "brown bodies" to make it worthwhile for the audience. In fact, the reviewer noted, a white actress who had put on dark makeup to play an "Indian" character, essentially doing "brownface," showed more skin.[22] The logic that followed was that if white women could be more erotic in brownface, what was the need for nautch girls? Audiences were not only disappointed by the lack of eroticism in the dancing but racialized the dancers because it was expected that women of color would show more skin than white women performers. As the reviewer from the *Gazette* alluded, Maggie Harold in *Zanina* was far sexier in brownface than Indian women ever could or would be: "Maggie Harold, who personates an East Indian Princess, and artificially browns her plump arms and bosom, shows more naked surface than do the four Nautch girls put together" (*Gazette*, January 30, 1881). So began a proliferation of nautch dancing by white women, who mimicked the dance practices of these Indian women.

Audiences had imagined Oriental bodies of temple and court dancers, swathed in jewels and rich silks, doing sexy, erotic dances to tantalize men. Women of color (particularly Asian women) were hypersexualized within the discourses of both orientalism and U.S. racialization. Indian dancers did not live up to that expectation because they remained more covered than expected.[23] While "otherness" had been an attraction before the dancers' arrival, the dark, unsexy Indian dancers proved not to live up to the terms of Oriental otherness.

The dancers who came to the United States were street performers from Bombay and Calcutta. Some were perhaps theater artists, since one of the men in their troupe was a theater manager from Bombay. It was also reported that they were part of a troupe that traveled to fairs and exhibitions to earn what they could (*Denver Tribune*, January 21, 1881), but this report seems to have been ignored by reviewers and audiences.[24] As dance anthropologist Pallabi Chakravorty (2008) and historian Sumanta Banerjee (2000) note, by the 1880s, and certainly by the 1890s and 1900s, court dancers had likely migrated to the urban centers of Bombay and Calcutta, after the British annexation of their towns and kingdoms. Some, stripped of their former courtly profession, had turned to prostitution, theater, fairs, and street dancing. The dancers who arrived to perform in America were therefore a contradiction: many were from those urban environments, far removed from courts and temples—if they had ever been there in the first place. These dark, urban, Indian dancing women, some of whom also happened to be traveling with their husbands (the musicians, jugglers, and snake charmers accompanying them), did not appease the appetites of white bourgeois theatergoers.

With respect to Indian bodies, the discourses of the commercial and political strands of orientalism conflicted with each other. The rhetoric of textual orientalism instilled in audiences the expectation of the Oriental dancing girl, the promise of exoticism from the desired other, but this desire remained unfulfilled in Indian women's performances in 1881. These warring strands of orientalism had to be worked out to reconcile the presence of dancing women from India on U.S. soil. But this reconciliation materialized in unique ways, and only when the brown woman's body was removed from the equation. This is precisely what theater impresario Daly did.

Removing the Body of the Brown Woman Dancer

Backers, financiers, and reviewers reminded Daly every day that his opera *Zanina* was a flop and that his debt was rapidly increasing. Costs were accruing on an astronomical scale. The show's failure and expense were laid at the feet of the nautch dancers. A reviewer noted, "If Mr. Daly had produced Zanina as an opera-bouffe, pure and simple, and had not been led astray into ways that are dark and tricks that are vain by the peculiar Hindoos, he would have made another fortune out of his profits. His mistake, however, is one that is very easily remedied" ("A Week of Novelties and Disappointments," *New York Mirror*, January 22, 1881, 6).

By February 6 (just a few weeks after their January 18 premier), Daly removed the Indian performers from *Zanina* and reworked the show. As noted earlier, Ala Bundi died February 2 of complications from typhoid malaria, and another, Bhoori, was inflicted with pneumonia. Instead of showing compassion, one reviewer reveled in their removal from the stage: "Mr. Daly still continues to present his generously mounted musical and spectacular comedy 'Zanina.' The Nautch girls one of whom is dead and the others already dying, have happily been eliminated from the spectacle" (*Evening Star*, February 6, 1881). Although complaining reviewers and audiences seemed pleased with this decision, the show's fortunes did not improve. For some critics, *Zanina's* extravagant costuming, staging, and spectacle could not compensate for an incomprehensible form and structure. Was it a play, a musical, an opera, or a comedy? It was too strange to be successful. Perhaps Daly had been trying to reproduce Indian theatrical styles that combined music, theater, dance, comedy, and drama; if so, that form was as unreadable to New York audiences as the nautch dancers were. *Zanina* was withdrawn February 12 and replaced with a revival of *Needles and Pins*, a show with a traditionally white cast (*World: New York Sun*, February 4, 1881). The swift end to the Indian dancers' run in Daly's theater had larger ramifications for the future of Indian dance in the United States.

Several reviewers had already suggested that Indian dancers did not belong on serious opera or theater stages. They were, after all, just curiosities

and spectacles, like other people of color who were being displayed on different stages, and should therefore be relegated to these "other" stages. In the
words of one reviewer, "The whole of the Hindoo [sic] show could be omit-
ted to the advantage of the play, and relegated to its place in an exhibition of
curiosities, where it properly belongs" (New York Clipper, January 29, 1881).
Another declared that the Indian dancers were not even good enough to be
curiosities and should be shipped back to India and fed to the tigers (Locke
1870–1920, 31). Interestingly, despite this brutal language, Indian dancers
found their way to the National Stage in Washington, D.C., February 1,
1881 (Philadelphia Times, February 1, 1881, cited in Brooklyn Daily Eagle,
February 13, 1881, 1). Yet, even with a good performance review of the
"burlesque" interlude of their performance in, they were not invited back to
the National Stage or any other theater or opera stage. Effectively, Indian
performers were sidelined to innocuous stages as curiosities and replaced
on theater stages by white women who were considered serious artists. This
displacement of Indian women dancers from "national" and "main" theater
stages to sideshows prefigures the movement to denaturalize Indians and prevent them from entering the United States after 1924. Just as women dancers were removed from center stage to the margins in 1881, and excluded
entirely from U.S. stages by 1907, Indian male laborers were denaturalized
and excluded from the nation decades later.

After this initial "failure" of Indian female dancers on the New York theater stage in 1881, Indian performers moved to the streets in P. T. Barnum's
circus shows and into dime museums and world fairs.[25] While the troupe
Daly had recruited in December 1880 apparently returned to India, in March
1881, a new group of performers replaced them. By 1884, Indian dancers
were performing with P. T. Barnum, along with jugglers, acrobats, and other
"Hindus" displayed in the show. Several advertisements for Barnum's show
during this period feature nautch dancing; however, it is impossible to determine where they were from, since nautch was a term used for all Indian and
even some Middle Eastern dance practices by this time.[26] Lithographs and
posters advertising the Barnum show depict North and South Indian as well
as Sri Lankan dancers (J. Davis 1993). By 1885, there were casual references
to nautch dancers on display in a dime museum in Boston (Wood 1885);
since no performers' names were mentioned, it is unclear whether these were
the same dancers brought to the United States by Barnum in 1884 or some
who stayed on after Daly's show closed in 1881. Periodically, Indian dancers continued to appear in P. T. Barnum circus shows, street performances,
sideshows, and world fairs in the 1890s, and on Coney Island from 1904
until 1907.

These troupes of Indian performers managed to earn some money exhibiting themselves and their performance techniques for a limited period of time. As John Tchen (2001) suggests, Asian people had been displayed as freaks, oddities, and exotics since at least 1831. It would be too simplistic to say that P. T. Barnum circus shows, theaters, and museums unilaterally took advantage of nautch dancers. It is possible that Asian performers knew how to sell themselves.[27] Much like other Asians who exoticized themselves to make a living in the mid- to late nineteenth century, such as Miss Pwan, Quimbo Appo, Chang and Eng (Tchen 2001), and even those in the Tong Hook Tong Chinese Theatre Company (Lei 2006), nautch women may have chosen to exploit American orientalist desire.

Asian practices were ultimately needed to help define and constitute the boundaries of whiteness and Americanness. As we have seen, however, while the labor of Asian bodily performance was desired, Asian bodies themselves were not. Therefore, white citizens in the United States simply performed these practices themselves.[28] Some middle- and upper-class white women in theater and popular dance forms echoed nautch dance, particularly in the establishment of Oriental theater and circus productions.[29] By March 27, 1881, about a month after the Indian women's departure from the New York stage, white women were mimicking nautch dancers (Odell 1939, 315). "The St. Felix Sisters and Four Nautch Dancers" were performing in New York by June 6, 1881, and continued their performance as "The Naughty Nautch Girls" until late August 1881 (Odell 1939, 317–318). Clearly, the latter performance of "Naughty Nautch" by white female dancers was designed to titillate audiences in ways the Indian nautch dancers never could. In the decades to come, large-scale dance performances such as *The Nautch Girl, Lalla Rook's Welcome,* and *The Man from Bombayo* (J. Davis 1993), to mention a few, would predate American modern dance in the twentieth century, which would have its own more hidden links to brownface minstrelsy (P. Srinivasan 2007). India and the Orient had to be "performed differently" to match the American palate; this reality led to the transplantation of Indian performance practices onto white, often bourgeois, female U.S. bodies.

As white bourgeois women absorbed and restaged dance practices from India, Indian performing bodies and their labor were no longer needed. The state cemented this exclusion with anti-Asian immigration laws. Thus, the kinesthetic legacy of nautch dancing women was absorbed by white artists such as St. Denis and rendered invisible within the North American modern dance project. Indian dancers were denied assimilation within U.S. citizenship discourses, even though their bodily labor was necessary and inherent in the evolution of U.S. modern dance.

Death of Citizenship

I return now to the deaths of Saheb's baby and Ala Bundi, which were so horrifically spectacularized in the papers. Reports and lithographs proliferated in newspapers immediately after fourteen-year-old Ala Bundi's death. The youngest and most beautiful of the dancers died a few days after her friend Saheb's baby passed away. This child was perhaps the first American child from Indian parents on U.S. soil, who then died as a brown American citizen. Ala Bundi, for her part, left her bodily remains on U.S. soil. For audiences who had seen the Indian dancers' performance onstage, and for many who had not, Ala Bundi's death and "wake" was yet another performance to be reviewed, recorded, and memorialized. Yet what is particularly important is the symbolic significance of their deaths. Ala Bundi was a failed dancer because her ill health prevented her from ever appearing onstage. She was also a failed immigrant in that she did not capitalize on her trip to the United States by gaining citizenship. Their sacrifices were manifold, and one could argue that they were for naught, at least in the nineteenth century.[30]

In the symbolism of the corpses of the Indian dancer and Saheb's Indian American child, we see the contradictory expulsion/inclusion of the Asian American subject reperformed. The child, born on American soil, a brown child of Indian descent, could not be reconciled with the needs of a national identity that privileged the white male Euro-American. Ultimately, no reconciliation was required because the child died, in effect expelling himself. What this child's corpse signifies is the border of the body—the national body.

Julia Kristeva, the Bulgarian French philosopher, contends that scholarship must give the materiality of the body primary importance. Kristeva's formulation works toward a material understanding of the body by connecting the body, complete with its drives, back into discourse. Bodily fluids and wastes also perform important functions. For Kristeva, the corpse functions as the fundamental bodily waste, which helps differentiate the subject from its object.[31] According to Kristeva, the threat posed by the corpse produces an abjection that reminds the living subject of her constant, unstable border position as a possible corpse, a corpse-to-be, and a body that is at all times near death:

> There, I am at the border of my condition as a living being. My body extricates itself, as being alive, from that border. Such wastes drop so that I might live, until, from loss to loss, nothing remains in me and my entire body falls beyond the limit—cadere, cadaver. If dung signifies the other side of the border, the place where I am not and which permits me to be, the corpse, the most sickening of wastes, is

a border that has encroached upon everything. It is no longer I who expel. "I" is expelled. The border has become an object. How can I be without border? . . . Abject. It is something rejected from which one does not part, from which one does not protect oneself as from an object. (1982, 3–4)

The question of the border of the body is obviously significant in understandings of selfhood and otherness beyond the psychoanalytic realm, particularly as it highlights the living subject's sense of embodiment and "liveness." This brings up questions of the "live" body, the material condition of this "live" body, and the discourses in which it is embedded and creates. The notion of the "abject," being without border, also alerts us to national borders and the framing of a citizen or alien. I find this concept particularly useful in examining the death of Saheb's baby, especially as it exposes the threat of the alien who gives birth on U.S. soil. I am concerned with embodiment and the materiality of the corpse and the "live" alien body. Paying attention to the movement of this "live" body enables us to examine the body beyond the static condition of "bodies," or even beyond the self-other dichotomy.

Karen Shimakawa (2002) argues that the Asian American body is in and of itself an abject body. The abject here refers to the expulsion of the corpse of the Asian body, dead after laboring for the nation-state. Shimakawa, drawing from Kristeva, uses this theoretical framework to think through the contemporary Asian American body onstage. I use this theory to rethink the two literal corpses of the Indian dancer and Saheb's Indian American child in symbolic terms. This contradictory expulsion/inclusion of the Asian American subject that is constantly reperformed is of particular relevance in understanding the wakes of Ala Bundi and Saheb's baby and what their corpses signify.

Seeing the corpses of two brown bodies, one Indian and the other American, created a crisis for white audiences. These bodies amplified the horror felt by white mainstream Americans when they came to realize that Indian dancers were not aesthetic bodies onstage but were material and thus could live and die. These living, breathing, and dying material bodies had entered the boundaries of the nation-state, rupturing the great orientalist fantasy. The material bodies of brown Indians thus had to be expelled to resolve the crisis.

The corpses and the reaction to the corpses by American audiences in newspaper reports thus foreshadowed the anti-Asian immigration policies that would mark the U.S. landscape in the decades to come. Asian bodies would have to be expelled even while their labored artistic practices would be absorbed. Yet the absorption of Indian dance practices by white female

bodies that followed was the other face of this abjection. There was an inges-
tion of Indian dance forms even while actual Indian dancing bodies were
excreted from U.S. soil.

By the time Indian women dancers disappeared from U.S. stages,
"Oriental dance" was reborn in a white American dancer: Ruth St. Denis.[32] A
few years after Ruth St. Denis absorbed the nautch dancers that she saw at
Coney Island in 1904, brown female Indian dancing bodies were deported.[33]
This is the epitome of the abjection of the brown Indian dancing body. The
ramifications of this absorption/expulsion are explored further in the next
chapter.

Conclusion

In the 1922 *United States v. Ozawa* case, the Supreme Court ruled that only
Caucasians could be naturalized, a ruling that denied citizenship to Chinese,
Japanese, and other Asians. Since Indians considered themselves Caucasian,
they believed they would not be subject to this ruling (Chan 1991, 93–94;
Takaki 1990, 298). However, in 1923, the landmark court case *United States
v. Bhagat Singh Thind* revoked all citizenships granted to Indians (Chan 1991,
93–94; Takaki 1990, 299). As mentioned previously, this culminated the
long debate on the question of race and citizenship for Indians in America.
Although the court considered Indians to be Caucasian in a "scientific" sense,
they nonetheless did not qualify as white. Indeed, according to Takaki, the
Constitution had to be reinterpreted to account for this anomaly:

> "It may be true," the Court declared, "that the blond Scandinavian
> and the brown Hindu have a common ancestor in the dim reaches
> of antiquity, but the average man knows perfectly well that there are
> unmistakable and profound differences between them today." The
> law "does not employ the word 'Caucasian' but the words 'white per-
> sons.' . . . The word 'Caucasian' not only was employed in the law but
> was probably wholly unfamiliar to the original framers of the stat-
> ute in 1790." The intention of the Founding Fathers was to "confer
> the privilege of citizenship upon that class of persons" they knew as
> "white." (1990, 299)

All naturalized citizens lost their citizenship overnight, and many Indians
were forced to leave the United States and return to India. This mandate
primarily affected Indian male laborers and students. By 1917, Indian women
were hardly in the picture because laws had already been enacted preventing
them from entering the United States.

The 1923 ruling need not have been such a surprise to Indian male labor-ers. Indians had already been deemed "not white" from the moment Indian women dancers stepped onto the U.S. stage in 1881. Debates over race were being worked out through the bodies of Indian women dancers in this "first encounter" on- and offstage. The various intersecting discourses of U.S. ori-entalism played themselves out on the bodies of Indian dancing women, and the violence of U.S. orientalism was manifest the moment Indian performing bodies materialized on the U.S. stage.

The Indian woman as artist/laborer in 1880 slid between laws that cur-tailed Asian women and men's immigration because there was little language in the United States to understand her racial position initially. She was Caucasian, but it was not until she arrived in the United States that she was assigned a position of color. Although Indian women initially had some free-dom to enter the United States and perform on national theater stages, audi-ence and reviewers' responses to their performances racialized the women and curtailed their movement between various "stages" soon after their arrival in New York. This shift in the U.S. understanding of Indian dancers demon-strated how Indians began to be racialized even before Indian male laborers arrived in great numbers.

Although the dancers were greeted with orientalist desire upon their arrival, the bodily materiality of their dark skins and the perceived lack of eroticism in their dances forced them off serious theater stages. The changing reviews demonstrate that part of the problem for viewers was to reconcile the imagined exotic Oriental dancing girl with the fleshy, moving bodies present in the U.S. nation space. The death and wake of one dancing girl and anoth-er's baby added to the negative materialization of Indian bodies in American minds. When the material, moving, bodily encounter with the imagined other occurs, especially in one's own backyard, the orientalist viewer must create distance from the disruption. The movement of Indian dancers to more lowly stages reflected white audiences' quick handling of this rupture, by reassess-ing the dancers' place in the hierarchy of U.S. performing arts.

Although Americans had already determined Indian performers' rightful position in the arts, it would take decades for the law to place Indian bodies within the hierarchy of citizenship. But the law was neither all-encompassing nor without loopholes. For instance, the arrival of Indian women performers contracted by Daly in 1880 predates the entrance of the first few contract Indian male laborers in 1882.[34] The women's arrival also violates the law barring the immigration of Asian women to the United States; in 1878, the U.S. government prohibited Asian women from entering the United States, and it often labeled those who did come "prostitutes" (Chan 1991, 105). Indian women dancers were initially racially ambiguous and not yet viewed as Asian, thus escaping detection. Indian dancers were circulating in the United States between 1880 and 1907 and escaped the boundaries of another law: the 1885 Alien Contract Law.[35] This law prevented the entrance of foreigners to perform "labor" but didn't prohibit performers, artists, and the like, who were not considered "laborers," from entering the United States.[36] Despite this law, Indian women performers came to the United States on limited contracts and were paid a wage for their labor (*Brooklyn Daily Eagle*, December 12, 1880, 3). Their performances escaped detection as labor because they were perceived to be doing the work of culture. Indian dancing bodies left traces through their dance practices despite having their bodies removed from the United States.

The simultaneous ingestion/excretion of dancing practices and dancing bodies offers insights into how female Indian dancing bodies peculiarly negotiated the terms of citizenship. These examples demonstrate how transnational female Indian dancers' bodies were negotiating immigration law that curtailed other Asian bodies, precisely because of their ambiguous racial and labor status, albeit for a short period of time.

What is particularly interesting is that the nautch women who arrived in 1880 were not the only dancers traveling to the United States. Some made even more spectacular impacts on U.S. culture, which have yet to be examined. The next chapter outlines one such interaction that occurred as more Indian dancers made the difficult journey across the ocean to reach U.S. shores.

3

Archival Her-Stories

St. Denis and the Nachwalis of Coney Island

I t was in graduate school during a classroom video presentation when
I first saw a *hamsasya* mudra formed perfectly on the right hand of a
white female dancer known as Ruth St. Denis (one of the three "foremothers" of American modern dance).[1] I was gripped with a thirst to know
how and why a white woman in a black-and-white film dating to 1941
could so expertly form a mudra, a hand position that had taken me quite
some time to master. I could tell by the tension and placement of her
finger on her thumb that she had imbibed the muscle memory of forming this mudra over time. Which Indian dance guru had trained her? As
the unruly spectator in her early years of formation, I asked my professor
how this was possible. Why was a North American Caucasian woman
credited as a "foremother" of American modern dance performing a movement located in Indian dance? I formed this mudra with my own hand as
I watched St. Denis doing so on the screen before me. I was even more
astonished when I was informed that *Radha*, the dance piece St. Denis
was performing, dated back to 1906 and was indeed the signature piece
that launched her career as a solo and independent artist. When I read
her biography by Suzanne Shelton (1981), I was led to believe that St.
Denis happened to see some Indian dancers but that she had not learned
to dance from them. Rather, she had conducted research in a library and
was further inspired by a cigarette poster of an Egyptian deity. But St.
Denis's hand, precisely forming the mudra, and her bodily movements,
lifting her skirt in spiral turns, told a different story. As a professional

Indian dancer, I could see and "feel" that St. Denis's training could not have come simply from library research. As the unruly spectator, I felt the kinesthetic traces of Indian dance training that were present in St. Denis's body. While I discovered later that much had happened to St. Denis between her 1906 premiere of *Radha* and the 1941 film of it, photographs and reviews of her 1906 performance led me to search for the bodies of Indian women dancers buried in the archive, who had so clearly inspired and given over their dance practices to St. Denis. This search ultimately became an ethnographic encounter between my body and those of the Indian women dancers documented in the archive. That encounter is staged in this chapter.

While the *nachwalis* discussed in Chapter 2 were deeply buried in the archives, the *nachwalis* discuss in this chapter were even more elusive and could only be excavated through a postcolonial, performative, and "ambivalent" reading of the biography, diary, and autobiography of St. Denis (Bhabha 1994).[2] I also examine the possibility that *nachwalis*' artistic labor was transmitted between bodies and can therefore be excavated through the basic dance principles of movement. These Coney Island dancers were temporary migrant workers visiting the United States for only a few years. Thus far, no photographs give a clear visual record of their presence. But it is this very absence that pushed me to write about them and thus create a dance "bodily archive."[3] Their performances were temporary, but the legacy of their dance remains in the transmission of movement. St. Denis's biographer Suzanne Shelton carefully details various dances performed by St. Denis. In particular, she describes St. Denis's turns and whirls in terms of nautch dance movements in her performance of *Radha*. It is therefore only through an engagement with turns, whirls, and dance movement itself that the labored hauntings of nautch dancers can be understood in terms of their contribution to dance, citizenship, and U.S. labor history.

Contextualizing Nautch at Coney Island

Early Indian dancers continue to find themselves written out of the archives of dance and cultural history despite having influenced several white female performers. White Caucasian female dancers such as Ruth St. Denis battled patriarchy to emerge as independent figures in their own right and claim rights of citizenship. While their work is recorded in multiple historical archives, laboring Indian female bodies that also contributed to American culture have disappeared. In attending to this labor of dance in this chapter, I, as the unruly spectator, am interested in how the terms of citizenship change for both Indian and white dancing women in the United States.

Although the encounter between *nachwalis* and St. Denis is mentioned briefly in dance writings, there are no accounts that lend much credence to this meeting, let alone that nautch dancers may have contributed to St. Denis's emergence as a choreographer. Countless writers confine St. Denis's beginnings to a single moment: an orientalist poster advertising cigarettes depicting "Egyptian deities" (see, e.g., Coorlawala 1992; Desmond 1991; Erdman 1996; Khokar 1961; Shelton 1981; St. Denis 1939). Assuming that St. Denis's creative flair could not have come from corporeal interactions with the nautch dancers she saw in Coney Island in the summer of 1904, and whose forms she imitated artfully in the years to come, dance writers have bought into the idea that St. Denis's dance ideas derived from library research and that her individual genius then emerged through the performance pieces she subsequently created.

St. Denis was concerned with reproducing the spectacle she had seen at Coney Island called the *Durbar of Delhi*. Using her interactions with nautch dancers and Indian male performers, she emerged as an economically independent woman choreographer. At the turn of the century, St. Denis and other white bourgeois women were for the first time taking center stage as choreographers and performers in their own right. Having been previously marginalized, white bourgeois women were resisting patriarchal dominance in a variety of creative ways. As Linda Tomko (2004) rightly points out, white bourgeois women were fighting for suffrage and the right to enter the public sphere in the early twentieth century. When white bourgeois American women are battling against patriarchal control over labor and for political, social, constitutional, and citizenship rights, they simultaneously seize representational and discursive control by using the laboring practices of people of color for "cultural capital" (Williams 1983).[4] Even though modern and postmodern dance historians fail to remember the nautch women whose labor prompted St. Denis's creation of *Radha*—the first elaborate piece she premiered after seeing the exhibitions in the Coney Island "spectacle"— St. Denis's white female body in performance highlights and testifies to their kinesthetic legacy.

As discussed in Chapter 2, nautch women have a history in the United States, and the Coney Island nautch dancers were not an anomaly. An unusually high number of Indian dancers were brought from Bombay to Coney Island by Thompson and Dundy in 1904.[5] Simultaneously, P. T. Barnum brought another group of dancers from South India and Sri Lanka for his New York shows, and another troupe from Sri Lanka were brought to the St. Louis World Exposition. It is the Coney Island troupe that is of concern in this chapter. It seems that the female dancers brought to Coney Island were primarily from northern India, although some were from Sri Lanka. Although the evidence is ambiguous, it appears that this troupe was dancing a precursor of the "classical" form known today as *Kathak*. In making some of these observations about the dance forms in India during this time period, I am informed by Pallabi Chakravorty's (2000) work on women dancers in Kolkata during the nineteenth and early twentieth centuries.

It is significant that Indian dancers traveled to the United States between 1880 and 1904, because dance in India was undergoing a massive transformation at the time. The Indian anti-nautch movement began in 1892 as Indian nationalists opposing the colonial government linked dancing girls to prostitution and urged a "boycott of nautch dancing at formal occasions" (Meduri 1996, 56). This culminated in the Abolition Act of 1947, although the colonial government had already issued an inquiry about the *devadasi* practice by 1872. Effectively, dancing women bore the brunt of nationalist negotiations with colonialist ideals, through which, ironically, the agendas of empire and nationhood became identical.[6] Although the dancing women were not valued, their dances were. Their dance was subsequently modernized, classicized, and reconstructed on the bodies of upper-caste and middle-class Indian women by the mid-twentieth century. Certainly, in the late nineteenth and early twentieth centuries, nautch women were not the most likely ambassadors of Indian culture to the West. It is not surprising, then, that nautch women who came to the United States during this time have been written out of both U.S. and Indian dance histories.

My argument in this chapter is threefold. First, I suggest that although dance scholars have begun to acknowledge the bodies of people of color who have contributed to American modern dance,[7] far more work needs to be done to examine the influence of intercultural connections. I contend that a reexamination of the inception of modern dance from Oriental dance reveals the labor of Indian dancing women and men, which has been rendered invisible. This calls the "national" and modernist project of American dance into question.[8] By attending to Indian female dancers as laborers, we can understand their contribution to American nationalist cultural practices in meaningful ways.

Second, I suggest that a focus on gendered bodily discourses and practices opens another archive in interrogating orientalism. Following the work of Edward Said (1979), discussions of orientalism that examine knowledge and power have largely focused on literature.[9] It is here, then, that I ask what happens to the theory of orientalism when corporealities are made central to the investigation of colonialism (in this case, U.S. imperialism), knowledge, and power. I argue that contradictions and racist overtones come to light that were previously sidelined in North American orientalist discourse. The violence of North American orientalism and its racist underpinnings have left

marks on bodies both through enactments of exclusionary immigration policies and through representational and discursive control. A close analysis of
St. Denis's early performances reveals a deep imbrication within the violence
of orientalist discourse. Rather than focus on only the spiritual, I ask what
an examination of the material can do for our understandings of St. Denis's
performance. Therefore, I am calling for an interrogation of dance and Indian
dancing bodies as they intersect with immigration law. In Chapter 2, I
argued that at the moment of contact between Indian dancers and New York
audiences in 1880, the racial formation of Indians was taking place, and anti-
Asian sentiment was already under way. Here we see the development and
material repercussions of the anti-Asian bias on the terms of citizenship for
both Indians and white Caucasian bourgeois women.

Third, I argue for an examination of kinesthetic contact among dancing
women, as well as the discourses of living, breathing texts produced by these
dancing bodies, rather than a narrow focus on the written record, which I
term the *bodily archive*.[10] The significance of bodily contact and the subsequent kinesthetic exchange between St. Denis and the nautch dancers must
be highlighted.[11] I suggest an examination of discourses by and through the
body by focusing on its corporealities, where bodily reality is not seen as a
"natural or absolute given but as a tangible and substantial category of cultural experience" (Foster 1995, xi). Such a focus on the performing body as
its own archive reveals alternate understandings of dance practices in North
America. Turning to the bodily archive also enables a look at how the terms
of U.S. citizenship were contested, lost by particular gendered and racial
subjects, and won by others. Examining this period between 1904 and 1924
allows us to track the shifting terms of citizenship as they played out and
were challenged by Indian women dancers and white women dancers.

I am informed by subaltern and postcolonial scholar Gayatri Spivak, who
argues that feminist historiography's key method is excavation but that this
process is always caught in a double bind. Spivak posits that the subaltern
woman whose story has not been told in the official archive is always outside
representation, and therefore, bringing her into representation evacuates her
subaltern status (1988, 1999).[12] In her essay "Can the Subaltern Speak?"
(1988), Spivak suggests that although the subaltern might speak, she is not
really heard. I acknowledge the impossibility of recovering or representing
nautch women as subjects in their own right. Rather, I take up the call of
subaltern postcolonial scholars such as Spivak, Gyan Prakash, and Dipesh
Chakrabarty to find the partial, fragmented, and hybrid subject within the
"colonial"—or "imperialist"—U.S. archive. For example, Spivak argues that
the subaltern subject emerges only when she is needed in the space of imperial production. As the historical record is created, who is dropped, and when

and why, is directly related to the imperatives of imperialism (Spivak 1988). Critical historical dance analysis is difficult at best because of the ephemerality of performance, but a focus on corporeality and kinesthetic exchange offers an opening for bodies that have been unaccounted for.[13]

I begin to tell nautch women's stories while acknowledging that these stories can only be partial, filled with half truths, and at times, fictive.[14] In the process I am not creating another originary moment, or faulting St. Denis for a partial history; rather, I offer an alternative to the singular dominant history of the dance encounter between St. Denis and Indian nautch women and men. I also acknowledge that it is through my own training as an Indian dancer that I interrogate the archive from a kinesthetic perspective. It is only after my own bodily reaction as a dancer when I saw Ruth St. Denis's hand forming a mudra in a black-and-white film that I began this journey.

Beginning with a critical analysis of dance scholars who have failed to account for the encounter between St. Denis and the *nachwalis*, I move toward an interrogation of this dance meeting between St. Denis and the nautch women, offering insights based on newspaper reports from New York and historical records from India and discussing the absent-present as it is enabled through a kinesthetic perspective.[15]

I suggest that an attention to bodily practices in terms of the bodily archive reveals the kinesthetic legacy that Indian dancers left on white bourgeois women, such as St. Denis, that enabled her to stage her entrance into the public arena and emerge as a "citizen" of the United States. This chapter, in effect, challenges current dance history accounts that do not allow room for the possibility that the kinesthetic interaction of multiple laboring bodies creates new dance forms, as opposed to an individual genius choreographer, who magically creates movement through library research or a spiritual reaction to an image on a poster. Accounting for this bodily labor ruptures simplistic, essentialist origin myths that aspire to pure beginnings and, instead, unearths the potential to rethink dance, women, and labor history in America as a complex, rich amalgam of forms and processes.

Ultimately, I suggest that the dance practices of Indian performers enabled Ruth St. Denis to enter the public sphere and stage the terms of cultural citizenship for white middle- and upper-class women. The singular citizen body was enabled by the labor of many bodies. Indian women performed as contract laborers and were forced to leave the United States because of racist immigration policies that targeted Asians. However, I suggest that their bodily practices left behind kinesthetic traces of dance culture. These traces enabled white women like St. Denis to obtain cultural capital and emerge as economically independent solo artists; it also enabled them to negotiate full political citizenship rights during the battle for female suffrage in the United States.

The Origin of American Modern Dance: A Cigarette Poster?

> The music becomes threatening, building to a furioso, as Radha rises and twitches her hips. Her skirt whips angrily from side to side. One elbow leads her into a spiral turn. Reversing directions, she turns restlessly until a *nautch* whirl possesses her. As she spins one hand makes its own agitated rotation . . . she writhes and trembles to a climax, then lies supine as darkness descends. (Shelton 1981, 61; emphasis added)

Dance scholars such as Uttara Coorlawala (1992), Jane Desmond (1991), Joan Erdman (1996), Deborah Jowitt (1989), Mohan Khokar (1961), and Suzanne Shelton (1981), to name a few, note that St. Denis saw nautch dancers at Coney Island in the summer of 1904. They dismiss this encounter as insignificant and focus instead on a cigarette poster as the proto-text that inspired St. Denis. I refer here to the cigarette poster featuring an Egyptian deity that has, metaphorically speaking, blown smoke over the nautch women themselves since it is the single, most cited explanation for St. Denis's emergence as a choreographer. Perhaps these writers were influenced by St. Denis's autobiography, in which the author attributes her initial creative stage to her reaction to the poster:

> I saw a modernized and most un-Egyptian figure of the goddess Isis. She was sitting on a throne, framed by a sort of pylon. At her feet were the waters of the Nile with lotus growing. . . . Lying on my bed, looking at this strange instrument of fate, I identified myself in a flash with the figure of Isis. . . . I knew that my destiny as a dancer had sprung alive in that moment. (1939, 52)

This passage suggests that individual genius sprang from an intense reaction to an advertisement, an orientalist poster purporting to depict an Egyptian god. Although the poster image is pure fantasy, St. Denis identifies with a god she considers to be Isis. While the poster may have inspired St. Denis, I contend that it was her bodily encounter with Coney Island nautch dancers that enabled her to create her first piece. Indeed, St. Denis returned to her original *Egypta*, inspired by the poster, only in 1910, after she had already completed *Radha*, *Snake Charmer*, and *Incense* in 1906.

The other wellspring for St. Denis's genius most often mentioned in dance literature is her library research—even though St. Denis admits the Coney Island spectacle captivated her, particularly the snake charmers and nautch dancers. In her autobiography, she admits, "When I reached home that evening I had determined to create one or two Nautch dances, in imitation of these whirling skirted damsels. . . . [W]ith these I was sure I would find some vaudeville bookings" (1939, 56). Suzanne Shelton, St. Denis's biographer, views the nautch dancers as non sequiturs who merely prompted St. Denis's research in the Astor Library.

> She had in mind something like the Indian dances she had seen the previous summer at Coney Island, where the world-famous durbar, or gathering of Indian potentates, was reproduced as an *East Indian sideshow, complete with rajahs, snake-charmers, and nautch girls.* Looking for information on India, Ruthie went to the Astor Library where, in true Belasco fashion, she *researched her ideas.* (1981, 50; emphasis added)

As this passage demonstrates, Shelton suggests that St. Denis researched her ideas from textual sources and emerged a genius in the performance piece she subsequently created. Nautch women's bodily encounter with St. Denis is marginalized in this account. Interestingly, dance critic Deborah Jowitt (1989) remarks that St. Denis admitted to a reporter in 1905 that she had been influenced by the Coney Island dancers (131). However, Jowitt seems to suggest that St. Denis did not believe this to be an encounter that was authentic enough to deeply influence her work. Dance scholars who focus on Indian dance, such as Mohan Khokar, Uttara Coorlawala, and Joan Erdman, support the view that the nautch women were insignificant in the development of U.S. dance. Instead, these scholars look to the influence that Western dance has had on the revival of Indian dance, particularly in the 1920s and 1930s. Since Indian nationalist history has sought to erase Western connections in Indian dance, Khokar's, Coorlawala's, and Erdman's contributions are significant in redressing this imbalance. However, in the process, Erdman ends up arguing for an originary moment for Indian dance in Western dance, which blocks the possibility of an exchange between India and the West before the 1920s. The privileging of the "classical" also informs Erdman's argument for the inception of Indian dance in Europe:[16]

> While it is true that twentieth-century Indian dance is a historical consequence of the idea of oriental dance, which did in fact originate in Europe, the dialogue between oriental dance (European) and

classical dance (Indian) was a complex interchange of expectations and discovery. Actual Indian dance influenced programs of western artistes only after their interest in the feminine divine principle and in the play of the gods provoked Ruth St. Denis and prima ballerina Anna Pavlova to seek authentic Indian dance and dancers in India in the 1920s. (1996, 290)

Erdman's account dismisses nautch women (perhaps because their dance would not be considered classical) and does not problematize Euro-American Oriental female dancers' practices. While Jane Desmond (1991) offers an insightful feminist psychoanalytic critique of colonialism, orientalism, and sexuality in St. Denis's work, she does not consider evidence of St. Denis's visit to the Coney Island show. Thus, Desmond, along with other dance scholars, has failed to examine the brown female bodies behind the smoke of the cigarette poster.[17] In rethinking dance scholarship regarding this encounter, I use a postcolonial lens to read the biography and autobiography of St. Denis with an ambivalence that, by privileging the corporeal dance encounter, allows for multiple possibilities.[18]

The Dance Encounter

During these days someone took me down to Coney Island. I was mildly intrigued by the sights and sounds, but my whole attention was not captured until I came to an East Indian village which had been brought over in its entirety by the owners of the Hippodrome. Here, for the first time, I saw snake charmers and holy men and Nautch dancers, and something of the remarkable fascination of India caught hold of me. (St. Denis 1939, 55)

Ruth St. Denis was one of the millions visiting New Coney in the summer of 1904. The nautch dancers did not take much notice of this one white woman among the throngs passing by and therefore never quite understood the impact they had made. They, too, eventually returned to India, never knowing they had helped to ignite American modern dance. Or perhaps they did. Did they know who St. Denis was? Might they have realized the impression they made on the millions of visitors who saw them at Coney Island (*New York Times*, May 15, 1904, 3)? Indeed, it is frustrating not to know their perspective. Because, after all, what remains is but a one-sided account of the encounter in St. Denis's diaries, autobiography, and biographies. Unlike the dances of the *nachwalis* who performed under Augustin Daly in New York, the performances of the Coney Island dancers were not viewed as legitimate art deserving newspaper reviews. What is possible, then, is a postcolonial reading of these fragments to account for the ephemeral bodies that graced these archives. But, more importantly, I pursue the idea that these bodies are moving in the archive; in effect, they are unlocatable, unfixable, and transitory. Just as dancing is ephemeral, and just as temporary Asian laborers are in transit while visiting the United States, so too is their danced labor transitory. It is from the perspective of dance that an account from the "other" side might be possible, not just through a postcolonial reading of absence but through a presence found in the principles of dance and bodily transmission. As the following passage from St. Denis's autobiography attests, she was significantly influenced by the dance movements she saw at Coney Island:

> When I reached home that evening I had determined to create one or two Nautch dances, in imitation of these *whirling skirted damsels*, and possibly a Japanese number, a faint echo of Mme. Sadi Yaco [*sic*]. With these I was sure I would find some vaudeville bookings and, with the money earned, produce *Egypta*. I was very happy over my decision, and went the next day to the Astor Library to do a little research in Nautch costumes. (St. Denis 1939, 55; emphasis added)

Although St. Denis's diary and autobiography record her encounter with Indian dancing girls in the summer of 1904, the accounts are brief. St. Denis describes the quality of the dancing and the costumes that she saw and, more significantly, admits that she was influenced by the event. It is important to note St. Denis's own admission that she experienced nautch dance practice and all its physicality firsthand and that this fueled a fascination, leading to her research of nautch costumes in the library. If we attend to what St. Denis actually says, we begin to understand the materialist dimensions of her desire. She encounters live dancing bodies, whom she blatantly desires to imitate for several reasons. She astutely recognizes that, fascination for India aside, she stands to make substantial economic gain by imitating these live dance forms for vaudeville audiences. Understanding the market for orientalia, she imagines herself becoming successful by performing her own orientalist desire for others and thus garnering cultural capital. In obtaining this cultural capital, St. Denis achieved stardom as a female status symbol, which was no small feat for a woman. St. Denis believed she was witnessing an authentic "East Indian village" of Indians who were not performing but in fact "living" as they would in their homeland.[19] Perhaps we can think of St. Denis as a dance anthropologist who was restaging "the natives" for widespread American consumption.

In her accounts of the creation of her dances, particularly *Incense* (1906), St. Denis admits she did not know how everything came together:

My first Indian dance was a jumble of everything I was aware of in Indian art, but with little sense of balance and continuity. Ideas came in a stream and from quite unrelated sources . . . *I thought in terms of scenes and not of technical virtuosity.* Mother and I moved our bits of toast about to indicate where the Indian water carrier came in and spoke to the fruit seller, where the merchant's stall was, and where the brass seller squatted to watch the snake charmer's exhibition. (1939, 56; emphasis added)

St. Denis acknowledges her ideas came from unrelated sources. Of particular note is her admission of interest in "scenes." These scenes reflect many elements of the Coney Island show she had viewed, yet she gives the source no credit. Newspaper reports of the time gush and revel in the exotic spectacle created at Coney Island and reflect the "scenes" that St. Denis describes:

There was the Vice Royal palace in the city that had been reproduced in miniature, and a pageant of Oriental splendor was presented. There were guilded chariots and prancing horses, and trained elephants and *dancing girls*, regiments of soldiers, and an astonishing number of *real Eastern people* and animals in gay and stately trappings. . . . In fact there was a charm about the streets of Delhi that kept the people spellbound until the exhibition ended. Five thousand people at a time saw this remarkable show, and then went back to see it a second time. (*New York Times*, May 8, 1904, 5; emphasis added)

There are only brief mentions of the nautch dancers. The spectacle as a whole, with animals and large numbers of costumed people, captured this journalist's interest. But for St. Denis, it was the nautch women who mattered most, even though she conveniently forgets their centrality and focuses instead on the broader show.

An interview with Frederic Thompson (an impresario of Luna Park) reveals that elephants and Indian performers had left Calcutta in April 1904 on ships that were expected to arrive in New York before the summer opening of Coney Island on May 7 (*Brooklyn Daily Eagle*, April 10, 1904, 5). It is remarkable that Thompson was able to secure a contract with these dancers to bring them to New York, particularly when "traditional" dance and dancers were under attack in India. Newspaper reports and firsthand accounts of *Durbar of Delhi* offer slightly different information about the whole spectacle. While some reports refer to the dancers as part of a procession, others suggest they were part of a separate show. Photographs of the procession offering partial views also suggest the order in which nautch performers might have been viewed. Apart from one or two brief accounts, we do not know what the dancing looked like or what was being performed. Using this piecemeal material, I offer a view of how the dancers might have been seen in relation to the larger event. In the next section I offer a deconstructive method that takes into account my own complicity in the project of an impossible recovery. I lay bare the notion that my representation of nautch women is an intersubjective, ethnographic encounter between my body and the archive.

The Staging of Nautch at Coney Island

The audience stands before a grandstand that faces a staged city street. The street is lined with bazaars selling spices and trinkets as would be seen in the streets of Delhi, and to one side is a mosque resembling the Taj Mahal (*New York American and Journal*, June 17, 1904, 16–17). The parade begins in the distance before a backdrop of the Himalayas. Six female nautch dancers lead the parade, "brilliant in reds and yellows, with sloe eyes and graceful bodies," and bend from side to side, swaying and moving slowly to the music (*New York American and Journal*, June 17, 1904). Following is a procession of elephants with their Indian male mahouts. The elephants are decorated with silk and velvet saddle-cloths (*New York Daily News*, March 20, 1904, 10). *Howdahs* from India are mounted on top and covered with more than two thousand brilliant lights, which sparkle and dazzle at night, but it is daytime now. Winding their way down the main street of Luna Park, steered by their mahouts and the "rajahs" seated on them, the elephants are followed by chariots, soldiers on horses, soldiers on foot, and then camels. Musicians, acrobats, jugglers, snake charmers, "artisans," and "yogis" bring up the rear of the procession, dressed in reds and yellows that match the color of the roofs and buildings of Luna Park (*New York Times*, May 8, 1904; *New York Times*, May 15, 1904; *New York American and Journal*, June 19, 1904; *Brooklyn Daily Eagle*, April 10, 1904). In performing for the *Durbar of Delhi*, the dancers would have created quite a scene (*New York Times*, May 8, 1904, 2; Shelton 1981, 50; St. Denis 1939, 55).

As the parade fills up the "streets of Delhi," the audience is treated to a short five-minute performance by dancers, musicians, jugglers, and snake charmers. In the background are "merchants" selling their wares in the bazaars. The dancers then stand in two rows and perform before the bazaars on one side. They trace rhythmic patterns with their feet, following the sound of the drummer who accompanies them. They start spinning, and their skirts fly out in the wind. They are indeed eye catching and together with the snake charmers seem to be the center of attention. All eyes are riveted on them (except for perhaps those of the children, who are distracted by the elephants trumpeting in line behind the performers). As the dancers finish their piece, they move into the background and mingle with the folks in the bazaar. The parade ends with elephants sliding down the chutes into the water below, thrilling the crowd (*New York American and Journal*, May 15, 1904).

It is possible that the dances the nautch women performed were simple versions of *tatkar* (rhythmic footwork) or *tukde* (combinations of rhythmic footwork, hand movements, and turns), which are aspects of folk dance and the *Kathak* repertoire.[20] One dance in particular involved rhythm and series of fast turns and spins, which is perhaps what caught St. Denis's attention and is mentioned in her diary and biography as the dance of "the whirling skirted damsels." The dancers were most likely wearing skirts that would fly out when they spun on their heels. Their hands formed mudras—gestures used only for aesthetic purposes. It is also unlikely that the dancers performed the more complex, expressional aspects of their repertoire, such as *thumris*, which are facial and bodily expressions that interpret sung text.[21] But it is possible that the dancers used facial expression and some elements of mime in their performance, and perhaps even interpreted a *bhajan* (a primarily mimetic devotional piece). This could explain St. Denis's conflation of Indian dances with spirituality, an interpretation that became a hallmark of her work.

Dance Labor and Bodily Transmissions

St. Denis's creation of the dance pieces *Incense* (1906), *Radha* (1906), and *Nautch* (1908) reflected many elements of the *nachwalis'* dances. While St. Denis may not have formally trained with these dancers, as a receptive audience member, she did have kinesthetic contact that influenced her creations. St. Denis was particularly articulate with her hands and fingers. Her performance was composed of posing, followed by turns, and a shuffling walk. Several aspects of what St. Denis saw among the Coney Island nautch dancers, such as the *tukde* along with the use of mudras and facial expression, repeatedly emerged in many of her choreographies, including *Snake Charmer* (1906), *Incense*, and *Dance of the Black/Gold Sari* (1913). As Shelton writes,

> Ruth had seen nautch girls at Coney Island, and she added her own hijinks to their basic dance. . . . Through the years St. Denis's Nautch

evolved into half-dozen different dances . . . but always the basic
ingredients were Ruth's character acting, her head-isolations, enticing
arms, skirt manipulations, whirling, drumming feet, and the tinkle of
ankle bells. (1981, 81)

She could not have easily learned these elements solely from her research
of orientalist texts. I am not arguing, however, that kinesthetic contact with
the nautch women is the only means through which St. Denis created her
dances. Clearly, her training in Delsarte[22] technique, her training in Genevieve Stebbins's work (also derived from Delsarte), her focus on yoga practice,
and her viewing of the Japanese artist Sadayakko Kawakami all contributed
to her creations, and all of these influences call attention to corporeal interactions as the basis of St. Denis's work.

The *nachwalis* most likely returned to India, and we do not know what
became of them.[23] The anti-nautch campaign was in full swing in India
as a result of colonialist and nationalist pressures, and soon most dancing
women were forced to leave their art form behind and turn to other profes-
sions. They simultaneously disappear from the North American and Indian
dance archives just as St. Denis's career takes off. In the orientalist tradition, St. Denis's performances were considered the creative imaginings of a
white bourgeois American woman. For countless American audiences of the
time and for subsequent dance writers, it was easier to imagine and desire
Indian dance as a foreign element coming from afar than as a firsthand bodily
encounter among women. Despite the presence of nautch bodies at Coney
Island, U.S. orientalism served to hide this face-to-face encounter behind the
imagined one that enabled St. Denis's career to thrive.

In her early performances, the press and audiences alike mistook
St. Denis for a Hindu princess, a Hindu dancer, and even a Native American
performer (Shelton 1981, 53). For example, when an eccentric and powerful
New York hostess invited St. Denis "and her Hindus to dance in her mansion"
in 1906, the press believed they were Native Americans (Shelton 1981, 53).
St. Denis used such orientalist misidentifications to aid her career, both for
economic profit and cultural capital, and performed the role of the "Hindu
dancer" extremely well. It is clear from her autobiography that St. Denis was
very aware of her participation in the racialized economy of the time. She
contributed to and marketed herself in this economy through her performance
in brownface at the start of her concert performances, in which she covered
her face, arms, and legs with brown paint. Far from contested, the brownface
show was embraced by the New York public (St. Denis 1939, 71).[24]

In the orientalist tradition, St. Denis seized control of the representation
of the Indian "others" and reconfigured their ancient dances through her

own framework. She participated in the rhetoric of mistaken ethnicity and played on these performance mis-tropes for her own ends. St. Denis, in her performances, conflated her own body with that of a brown Indian woman, collapsing the character she performed onstage with herself. Interestingly, it was her mother who reminded St. Denis that she was an American dancer, not an Indian one.

> Up until now we've called you Radha. But as you're going to do other things, I think you ought to use your own name. After all, *you are an American dancer, and not an East Indian*. What was it that Belasco used to call you? Wasn't it Saint Denis?" (St. Denis 1939, 68; emphasis added)

Mother Denis rightly suggested to St. Denis that she had the ability to stage various kinds of Orientals and should not risk being associated with one type over another. This set the stage for St. Denis's other Asian pieces. Throughout her career, St. Denis staged dance practices from Japan, China, Thailand, and Indonesia, to name a few. Like other orientalists who collect Asian objects (Yoshihara 2002), St. Denis became a curator of Asian artistic practices, but unlike other collectors, she housed, displayed, and rechoreographed her collection in, on, and through her body.

For Indian dancing women, orientalist state policy in the form of racist immigration laws did not allow for contestations of dance representation, at least not until the 1940s, with the arrival of traditional female Indian performers such as Varalakshmi and Bhanumati,[25] or, one could argue, even more significantly, not until the 1960s, with the performances of Balasaraswati.[26] But by the 1930s, Oriental dance had metamorphosed into modern dance, and St. Denis's students, including Martha Graham, Doris Humphrey, and Charles Weidman, were performing under its new name. Oriental dance produced another offshoot, ethnic dance, which encompasses dances of the world. Ethnic dance was also propagated by white American dancers such as La Meri. Thus, the kinesthetic legacy of *nachwalis* was absorbed and rendered invisible in North American modern dance.

The multiple valences through which the discourse of orientalism operated perhaps enabled St. Denis to perform as an "authentic" Indian dancing girl because it was easier to imagine the "native" through the white American woman's body than through the "authentic" nautch herself.[27] St. Denis familiarized the unknown by domesticating the foreign, even polluted, body[28] of the Oriental "other" and thereby made her performance safer for American audiences. This removed the need for brown Indian women's bodies to represent "India" aesthetically or literally and left the field open for white female performers to stage "India" for American audiences. St. Denis, however, did not do this alone. She was aided by Indian male performers, whose contributions to her career have also remained unacknowledged. Capitalizing on the desire for Asian goods and philosophies by using her body as a locus for Oriental desire, and aided by several Indian men to authenticate her work, St. Denis enabled white North American audiences to experience the Indian "other" in a safe way. I explore this idea in more detail in Chapter 4.

Nachwalis' labor was effectively effaced through St. Denis's kinesthetic absorption of their dance practices. While Indian women dancers disappeared, their dance forms did not. Their dances helped St. Denis stage herself as a solo, independent female choreographer. Viewing Indian women dancers as laborers helps us understand that while Indians were made into noncitizens, nonimmigrants, and nonlaborers in the United States, their dancing bodies left archival kinesthetic traces that were absorbed by white women dancers. This transfer of cultural practices enabled an accumulation of cultural capital for white women dancers who were then able to assert the terms of their cultural and political citizenship.

Conclusion

> Cawnpore [*sic*], March 10. We are seated in a cool, rather dark room in our bungalow, waiting. Presently, along the corridor, comes the conjurer we have summoned. . . . To our amazement, he says he was in the old Thompson and Dundy performances at Coney Island! He must, then, have been in that troup [*sic*] of jugglers and snake charmers who started me off on this wild career of Indian dancing. (St. Denis 1939, 289)

As this passage suggests, years later when St. Denis visited India, she admitted the contribution of Indian bodies to her dancing. While she does not name particular women dancers, she suggests that the troupe ignited her career in Indian dancing. In this chapter, I have focused on the gaps in St. Denis's biography and autobiography. I have attempted to locate *nachwalis'* moving, dancing bodies in between the accounts of St. Denis's dances and her life. It is their subaltern bodies moving within the spectrum of visibility and invisibility that is key in this discussion. St. Denis's performances, photographs, films, and writing attest to the absent presence of Indian dancers. But these archives need to be mined using dance methodologies and choreographic analyses before these dancers can be made visible and seen moving in these in-between spaces.

4

Legal Failures and Other Performative Acts

1909: Mohamed Ismail [sic] is suing Ruth St. Denis, the dancer, in the City Court for $1250 for services rendered. Mohamed Ismail asserts he originated an Oriental dance which Miss St. Denis is performing at a local theatre, and taught her the steps. Miss St. Denis enters a denial. ("Sues Ruth St. Denis: Mohamed Ismail Says He Originated Her Hindoo Temple Dance," *New York Times*, November 27, 1909, 9)[1]

1911: It was during this tour of the South that one of the Indian boys tried to run away. (St. Denis 1939)

1916: Mogul Khan has married my maid Mary. (St. Denis 1939)

W hen I first saw photographs of St. Denis performing *Radha*, my attention was immediately drawn to the bodies at the edges of the photographs. Most of the photographs show St. Denis front and center, posing in dramatic gestures with her skirt flying, while costumed brown Indian men sit on the peripheries. Their gazes are directed at St. Denis, and their bodies are slightly bent over. They are supposed to function as "Hindu priests." In the 1941 film of the dance piece, however, there are no Indian men on the peripheries while St. Denis is dancing. The film depicts St. Denis as the sole star at center stage, and the men have disappeared. The original function of the men on the stage and their subsequent disappearance piqued my curiosity.

Clearly, St. Denis was informed by many corporeal encounters with Indian male performers who have also remained unaccounted for in dance scholarship.[2] St. Denis's autobiography and Shelton's biography reveal that St. Denis had sustained encounters with Indian male performers who not only helped her create her initial production of *Radha* in New York in 1906 but also other performances. St. Denis hired several Indian "boys," as she called them, to tour with her across the United States between 1909 and 1914, and many records of her performances exist, including several with references to the Indian men who accompanied her. Some of them are noted by name, including Mohammed Ismail, Mogul Khan, and Inayat Khan (the last was a musician who accompanied St. Denis's performances). But many of these men remain anonymous, including several Columbia University students and one performer who tried to escape her tour.

Locating the Indian men who performed with St. Denis in the early decades of the twentieth century not only enables us to view the stagings of deeply racist debates over Asian immigration and labor but also transforms current understandings of it. In other words, a critical consideration of the white female bourgeois body of St. Denis in performance reveals her as a consumer of Indian male labor. In particular, the actions of three male performers (Mohammed Ismail, an anonymous escapee, and Mogul Khan) mentioned in St. Denis's autobiography, but not necessarily in relation to their performances, must be contextualized as labor that goes unrecognized and unacknowledged. However, it is only through an examination of their bodily acts in the archive that their labor can be understood.

While these Indian men fought the systems of power that denigrated and assaulted them, they were unsuccessful in legal terms. For example, Mohammed Ismail's suit against St. Denis seeking $1,250 on the grounds that he had taught her some of her dances was dismissed. The "boy," who I will call "anonymous," who literally and figuratively attempted to remove his racialized body from St. Denis's tour, was forced to serve out the time on his contract as a dance laborer, like other Asian indentured laborers of his time. Mogul Khan, for his part, tried to work the U.S. judicial system and its unfair immigration laws by marrying St. Denis's maid to obtain his citizenship. But he, too, failed in his attempt to stay married and remain a U.S. citizen because of the 1917 antimiscegenation law that rendered his efforts fruitless. Thus, the three men's acts, suing, escaping, and marrying, all failed in a legal sense. However, they also function as performative gestures on the parts of noncitizens, aliens, and colonized subjects, who apart from these brief appearances are otherwise quiet figures in the dominant archives. These performative gestures highlight the labor that otherwise remains unacknowledged by St. Denis. Furthermore, although they ultimately failed to remain citizens and stay in the United States, their actions demonstrate a negotiation with the terms of U.S. citizenship. Attending to their failures enables us to view of them as "actors," and their actions serve as "performances" that did not passively disappear into the archives.

There is kinesthetic value in their bodily performances. The attention to failure rather than success in this chapter involves a particular critique of dance studies that tends to focus on successes. Apart from the work of a few dance scholars, such as Nadine George (2000), Jacqueline Shea Murphy

(2007), and Anthea Kraut (2008), a focus on "star" choreographers as they perform on modern dance stages has been standard. Critical race-theory literature is often built on failures through deviant subjectivity, as the works of George, Shea Murphy, and Kraut exemplify. I build on their work and argue that the stage need not be the primary focus to understand alternate subjectivities, since it is often "backstage" work that goes unnoticed.

I am particularly interested in the conditions that permit these legal failures of claims of citizenship. For this purpose, I investigate what it means to consider the Indian male transnational colored body in performance with St. Denis and, in particular, how his labor became racialized in the United States. I frame these questions around the larger virulent and violent debates over Asian immigration. Indian men were undesired transnationals in the early twentieth century, finding themselves at the nexus of the racialized discourses and practices of British colonialism and U.S. imperialism. Ironically, in the United States, it is the trope of labor that makes Asian bodies visible as subjects (Lowe 1996). Asian bodies have been laboring for white capital for centuries in the United States. The court cases I examine in this chapter highlight that Indian and Asian men were framed through the trope of laborer and predominantly as transient immigrant laborer. It is through the trope of "Asian labor" that Indian men even become visible as subjects in law and in discourses of citizenship (Shah 2005).[3] Their experiences are indeed similar to those of other Asian male laborers at the time, but because South Asians considered themselves members of a different race than other Asians and African Americans, they did not always understand the terms of their racialization.[4] I use the trope of "Asian labor," however, to ask questions about Indian men not as day laborers but as artist-laborers, and therein lies the crucial distinction. What is gained from asking questions about the Indian artist-laborer in relation to other forms of gendered Asian and South Asian male labor at the time? For example, Vivek Bald (2006) maps out a range of work performed by South Asian men, including their role as British maritime workers traveling to Britain, the United States, the Middle East, and Asia as they moved through the circuits of the British Empire, as well as their positions as street peddlers, merchants, and shop owners.

In this chapter I suggest that attending to the question of the Indian male dancing body as a laboring body allows us to examine anti-Asian immigration laws as neither nonnegotiable nor all-encompassing. I thus take a view of subversive acts in the archive using Michel de Certeau (2002). I offer the perspective that examining the "practices of everyday life" of Indian performers reveals microlevel tactics that do not necessarily transform law but demonstrate the strategies that the oppressed use to negotiate power. I am interested in how anti-Asian immigration laws become enacted and how they become contested by Indian performers.

Since almost no books, diaries, letters, or other personal archival materials from these men remain (as with the *nachwalis* noted in Chapter 3), I am working primarily from St. Denis's manuscript collection, using a postcolonial perspective to locate these male bodies ambivalently within the dominant texts, with the understanding that their recovery can only be partial. I argue that key laws pertaining to Asian exclusion must be placed in relation to performance dates to understand changing discourses over time. In addition, I highlight the rise of St. Denis's career in conjunction with anti-Asian immigration law, as this demonstrates how Indian men and women lost legal battles over citizenship even as white women began to win their rights of citizenship.

In Chapter 3, I suggest that early-twentieth-century Indian women dancers entered immigration and dance archives corporeally and left kinesthetic traces of their performance practices. Here, I argue that these three men enter the archive only through their bodily acts, since there is little written record of them. But I investigate the nature of their corporeal entrance onto the archival stage in a different manner. I suggest that the men's labor can be understood through the various bodily actions they perform. These must be read in dialogue to better comprehend the intersection of the racist political economy of immigration law, St. Denis's own participation in this discourse, and the inception of American modern dance. Thus, I contend that various kinds of feminized Indian male dancers' labor must be accounted for in St. Denis's citizenship making.

Sikhs, Swamis, Students, Spies, and Performers: The Conditions of Indian Male Labor

In the early twentieth century, Indian men traveled to the United States for many reasons. As Harold Gould (2006) explains, these men were then variously categorized in the United States as Sikhs, swamis, students, or spies. The term *Sikh* references the earliest immigrants from India, who were Sikh men from the Punjab region. Since Indian orientalism was popular in the United States, several renowned swamis, or guru figures, traveled to America to teach yoga and spiritual mysticism. Many Indian men came to attend major U.S. universities. Finally, many Indian men were also thought to be spies. Because of the formation of the Ghadr Party in California—an organization that aligned working-class farmers and laborers with university students to protest unfair immigration treatment and the British colonization of

India—the British government believed that a number of Indian spies had fled to the United States.

In the first three decades of the twentieth century, Indian independence leaders such as Lala Lajpat Rai and Har Dayal did indeed make their way to the United States, believing it a safe haven from the British. But they soon found that British colonialism and its denigration and racialization of Indian laborers as inferior subjects, noncitizens, and black (within a U.K. context) had begun influencing U.S. immigration policy as well. Although initially U.S. immigration policies seemed more open to Indians, by the second and definitely the third decade of the twentieth century, it was clear that the definition of Indians' race had changed, and they were denaturalized along with all other Asians entering the United States. As mentioned in Chapter 1, until 1923 Indians (primarily male) contended that they were "Caucasian" by race; however, a Supreme Court ruling declared that this term could not be used to define Indians in the same way it was used to define Europeans. In a sense, British colonialism and U.S. imperialism had colluded to render Indians in America black, and they were declared noncitizens of both the British Empire and the United States. They thus came to represent a category of undesired transnationals.

The Indian male performers who worked with St. Denis were also a motley crew of men from different caste, class, religious, and working backgrounds who found themselves becoming undesired transnationals. The only difference was that their undesirability was being staged, managed, and performed for U.S. audiences right next to the white female body of St. Denis. I am therefore interested in examining the contexts that surround the creation, staging, and reviews of St. Denis's early performances to determine how the corporeality of the undesired transnational reveals new insights into issues of race and citizenship in the early twentieth century. I juxtapose the performance of the three Indian men onstage with their performative acts: suing, escaping, and marrying.

Seizing Representation: The Brown Male Bodies beneath the Smoke

By now, as you will see, I had expanded my plans to include supernumeraries. . . . They would sit on the floor and answer in a chorus the questions that I had flung at them. . . . When our evenings came to a close and the boys had drummed for me to dance until I was sure the neighbors would pound on the walls, we went off, very loud and gay, into the kitchen, where the boys made great dishes of curry while

I perched where I might and continued to harry them with questions.
(St. Denis 1939, 56)

As evidenced by reviews and her autobiography, St. Denis often performed
with an entourage of "natives." These men were essentially part of the set
design to bolster the myth of authenticity as she moved between different
stage spaces.[5] Yet official records of St. Denis's performances mark her as a
solo artist until she met Ted Shawn and formed a dance company.[6] For example, Christena Schlundt's (1962) chronology of St. Denis and Ted Shawn's
performance lists all of the former's performances as solo events until she
met the latter in 1911. Although Schlundt includes a photograph of St. Denis
with three Indian male performers on stage, Schlundt still bills St. Denis as
a soloist: "American Tour of East Indian Dances, 1909–1910: Ruth St. Denis,
Soloist" (14).[7] Thus, the Indian men are not seen as performing bodies, let
alone artists, in most accounts of St. Denis's performances.[8]

As nautch women disappeared, Indian male performers began appearing
in St. Denis's shows. St. Denis herself explains that some Hindu, Buddhist,
and Muslim men were picked off the streets of New York, along with male
jugglers from Coney Island, desk clerks, university students from Columbia,
and her brother's friends, who stayed behind and even helped St. Denis stage
her first show, Radha, in 1906 (Shelton 1981, 51–52; St. Denis 1939, 56).
These were men who St. Denis admits she consulted in creating both her
performance and lavish sets that featured the imagined inside of a Hindu/
Buddhist temple. Made up to look like "priests" in the show, these men were
hardly priests, even though they were marketed and represented as such by
St. Denis. They appear to have come from a range of classes, castes, and
religious and educational backgrounds. Everything about them seems to have
been a performance, including their hyperexoticized names.

It is interesting that St. Denis used these men rather than nautch women
to help her with her production.[9] I suggest that this is because white bourgeois women like St. Denis could keep up their artificial—but, at the time,
more culturally palatable—version of the Orient better than the tangible
bodies of female nautch dancers could. Nautch women's bodies were also
dangerous to St. Denis's claims to authenticity in the early years of her performance.[10] Authentic nautch dancing bodies would compete with St. Denis's
onstage, whereas "passive" male Indian actors would not offer competition.
Indian male bodies thus became the substitute for India and Indian dancing
women.

The men added dimension to St. Denis's performance as research subjects and as "native informants" for staging her Oriental dances. By her own
admission, conversations with the Indian men were vital to her creations.

Shelton notes that these conversations were lengthy, contentious, and significant:

> During the autumn of 1905 she attracted a small company of Coney Island Indians, clerks from the Bhumgara store, and Columbia University students and friends of her brother's, an indiscriminate mix of Moslems [sic] and Hindus that turned her rehearsals into religious wars. . . . Ruthie's tiny New York apartment on Forty-second Street, between Eighth and Ninth Avenues, must have seemed the center of strange activity that autumn: streams of Indian visitors, arguments that lasted into the night, the smell of curry and incense, the sound of tinkling bells, the fall of dancing feet. (Shelton 1981, 51–52)

St. Denis herself admits she had a great deal of contact with the Indian men, many on a daily basis. Her autobiography reveals that she used the knowledge provided by the "native informants" to assert her own authority in terms of economic and cultural capital. She thus used them as a dance anthropologist would. Except that they are not credited for their contributions. It was the question of acknowledgment and monetary compensation that Mohammed Ismail took exception to and filed suit over. While few details are available regarding this court case, there exists a deeper, more layered, and hidden archive surrounding this lawsuit. Why was Mohammed suing St. Denis? There had been no legal precedents establishing copyright or "ownership" of dance steps (Kraut 2008). On what grounds was Mohammed suing St. Denis? Did he really think he could win such a case? In one account, he sued her for $1,250; in another it was $2,000. Whatever the case, Mohammed was forced to withdraw his action, and the judge dismissed the case:

> Ruth St. Denis, the barefoot dancer, successfully defended an action yesterday brought against her by Mahomet Ismail, a Hindu who sued her in the City Court, before Judge Lynch, for $2000, alleging that he had taught her some of her East Indian dances. Ismail, accompanied by many of his be-turbaned fellow-countrymen, made a picturesque spectacle in Part IV, of the City Court. But after he had undergone a searching cross-examination about his past as a cook, waiter, and house servant, and had heard Miss St. Denis and various other witnesses testify that she had danced her Oriental dances long before she ever saw him, Ismail asked to be allowed to withdraw his action, and Judge Lynch dismissed the jury. ("Hindu Didn't Teach Her: Ruth St. Denis Successfully Defends His Suit for a $2000 Fee," *New York Times*, May 3, 1910)

The case was indeed a failure in numerous ways. Mohammed (who was a Muslim and not a Hindu, as mistakenly reported) was demeaned in court for being a cook, waiter, and servant, and therefore his authority as a dancer, dance teacher, and choreographer was put into question. In other words, Mohammed was pigeonholed into the stereotype of Asians and Indians as manual or day laborers. Mohammed could not prove that he was qualified to teach St. Denis. Because he was a racialized immigrant Asian laborer, his defense was disregarded, and while being cast into the trope of laborer, Mohammed entered the legal archives.

What was Mohammed's profession? This was the $1,250 or $2,000 question. He was not a "professional" performer, musician, dancer, or artist. When Mohammed had to take whatever jobs came his way to earn a living, he could not justify his profession as an artist. He failed to make the court understand that since dance had fallen into disrepute in India, there was little work for men in the dance profession. He could have told them that in Indian dance tradition, drummers are often part of the dancers' entourage and know and understand dance movements themselves. He might have been the son of a dancer in India and trained there from a very young age, but he failed to say any of these things. Despite being emboldened enough to sue St. Denis along with the help of his fellow "be-turbaned countrymen," Mohammed's discourse fell through the cracks precisely because of the anti-Asian sentiment and unfair immigration laws prevalent at the time. He was silenced by the logic of whiteness, privilege, and power. His labor as a dancer, teacher, artist, or choreographer could not be recognized within the matrix of these discourses of power precisely because within an American context, an Indian cook, servant, or day laborer could never become an artist or "genius" choreographer. Or like other men and women of color, Mohammed and other Indian men were only doing what was "natural." They were not "performing" as such, and therefore there was no artistry involved. In other words, the male Indian body onstage was performing only its "natural" self and was incapable of creating anything "new." Furthermore, since Asian bodies were viewed in the American context as only manual laborers, there was no room for Mohammed to be recognized as an artist. The court pronounced its dismissal of Mohammed precisely because of the way Asian bodies were being classified—as day laborers and nothing else.

Only a white bourgeois woman such as St. Denis could be seen as a creator of "new" performance, because only such a person was viewed as capable of willfully constructing performances. Her labor was made visible while the Indian men's labor was simultaneously made invisible. St. Denis was thus the only body that could take on the role of a professional artist and seize power from "authentic" male Indian bodies, who were ironically rendered "inauthentic" by profession. In other words, the Indian men could only ever serve St. Denis, onstage and off, as laborers. It was their very labor that was effaced by St. Denis and masqueraded as her labor.

However, Mohammed's bodily act of entering a U.S. courtroom to sue did get recorded in several archives, including small mentions in newspapers and one mention in St. Denis's biography. Interestingly, St. Denis never references the lawsuit in her autobiography; it is Suzanne Shelton, her biographer, who briefly refers to it but then dismisses it as a native's avaricious attempt to steal St. Denis's increasing wealth and fame (1981, 95–96). Mohammed's bodily movement from the stage to the courtroom demonstrates his willingness to sue despite knowing that he would likely fail within the U.S. court system of 1910.

We can never know exactly what Mohammed and the other Indian men did or did not teach St. Denis since we are not privy to what aspects of the dance she gained from her "boys," who drummed for her and prepared curry dishes for her as she questioned them. What we do know is that many of them not only served as her "native informants" but also performed onstage with her and labored for her in many other ways. For example, some greeted audience members before the show, others provided drinks and bowed to all the guests, and still others helped set up and take down her large stage decorations. Some were musicians; others quiet attendants offstage. Many were "priests" sitting stoically onstage as St. Denis danced.

The racism that prevailed in the silencing of Mohammed was present in St. Denis's performances. St. Denis admits that when she performed with the men onstage, she received racist heckling:

> I imagine that many of the turns that followed me were concerned with ribaldry and not art, for when the curtains rose and one of the Hindus entered the temple bearing an incense tray on his upturned palm it was too much for this audience and one of them, in a rich Negro dialect, called out, "Who wants de Waitah?" They roared at this and I could see my Hindu priests *stiffening under this ridicule*. (St. Denis 1939, 65)

When St. Denis mentions in her autobiography that her "Hindu priests" stiffened under the ridicule of racial epithets, denigrating them in African American terms by white audiences, she knew and understood what was going on. In other words, when a brown Indian man entered the stage carrying an upturned incense tray, despite whatever Oriental imaginings St. Denis had hoped for, the Indian's brown male body was only understood in terms of the framework of race in the United States. The Indian man was thus viewed as blacks were viewed in the United States at the time. It was the corporeal presence of the moving Indian body that set the discourse for this racialized framing as opposed to the imaginings of orientalist discourse.

As St. Denis herself mentions, the Indian men were aware of the racial politics of the time and stiffened under the "ridicule" of being conflated with African Americans. Fearing for their own tenuous immigrant positions as laborers, and playing off recent orientalist scholarship[11] that had been translated into German and English, they often worked in opposition to other people of color and went to great lengths to define themselves as Aryans and therefore Caucasian cousins of Europeans (Takaki 1990, 294). But not all Indian men fell into this category. As Vivek Bald (2006) persuasively argues, many South Asian men married Puerto Rican and African American women, particularly in the 1930s, and were aware of their racialized status and position. The men who performed with St. Denis were racialized as black men and thus fell into the racial frameworks of mainstream U.S. culture, and although she seems keenly aware of this, they do not seem to be quite as aware.

At least in the beginning, when she premiered *Radha* in 1906, St. Denis knew and acknowledged that racialized tropes were being used to interpret her performance. "The critical reception broke the next day. To the *New York Telegraph* the dances were nothing more or less than a wow! A 'mixture of hoochee-koochee and cake walk'" (St. Denis 1939, 71). Interestingly, a Middle Eastern dance form that became known as the "hoochee-koochee" and the dance form called the "cake walk," made famous by African American dancer Aida Overton Walker, are collapsed to describe St. Denis's performance. Both Walker and "hoochee-koochee" dancer Little Egypt were performing around the same time as St. Denis. It is through these terms that Middle Eastern and African American dances were known and through which nautch dances and St. Denis's performances could be understood. As Shannon Steen (2010) argues, "Race is a system through which multiple racial categories are created, and then combine, split off, and interact dynamically with one another." Particularly in North America, nautch dancers and St. Denis's creations were operating within an ever-changing racialized economy. This economy was one that had denigrated, assaulted, and seized representations of bodies of color for at least a century and was beginning to be questioned in the late nineteenth and early twentieth centuries by African American and Native American performers.[12] However, this was not the case for Indian dancers for a variety of reasons.

Just as the "Cult of Authenticity" was becoming an important discourse for racialized performers, St. Denis was able to overcome the issue and continue her brownface and yellowface acts between 1906 and 1930. After the first few years, however, St. Denis dropped the brownface in her perfor-mances and adopted what Susan Manning terms "metaphorical minstrelsy." (2006). This meant that she stopped using brown paint on her body but continued her imitation of Indian and other Asian dances. But St. Denis's performances were viewed as neither minstrel acts nor metaphorical min-strelsy because Indians did not and do not function in the North American imagination as American citizens who can contest the framing of their own representation.[13] This is partly because Indians and other Asians were subject to anti-immigration laws, but it is also because they have always remained "foreign," even after several generations of presence in the United States.[14] Unlike European immigrants, who can become "white," Asians can never assimilate racially (Okihiro 2001; Chan 1991). St. Denis thus relied and capitalized on what these particular male colored bodies represented onstage in relation to her own white body for a North American audience. She played on the racial and sexual threat the men posed.

Racial Distancing

St. Denis toured a large part of the United States between 1909 and 1913. Many of the Indian men traveled and performed with her, accompanying her onstage as a multitude of "actors" and musicians, providing a contrasting backdrop for her singular white "dancing" body. While touring, the Indian men were subjected to considerable hostility from railway and streetcar con-ductors. They could not sit with St. Denis or stay in the same hotels as she, even in the more progressive northern states (Shelton 1981, 95–96). Indian men were viewed as "colored," as were African and Chinese Americans, for example.[15] St. Denis admits that she was afraid of the ban on mixed-race theatrical companies, particularly in the southern states. She knew that her "Hindoo men" were viewed as "colored" and told reporters she was afraid of booking her company in the southern states. Despite the race problem, St. Denis managed to secure many tours over the years. But it may have been the extreme racism that the Indian men faced on a daily basis that led one of them to try to escape the tour in 1911.

This Indian male performer's escape attempt highlights the immigration debates, particularly as they played out in St. Denis's company. St. Denis notes with frustration in her autobiography that they were able to drag the escapee back to complete the tour with the help of the Indian consulate (then controlled by British officers). She suggests that the Indian man left her tour because he wanted to remain illegally in the United States. Doing so was quite difficult for Indian men in the early twentieth century, because of racism and the highly restrictive immigration policies; thus, it is unlikely that the performer left her company midway through the tour for this reason. Perhaps the performer was tired of working for St. Denis or of the low wages he received and left to seek other options. Perhaps he wanted a vacation from the rigorous performance schedule that St. Denis had set up. Whatever the case, he was quickly and forcibly brought back to finish the tour with the company. As St. Denis explains, he had to complete his contract! In other words, he was a laborer just like other Indian men who were working on farms and railroads at the time and was forced to finish his contractual obligations. Because of his subversive bodily act to elude his employer, this anonymous performer entered the archive of St. Denis's diary and autobiography. Furthermore, his actions demonstrate the ways that immigration law wrote itself onto performing racialized bodies. His labor contract thus made visible this part of St. Denis's performance discourses, which would have remained invisible. In other words, art and dance are often seen as esoteric and in the realm of the aesthetic—acts that exist purely onstage. Labor contracts and the legal terms of power that are involved in negotiations between choreographers, managers, and performers often remain invisible. St. Denis's diary, autobiography, and biographies do not make clear the unequal distribution of power between herself and the performers she employed. By attempting to escape from St. Denis, the Indian performer rendered visible the unequal distribution of power inherent in his contract.

Therefore, it is important to remember this attempted escape within the context of St. Denis's racialized tours. Imagine the impact of St. Denis's white female dancing body surrounded by dark brown Indian men in towns and cities from New York to San Francisco.[16] Five years after their initial performances in New York, and the overtly racist viewings in which the Indians were conflated with African Africans, newspaper clippings from 1911 reveal different readings of the troupe during their tour:

> In one instant as it were, the audience is taken a thousand, nay, 10,000 miles away from Occidental civilization and back into the strange country whose dance is so well described in the sonnet of the little known Francis Saltus. It is not alone that Hindu dances that are presented. *It is a vision of India, not the India of Rudyard Kipling and Flora Annie Steele; not even the India of the burning love poems of Laurence Hope but the native India of the worshipers of Krishna,* presented in scenes of street, and home, palace and garden, forest and temple.
>
> Ruth St. Denis, who evokes this vision and makes it for the afternoon a reality, is an artist in every sense of the word. Aided by such extraneous things are splendid and accurate stage settings, languorous,

haunting, *melancholy Hindu music, chanting Hindu natives, the smell of incense, the tinkle of the strange bells, the throb of native drums,* she takes her audience completely captive by a combination of pantomime and dance that is unlike anything ever before seen on the American stage. ("Visualizes of Motion: Ruth St. Denis Presents Remarkable Series of Allegories at the Mason," April 25, 1911, Denishawn Clippings File, The Dance Collection, New York Public Library of the Performing Arts; emphasis added)

The following writer expresses a strong opinion about the function of the "almost naked Orientals" who accompanied St. Denis:

In the east, incense is a symbol of devotion, and the Spirit of Incense dance is expressive of this thought. Wreathes of pale blue incense smoke quiver in the atmosphere; *clean-limbed, nimble-footed, almost naked Orientals animate the scene, who now stand mute and stoical, and now exchange vivacious greetings.* ("Amusements," 1911, Denishawn Clippings File, The Dance Collection, New York Public Library of the Performing Arts; emphasis added)

There is no doubt that the "natives" produced excitement and tension in audiences, but it is St. Denis's white female body that relieves the situation for audiences. Robert Lee (1999) persuasively argues that in the case of Chinese men, their increasing numbers in domestic service sectors (as, for example, household servants) fueled anxieties about the sexual threat they presented toward white female bodies and the underlying threat of miscegenation. In the case of these Indian men, St. Denis domesticates the alien threat and makes them safe for white audiences:

Miss St. Denis has gathered about her a bit of the east itself and transplanted it to the American stage. *Her attendants and very capable supporters are for the most part natives of the lands she depicts in her dancing.* The musical mantle that goes over it all is so sweetly strange that it disturbs the listener's peace of mind and *produces an uneasiness that is only satisfied when the beautiful dancer flits onto the stage* and melts into the melody as though she herself were the creator of it. (Denishawn Clippings File, n.d., The Dance Collection, New York Public Library of the Performing Arts; emphasis added)

There are several features to note in these three passages that connect to how orientalist discourse operated in the viewing of this performance. In the first passage, it is the corporeal "liveness" of the orientalist spectacle that brings such an overwhelming response for white American audiences. The reviewer bases his reading of St. Denis's performance on extratextual information about India gleaned from literary sources that inform his understanding of the spectacle before him. But the live bodies of the "natives" in contrast to St. Denis are what captivate him. Classic tropes of orientalism suggest that the East is rendered passive and feminized in opposition to an active, masculine West. Similarly, the writer of the second passage describes the natives as at times stoic, passive, and essentially inactive, in opposition to St. Denis's authorial, moving, "speaking" body of the first passage. Perhaps it was the visceral and striking presence of the Indian men, albeit feminized, who stood in contrast to St. Denis's white female form that further authenticated and enhanced her performance in contradictory ways. On the one hand, these men were portrayed as barbaric, which made St. Denis's performance dangerous (at least in a staged and controlled way). Audiences were always aware St. Denis was in control over both the actual Indian male bodies and their representation, but the men still represented the danger of the unknown. On the other hand, her performance was less dangerous because she maintained a clear difference from the men even as they assisted in rendering her performance "authentic," as implied by the third passage.

They rarely came close to her or touched her in performance. St. Denis was always literally and symbolically separate from these men; she performed at center stage, while they existed only on the peripheries of the stage and performance. She never performed for these men since they could not be sexualized beings. They were feminized as other Asian men were, conferring power to St. Denis. Thus, it is St. Denis's body in performance that mediates between East and West. By centering her own white female body and contrasting it with the Indian men, St. Denis thus maintained control and mastery over the unknowable, dangerous Orient. St. Denis's white body allowed the desire for the unknowable and mystical to exist in ways that were safe. By assuming patriarchal control over the representation of India and therefore of Indians themselves, St. Denis stabilized audience fears of the essentially unknowable Orient.

At a time when anticolonial dissent was fomenting in India and the United States and anti-Asian immigration laws were unfolding in the United States, a white woman was assuming patriarchal control over the representation of India and therefore of Indians themselves onstage. As seen in the reviews of St. Denis's 1911 performers, these men evoked India through their corporeal presence onstage, thereby authenticating St. Denis's performances. But when white women could perform the exotic and become the choreographers of staged "live" orientalist visions, the danger of Oriental bodies polluting the American landscape could be laid to rest. St. Denis's show thus surpassed anything an audience could see at Coney Island or in other displays of female Indian dancers themselves, because it is only through the illusion of a white woman performing the Orient that its mystique could be maintained (Yegenolugu 1998).[17] The presence of actual Indian dancers and performers center stage would rupture the mystique of the Orient. During her 1911–1914 tours, St. Denis was benefited by the anti-Asian immigration debates and was effectively staging these ongoing debates over labor and immigration that plagued Indians at the time.

The Disappearing Indian Bodies

I argue in this section that, far from being a benign discourse, North American orientalism manifested in a violent, racialized economy accompanied by anti-immigration laws that enabled a white woman such as St. Denis to perform Indian dances of sorts without opposition or question.[18] Thus, the quixotic love-hate, desire-repulsion, excitement-fear binaries were ever present in the relationship between white Americans and various Asian "others." It was through this complex prism of relationships that St. Denis gave herself and countless numbers of her white female students the discursive, corporeal, and representational power not only to control but also to choreograph how Indian dance would be viewed for decades to come in the United States.[19]

As white women absorbed nautch women's practices, the state played out its irreconcilable and contradictory desire and loathing for Asians in racist immigration policies that curtailed Asian women, including Indian women, from entering the United States (Leonard 1992; Espiritu 1996). Despite a desire for Indian and Asian goods, philosophies, and products, actual Asian bodies were often unwanted.[20] By 1910, Indians had been declared racially unassimilable, although they had actively been recruited for their labor by the U.S. government until this point. From 1909 to 1911, up to 50 percent of U.S. visa applications for Indians were rejected, and the statistics grew steadily worse as the British government pressured the United States to further curtail Indian immigration. From 1907 until 1917, when Congress prohibited immigration from India, 6,400 Indians, mostly Sikhs and farmers from Punjab, came to America's West Coast, and less than 1 percent of them were women (Chan 1991, 18–23; Takaki 1990, 294). The North American immigrant landscape was dramatically transformed for Asians, and Indians were effectively denied a consolidation of community and cultural practices.

In the first two decades of the twentieth century, immigration law prevented Indian men from bringing their wives because bosses thought they were more efficient as a workforce without family distractions, and the law

did not permit women to enter the United States on their own as laborers. The gender differential in immigration policy led to various actions.[21]
It became clear between 1917, when immigration law barred Asians from
immigrating to the United States, and 1924, when Asians were denaturalized
and deprived of citizenship, that although the United States needed Asian
labor, it did not want the permanent presence of Asian bodies. Leonard suggests that systematic racism took place over time:

> There was a rising rejection rate of Asian Indian applicants by the
> Bureau of Immigration and Naturalization. Before 1907, fewer than
> 10 percent of applicants for admission were rejected; in 1907, 28 per-
> cent were rejected; and in 1909, 1911, and 1913, 50 percent or more
> were rejected. (1992, 31)

Indians, who had previously been seen as a solution to the Chinese and
Japanese problem, now became an issue.[22] Racial assimilation was viewed as
impossible because of the different "habits" of the "Hindus":

> The civic and social question concerns the ability of the nation to
> assimilate this class of Hindus and their probable effect on the com-
> munities where they settle. Their habits, their intense caste feeling,
> their lack of home life—no women being among them—and their
> effect upon standards of labor and wages, all combine to raise a seri-
> ous question as to whether the doors should be kept open or closed
> against this strange, new stream. (Takaki 1990, 297)

As Takaki notes, even high-profile[23] Indian visitors, who had no intention of
permanently settling, were not welcome in the United States. Finally, the
1923 Supreme Court ruling against Bhagat Singh Thind proclaimed that
Indians were not "Caucasian" in the popular understanding of the term. In
other words, they were not "white" and were therefore unassimilable. They
became undesired transnationals, noncitizens, and aliens.

In an increasingly hostile environment before 1923, Indian men
had few choices for obtaining U.S. citizenship. Mogul Khan, one of the
last Indian members of St. Denis's troupe, disappeared from her performances by 1918. Mogul Khan had by far the longest relationship with
St. Denis among the Indian male performers (Shelton 1981, 132). Most
likely this was because Mogul Khan had married St. Denis's maid Mary in
1915 and continued performing with the company long after most other
Indian men had disappeared from her troupe. But after the enactment of
the antimiscegenation law preventing white women from marrying Asian

men in 1918, Mogul Khan disappeared from St. Denis's performances and writings.

While Mogul Khan's efforts to stay married to Mary ultimately failed, we are forced to consider his marriage act an important one. Many Indian men married white American women in the second decade of the twentieth century in part because Indian women were prevented from immigrating to the United States. They also married white women because it enabled them to become U.S. citizens. However, after 1918, this was no longer possible, and as Karen Leonard (1992) argues, some Indian men turned to Mexican women instead. In the case of Mogul Khan, we know little except that his marriage to Mary would have been declared null and void after 1918. But it is his performative marriage act that garners his entrance into the archive and causes him to disappear again because of anti-Asian racist immigration policy. He had to stop laboring for St. Denis precisely because of anti-Asian immigration policies. This turn of events then forced St. Denis to bring more white men and women into her company and move away from all Indian performers.

It was amid the implementation of anti-Asian immigration policy that St. Denis's career began to soar; in 1915, she formed a partnership with Ted Shawn and established the Denishawn School and Company. Creatively, St. Denis had a powerful and prodigious choreographic streak from 1906 to 1918. St. Denis began branching out from her repertoire of Indian-themed pieces in 1910 when she choreographed and performed *Egypta*. This was followed by many Asian-themed pieces. A direct comparison of St. Denis's career to immigration issues during the time demonstrates the importance of anti-Asian laws in enabling her career to thrive.

In 1906, St. Denis premiered *Radha,* in company with several Indian male performers.[24] In 1907, Indians were feared as labor competitors by white workers and were frequently victimized by white working-class antagonism and violence. In one case, several hundred white workers invaded the Asian-Indian community in Bellingham, Washington, and drove seven hundred Indians across the border into Canada. That same year, St. Denis left on her tour of Europe. In 1908, the Asiatic Exclusion League, formed several years earlier, discussed the "Hindoo problem." St. Denis created a Japanese-inspired piece called *A Shirabyoshi* in the same year. In 1910, Mohammed Ismail attempted to sue St. Denis for using his choreography without credit. His case was dismissed. The same year, St. Denis premiered *Egypta*, a piece that branches away from Indian themes, and she studied with a geisha in Los Angeles for a few weeks. In 1911, while touring the United States, one of her Indian performers attempted to escape from St. Denis's troupe, but he was caught with the help of the Indian consulate and forced to return to St. Denis's company. In 1913, St. Denis premiered a duet with Ted Shawn called *The Garden of Kama* and a solo piece called *O-Mika*, a Japanese-inspired number, heralding the beginning of many of her Asian-themed pieces beyond India. She also created *Bakawali*, "A Hindu Love Tale of Indra's Heavenly Court," which included four new dances: "Dance of the Gold and Black Sari," "Jewel Dance before the God of Heaven," "Dance in the Forest of Ceylon," and "Dance of the Blue Flame." In 1914, there were few Indian females in the United States, the ratio of Indian men to women being seventy-five to one at its most favorable. That year, women represented only 24 percent of the five thousand Indians in California, and St. Denis created *Legend of the Peacock*. In 1915, the Denishawn School was established in California. In 1916, St. Denis performed her solo *Kuan Yin*, and she and Shawn premiered their commissioned work at the University of California–Berkeley. Mogul Khan was part of the troupe and had married St. Denis's maid Mary. By 1917, an immigration law preventing Indian male laborers from bringing their wives to the United States was enacted. Antimiscegenation laws were also enacted, and Indian men were denied the right to marry white women. In 1918, St. Denis created the *Royal Ballet of Siam* as *United States v. Ozawa* ruled that only Caucasians could be naturalized. Indians believed that since they are Caucasian, they would be granted citizenship. The Denishawn School was thriving and prosperous in California, although St. Denis (1939, 255) suggests that she and Ted Shawn remained poor because they footed the bills for their extravagant shows. Both St. Denis and Shawn took up teaching their repertoires to young working-class and bourgeois white girls and also toured across the United States. In 1923, the case *United States v. Bhagat Singh Thind* ended with the decision to revoke all citizenship granted to Indians. This was the culmination of a long debate on the question of race and citizenship in America. Although Indians were considered Caucasian, they were not deemed to be "white," and the Constitution was reinterpreted to account for this anomaly. In 1924, the Immigration Act preventing all Asian immigration and the right to citizenship was enacted. In 1926, St. Denis created *White Jade* before launching her tour of the Orient.

As the Asiatic Exclusion League systematically worked to prevent Asian bodies from having equal immigration and citizenship rights, the Indian troupe of clerks, students, and sideshow performers began fading out of St. Denis's performances. Thus, the Indian male performers who had worked with St. Denis beginning in 1906 and had accompanied her on tours until 1911, had mostly faded away by the 1914 tour.[25] Friends of St. Denis and Shawn, and students from the Denishawn School whom they had trained, began replacing the Indian men onstage. With the absence of Indian women and only a few Indian men remaining, most of whom were working-class laborers, there was no one to contest St. Denis's appropriation and staging of Indian cultural and dance practices in the United States.

In sum, the white American bourgeois female body assimilated all varieties of racial difference in the modernist project in a safe way for white audiences, thereby relieving patriarchal anxieties over miscegenation, racial mixing, and cross-racial desire. St. Denis consumed the labor of her Indian male performers, thus making the white bourgeois female body an active enabler of patriarchal order. She artfully staged this order for visual consumption and kinesthetic pleasure. There was never any doubt that St. Denis was the star, the choreographer, and the author, who carefully maintained white patriarchal order; thus, Indian male "laborers," like their immigrant counterparts who labored in the fields, continued to labor in St. Denis's performances as extras and attendants. The racial division of labor evidenced through racist immigration policies was restaged through the body of St. Denis in performance. An analysis of the bodily acts of these Indian male performers provides insight into the debates over Asian labor and the ways in which the terms of citizenship were contested, even though there were legal failures in this process.

Conclusion

What is troubling is that, despite a recorded visual presence in St. Denis's performances, the Indian men who performed with her have faded into the background. Although right in front of our eyes, they seem invisible, unimportant in comparison to the primacy of St. Denis's white female body. Their labor appears to have been for naught. But it is their legal failures that call attention to their corporeal presence and bodily labor. An alternative reading of archival data, performances, and photographs in relation to these failures thus allows us to acknowledge their labor. The Indian men who labored for St. Denis first gave their intellectual, creative, and cultural labor to her in her apartment to help create her dances. Second, their laboring bodies onstage helped evoke an "authentic" India even as St. Denis stabilized audience fears of the essentially unknowable Orient. Third, although they could not overcome the racial division of labor in the performances with St. Denis and in everyday life, at least three of the men called attention to their bodily labor through performative acts.

Despite the power differential, Mohammed attempted to sue St. Denis, asking for recognition of his labor in teaching her and calling attention to the ownership of the material she was performing. He put an exact monetary value on it precisely because St. Denis did not. The Indian man who attempted to escape from St. Denis's tour also deserves recognition for making visible the contractual labor agreement between the men and St. Denis. Mogul Khan in his marriage to Mary and its subsequent dissolution also demonstrates how racist immigration law deeply affected St. Denis's company. What these three men's bodily acts also offer is an alternate understanding of labor and the contestations of citizenship. They ask us to consider their performance labor on- and offstage as material and political.

In conclusion, I turn to Mohammed. Knowing that his immigration situation was precarious, that he was giving up a livelihood in touring and traveling with St. Denis, and that he might be expelled from the United States, Mohammed still had the courage to record his dissent. I view this dissent as a performative act because Mohammed was no doubt aware of the racist court system that denied a voice to immigrants and other men and women of color. Yet he still recorded his complaint in the official archives, believing he was within his rights to do so. Although Mohammed's suit against St. Denis failed, his dissent is recorded in the dominant archive. His act therefore not only calls attention to labor that otherwise would have remained unrecognized but also creates the possibility of remobilizing St. Denis's transnational co-performers.

What this chapter ultimately reveals is that white dominance in the form of patriarchy is enacted through the body of the white bourgeois woman, but not without contestation. The white bourgeois woman enacts the imperatives of the state by seizing representational and discursive control of Indian male and female dancing bodies through cultural capital. She is taking control of Indian bodies of color and representing them onstage in the process of combating the power of white patriarchal dominance as it is being enacted upon her. St. Denis is able to do this precisely because of anti-Asian immigration laws. Wielding legal power in court against Ismail Mohammed and on the dance stage effectively enables St. Denis to establish herself not only as a solo artist with enormous cultural capital but also as economically independent. However, those who control representations of Indian dance shift dramatically along with Asian immigration law.

I have examined the possibility that accounting for the labor of Indian male performers enables us to see more clearly the tensions and contradictions within anti-Asian immigration law. Indian performers did not simply let themselves be acted upon; rather, they attempted to act against dominant and powerful legal forces. Despite failing to transform any laws, they nonetheless demonstrate the possibilities of Asian laborers' bodily negotiations with the terms of U.S. citizenship as artists and not just as physical and manual laborers. A focus on corporealities and of bodies performing and acting in the archive offers us new ways of thinking about the violence of American orientalism as enacted on and contested by laboring feminized male bodies and new ways of thinking about the performance of citizenship, even as the terms of citizenship are being denied to them.

5

Intermission and Costume Changes

This chapter addresses the intersection of American modern dance at midcentury with U.S. immigration policy and the effects of this on the movement of Indian dancers to the United States. It functions as an "intermission" to address the so-called gap between two key immigration laws pertaining to Indians in the United States. Using Indian dance and its legacy as the central focus, I theorize that the gap between the 1924 immigration exclusion law and the 1965 Immigration Act reopened America's doors to Asian professional immigrants. Focusing on Indian dance during this period reveals the transformation of the terms of citizenship for Indians in America. While the 1965 moment has been fetishized in Asian American history as the beginning for Indian immigrants, Vivek Bald (2006, 2007) and Karen Leonard (1992) persuasively argue that it is not as if all Indians had left the United States between 1924 and 1965; many actually intermarried and remained behind. However, in terms of Indian dancers, there was a marked difference in the kinds of performers visiting the United States during this period.

Using the prism of dance, I argue that as American modern dance severed its ties to Indian dance in the 1930s, 1940s, and 1950s, the binary between modern and ethnic dance became established along with the binary between the American citizen and Asian ethnic (citizen but not quite). Focusing on the transformation of Oriental dance into modern and ethnic dance reveals how the terms of U.S. citizenship were formed even before the 1965 act was put in place. Venues such as Jacob's Pillow—one of the first international

dance theaters in New York, created by Ted Shawn (of Denishawn fame)
now turned impresario—contributed to the construction of the ideal ethnic
dancer. I suggest that the constructed binary between modern and ethnic
dance paved the way for Indian dance to emerge as an ethnic minority form
and paralleled the development of Indians as "model minorities."

In this chapter I examine the rhetoric of modernity as it developed in the
United States between 1930 and 1965 and as it relates to the transformation of Oriental dance into modern dance. I suggest that this development
reflects the changing terms of American citizenship for white women choreographers and dancers who attempted to perform their purist versions of
what Americanness might be, without acknowledging the hybrid history of
the forms they practiced. An acknowledgement of the hybrid history of their
dance and its specific history of racialized labor would have complicated
and unsettled Americanness and citizenship from a purely white endeavor,
into which it had been rendered, especially with the 1923 ruling that had
denaturalized Asians from American citizenship. I then examine how the
invention of tradition in India during this period enabled the creation of the
classical form of Bharata Natyam, and how it became intertwined with anticolonial and nationalist projects in India. This chapter thus paves the way
for an examination in the next two chapters of the changing and contradictory cultural practices of Indian minority communities in the United States.
This develops themes from previous chapters, which have focused on Indian
dancers before 1924 and their negotiations with U.S. citizenship. The changing class structures of Indians and Indian dancers is the key to understanding
this transformation.

Intermission: The Rhetoric of Modernity

At the end of the 1920s and the beginning of the 1930s, Bharata Natyam
and modern dance emerged as dichotomous forms, the former ancient and
classical, the latter new and innovative. White women gained suffrage in the
United States in 1920, and their right to vote shuttled them into the modern
age, giving them the full rights of citizenship for the first time. American
modernity emerged in part from the creations of independent white women
choreographers during this time. Modern dance clearly materialized in relation to Oriental dance, as many of the new generation of modern dancers
were members of the Denishawn Company, including Martha Graham, Doris
Humphrey, Charles Weidman, Pauline Lawrence, Jane Sherman, and others. As Tomko (1999, 135) explains, however, both Graham and Humphrey's
rhetoric suggests their modernity emerged from individual "genius," thereby
severing ties to their Oriental pasts.[1] Further, critics such as John Martin and

Walter Terry, and dancers like Humphrey and Graham, supported the notion that the "new" dance was a complete break from the past. What is unclear is why this presupposition remained largely unquestioned. When Humphrey and Graham denied stylistic and aesthetic ties with Oriental dance in their own "modern" constructions, none doubted them, and the rhetoric of modernity has ideologically taken into its fold numerous dancers, critics, and writers who have not investigated the possibility that modern dance was not actually a complete break from what came before.

The narrative of American modern dance choreographers and writers that espoused an epistemic break was in effect only arbitrary. It served to construct several binaries: modern dance and traditional or ethnic dance, Americanness and foreignness, white and nonwhite. In effect, this was the most powerful orientalist maneuver: to classify all other practices, particularly Asian ones—including St. Denis and Denishawn—as backward in time, traditional, repetitive, and old, while simultaneously rendering the white "self" as brilliant, new, and modern, thereby setting up a problematic schism between modernity and tradition. This schism continues today. It denies the kinesthetic history and bodily memory of these choreographers. By not acknowledging their bodily training with Denishawn and the impact of their "gurus" St. Denis and Shawn, Graham and Humphrey denied their bodies and, therefore, their own muscle memory in favor of the rhetoric of newness.

Humphrey was clear about why she needed to leave Denishawn:

I think everybody who has ever been with Ruth St. Denis has come away with a little of her vitality and her spark. . . . But what we did gain from her was vision. . . . It was like a university of the dance at Denishawn; we did absolutely everything. Any kind of dance that they could lay their hands on we had some part of, which included American Indian, Spanish dances with roses and a black wig, and Hopi dances with squash blossoms and the legs all done up in white wrappings, and American folk dancing, Japanese, Siamese, Burmese, the world's dances. After a while it began to seem a little scattered. *I felt as if I were dancing as everyone but myself.* I knew something about how the Japanese moved, how the Chinese or Spanish moved, but I didn't know how I moved or what the *American heritage* should be. But it came to me and, I think, to a good many others who were with them, that it was imperative to find out what we were as *Americans* and as contemporary dancers. This led to *a break*, of course, and to a completely *new start*. (Cohen 1972, 265–266; emphasis added)

Humphrey expresses a fear of losing her Americanness in the performance of other cultural forms. She does not view Americanness as a hybrid construction, which it is and always has been. Rather, Humphrey reiterates the common misconception that Asian dance practices, among others, could not possibly reflect an American identity.[2] Humphrey thus negates Denishawn's work as an American project and instead views it as an imitation and/or "inauthentic" rendition of Asianness.

This rhetoric ignores more than fifty years of interconnections between dancers, performers, and people of Asia and America in the American landscape. Interestingly, Tomko suggests, "through appropriation of 'other' dance cultures . . . [St. Denis and the Neighborhood Playhouse] attempted to alter American perceptions of dance as a native endeavor," but this was not successful because "appropriation served at best as an interim strategy," and the exoticization of others no longer worked (1999, 135). Tomko argues that Oriental dance and theater served as a point of departure for modern dance. I suggest that orientalist discourse continued to invoke its presence, albeit in an altered fashion. American dance had already swallowed the artistic practices of other cultures, including Native American and African American (Shea Murphy 2007; Manning 2006; Kraut 2008), and the rhetoric of modern dance masks this fact. This is a continuation of the orientalist discourse that hides the white American desire to borrow from the Asian other. Humphrey's statement above alludes to the idea that Americanness, and therefore American dance, must be a white "native" endeavor, simultaneously suggesting that only Asian people could perform "authentic" Asian dances.[3] This clearly signaled a shift from the late nineteenth and early twentieth centuries when only white women could "authentically" perform Asian dances and Asian bodies were not required.

Martha Graham, who became the new face of American modern dance in the 1930s by offering a break from her past in Denishawn, still had kinesthetic ties to the Oriental dances she learned from Ruth St. Denis and Ted Shawn. Most writers of the time, including John Martin and, later, Graham's biographer Agnes De Mille, contended that Graham's modern dance was unlike anything that had come before. Thus, the binary that set modern dance apart from Oriental dance denied the connections between the two and enabled the neglect of their intertwined history. But bodily connections do not lie. In the following passage, De Mille argues that Graham used yoga as a base for her modern dance constructions.

Consciously, I believe, Martha drew on this simple flowerlike unfolding for many of her basic root positions in the floor exercises. A kind of special ritual, St. Denis's *Yogi* is a kindergarten exercise compared with Graham's floor exercises, which begin all her classes. "Where a dancer stands," says Martha, "that spot is holy ground." Martha sat. It was more basic and it was more oriented. But she did not sit in the lotus position. Martha sat with one leg opened with crooked knee before, the other open with crooked knee behind. It became known as the swastika position and it necessitated an absolutely sprung crotch. (1956, 96)

While De Mille admits to some Denishawn traits in Graham, she foregrounds Graham's work as complex and tough, and denounces Denishawn as simplistic, like a "kindergarten exercise." She renders Denishawn's technique, and thus the Asian forms from which they drew, as simplistic compared with the technologically advanced techniques formed by Graham. The irony is that Graham continued to build on the yoga practice that she began with St. Denis, and this informed her work in the decades to come, especially her warm-up exercises.[4] While De Mille claims that Graham's basic yoga position was fundamentally opposite to the "lotus position" that St. Denis used, the description above is not that different to basic yoga postures that also require an "absolutely sprung crotch."[5] De Mille presses her argument by positing that Martha left behind all the orientalism and exoticism of Denishawn, yet she does not explain Graham's penchant for turning from one Asian exoticism to another.

While Graham stopped wearing saris after leaving Denishawn in 1928, this did not end her fascination with other Oriental goods, costumes, or products. According to De Mille, Graham began wearing kimonos and became extremely interested in Japanese design, aesthetics, and culture (1956, 93).[6] She did not tire of Hindu philosophy or Indian practices such as yoga, particularly kundalini yoga. It is remarkable that modern dance scholars either ignore or refuse to study Graham's deep belief in Hindu ideas, a clear continuation of her orientalism. How is this orientalism, this fascination with a branch of Hindu spirituality and yogic practice, different than St. Denis's? Graham's justification that she was developing a new form of dance completely divorced from that of Denishawn denies her own deeply rooted connections to yoga.[7]

Graham discarded Denishawn's overt mimicry in favor of a more subtle, hidden appropriation. This became the new face of orientalism, couched in the rhetoric of modernity. Asian influences remained unacknowledged. In asserting their modernity, individuality, and unique brand of feminism, both Graham and Humphrey were reacting to the new notion of what Americanness meant. Both choreographers focused on the vision of the individual while negotiating male dominance in America and emerged as pioneer women who created their own independent careers on American stages. However, their success was largely restricted to themselves; at the time, their independence did not extend opportunities to large numbers of women, although for some, a modest career as a dancer was possible within the companies of Graham and Humphrey. The vision of American modernity led them to turn a blind eye to the disparities of a new nationalism spreading in America that ignored the plight of Asian immigrants and people of color.[8]

From Modern to Ethnic: Who Gets to Be Authentic?

Another factor at play in the changing status of Oriental dance was the fluctuation in immigration law. I argue that Oriental dance succeeded in the United States precisely because of the absence of significant numbers of brown Indian female performing bodies—bodies that might question or negotiate with the white female performer's imagined Orientals and their dances during the early part of the twentieth century. Thus it was relatively easy to co-opt and perform Oriental dance without either the dancers or audiences having to face the unwanted body of the Oriental. After 1931, however, the increasing number of performances by Asian Indian dancers who had entered the United States temporarily on visitor visas complicated things. The orientalist narrative, thus, continuously changes especially with the increasing presence of Asian bodies on U.S. stages. The emergence of Indian dancers in the 1930s, such as Uday Shankar, who was increasingly viewed as "authentic" (Erdman 1996, 89), disrupted the orientalist narrative previously constructed on the bodies of white women such as St. Denis, whose dances became "inauthentic." Sal Hurok, the great impresario, invited Uday Shankar and his company to tour the United States in 1932, 1933, and 1934.[9] This twist empowered Shankar and disempowered St. Denis, although the orientalist gaze also feminized him. But there was a new term that emerged to account for the scores of Oriental dancers on stage.

It was the dance critic John Martin who coined the term "ethnic dance" in 1939;[10] however, La Meri also uses the term in her program notes in the 1930s (Hughes 1977), around the same time as John Martin.[11] The term initially suggested that the transition from Oriental to ethnic dance was a natural progression because modern dance was viewed as an epistemic shift from Oriental dance. Thus, Asian dances became "model" but ethnic minority forms.[12] As Rebekah Kowal (2009) notes, Asian dances became ethnic forms right around the end of World War II with America's establishment as a world superpower. The entrance of "authentic" Indian dancers such as Shankar helped create these divides. Several other dancers who performed under a new form labeled *authentic*, took center stage. As mentioned previously,

Shankar first came to the United States between 1923 and 1924 with Anna Pavlova and later with his own company in 1932 (Erdman 1996, 79, 90). Ram Gopal, another male Indian dancer, also came to the United States and performed in New York in 1938 (Abrahams 1974, 129). Bhanumati and Varalakshmi arrived to perform in 1942, Vashi Nataraj in 1947, and Sujata and Asoka in 1949 (La Meri Papers, 1912–1954, The Dance Collection, New York Public Library of the Performing Arts; Abrahams 1974, 142–144). These performers were again only temporary migrant workers often with short-term contracts who did not attempt to gain U.S. citizenship or any kind of permanent settlement in the United States. They were aided in their travels by Indian nationalist reconfigurations of traditional Indian dance forms.

American women choreographers were not the only ones to create and maintain the binary between modern and traditional dance. Just as modern dance emerged in America, Rukmini Devi, with the help of orientalists and nationalists in India, "invented" traditional dance, although she did not label it as such right away. The new traditional form masked its modernity in postcolonial reconstructions of a "pure" and "authentic" national identity, casting itself as the antithesis of modern dance (Meduri 1996, 2005; O'Shea 2007).

The "Invention" of Tradition

What had previously been viewed as Indian, Hindu, or Oriental dance stemmed from Western exposure to nautch dance. As mentioned earlier, *nautch* was a broad term the British used to cover dances from all over India. Generally, the dancers who came to the United States in the late nineteenth and early twentieth centuries seem to have come from Bombay, Delhi, and Calcutta. The brief descriptions of their forms and their subsequent appropriations suggest they were probably performing the precursor of the form known today as *Kathak* and a mixture of what is now termed folk dance. By the early 1930s, dance in India underwent a transformation, particularly with the work of a Brahmin woman, Rukmini Devi. Married to theosophist George Arundale, she was very much a part of the Theosophical Society in India (Meduri 1996).

Sadir had been practiced in South India by *devadasis*, or women married to a temple deity. The practice had come into ill repute, and it was Rukmini who was credited with rescuing the art by restaging it from the temple to the theater. Having been enamored with ballet after witnessing Anna Pavlova's performance, Rukmini decided to study under Pavlova's student Cleo Nordi. Pavlova, however, advised Rukmini, as she did Shankar, to find her own dance form from the rich traditions already present in India (Sarada 1985). It was not until Rukmini witnessed *devadasis* performing in Madras several years later

that she decided to study with traditional male gurus.[13] Far from simply mimicking *sadir*, Rukmini completely transformed it into a modern form. However,
this modernity was of a different type than that of American modern dancers.

Unlike modern dancers such as Graham and Humphrey, who did not
credit their forebears, Rukmini Devi offered both a break from and a link to
sadir, to simultaneously maintain distance from the bodies of *devadasis* while
focusing on their forms in order to access their "authenticity." Despite the
transfer of the form from temple and court to theater and the restructuring
of the repertoire, Rukmini Devi's postcolonial modern form masquerades as a
traditional one; this maneuver is possible because of the linkage of the form
to an essentialized iconic spirituality. Rukmini's motivation, in part, reflected
the current conditions of the political climate she found herself in, which
included nationalist movements, women's reform movements, and orientalist consolidation in the form of the Theosophical Society, among others. It
could be argued that, as the Indian nation formed, Rukmini Devi created
productions that changed over time, reflecting certain nationalist agendas
while refuting others.

Nationalists in India had configured *woman* as representing the private
sphere. The role of women in the new independent nation was to maintain
tradition through a different kind of cult of domesticity. Rukmini Devi broke
through the role assigned to her as a Brahmin upper-middle-class woman.
She used the male-dominated nationalist frame to renegotiate a space in
the public sphere for herself and other middle- and upper-class and caste
women. However, she did this as Brahmin women who were newly emerging as solo and dramatic artists displaced the *devadasi* women before them.
Middle- and upper-class women, assigned to the domestic sphere, seized a
space in the public sphere onstage at the expense of the *devadasi* women,
who had always been "public" women. The forms that Rukmini Devi constructed changed over time.

She simultaneously resisted confining women to private spaces (even
while arguing for the importance of women's high morality), rebelled against
the power of male gurus by creating her own traditions, and refused to accept
modernity on Western terms. To ignore her contribution would be to ignore
one of the most creative artists of the twentieth century in India. Many con-
tingent factors shaped her invention, including the development of modern
dance in America.

Consolidating Modern Dance and Its "Others"

Several dancers in New York performed Indian dance under its new name,
Bharata Natyam, including Ragini Devi in 1937, Ram Gopal in 1938,

Varalakshmi and Bhanumati in 1942, Rukmini Devi in 1953, and Balasara-swati in 1954 ("La Meri Papers" 1912–1954; Abrahams 1974, 125–145). In the United States, Bharata Natyam empowered the emerging dancers who laid claim to the marketing of Asian, and particularly Hindu, spirituality. The emergence of Bharata Natyam as the classical and "traditional" form now rendered Uday Shankar's dance "neoclassical" and other Oriental dancers as "inauthentic," thereby shifting the focus onto the binary paradigms of high/low, authentic/inauthentic, and traditional or Oriental/modern. *Devadasis*, as well as new middle-class Bharata Natyam and other classical dancers who asserted their authenticity by invoking the notion of tradition, displaced Shankar. Shankar had returned to India by 1938 to set up an institute he called Almora (Khokar 1983, 112). Although he created some unique ballet productions, he had to close Almora in 1944 and turned to film until 1948.

Simultaneously, white Oriental dancers had to find new strategies for selling themselves and continued to be inventive in their own way to survive economically. This is when the term *ethnic dance* seems to have emerged. Some, like St. Denis and Shawn, became impresarios, touring "authentic" dancers from Asia in the 1940s, 1950s, and 1960s, through the Jacob's Pillow Festival and other venues (Abrahams 1974). Other dancers, like La Meri, Hadassah, and their students, traveled to India and other Asian countries to learn "authentic" dances and came back to form schools of ethnic dance as early as 1942 (Hughes 1977).[14] *Ethnic dance* then became the new moniker for *Oriental dance* in America, setting up a fictive polemic with modern dance. La Meri was different in that she traveled to India to receive formal training.[15]

La Meri learned the newly transformed *sadir* as Bharata Natyam in Madras in 1937. She claimed that because of her innate talent and stamina, she had mastered the form in three months under the tutelage of Vadivelu Pillai, the guru of the *devadasis* Varalakshmi and Bhanumati and even learned finer aspects of *abhinaya* from the famed *devadasi* Mylapore Gowri Ammal. La Meri eventually performed in Madras (now Chennai) with Bhanumati and Varalakshmi and, according to her own recollections, seems to have been well received. Eventually, La Meri brought Bhanumati and Varalakshmi to the United States, and they performed in New York to appreciative audiences in 1942 ("La Meri Papers" 1912–1954). Two *devadasis* had returned to New York approximately thirty-six years after their nautch sisters had performed in Coney Island and sixty-one years after their other sisters had arrived in New York with snake charmers. The circumstances were now different, but they were still only temporary migrant workers who had to return to India once their performances were over.

When La Meri established the Natya School of Dance with Ruth St. Denis in 1941, a new era had begun, and in October 1942, this became the School of Ethnologic Dance Center. This era included the recognition of Indian dancers as "traditional" and "authentic" in America, while the construction of ethnic dance as a category alleviated anxieties of "inauthentic" dance for white female dancers such as La Meri, Hadassah, and others. The term *ethnic dance* gave the legacy of Oriental dance another way to continue its trajectory, albeit by accounting for the variations of modernity and tradition that came alongside it. This was consolidated particularly in the 1950s with Ted Shawn's Jacob's Pillow Festival.

After Shawn split from St. Denis, he formed his troupe of male dancers instituting a place at Jacob's Pillow to try out his new ideas. Even though the company disbanded, the popularity of Jacob's Pillow performances grew. Shawn established yearly festivals to promote "modern" and "ethnic/traditional" dances, where he became the curator, especially for performers from the East. Shawn was very particular about bringing dancers from the East to perform at the Pillow, juxtaposed with Martha Graham's company and ballet performances. He labeled each performance under distinct categories of "modern" or "ethnic" and placed them in opposition to one another. This classification in programs and performances at the Pillow clearly highlighted the differences of the native versus the foreign dancer and it was Shawn himself who was now making those distinctions. The difference between citizen and noncitizen was being staged at the Pillow through dance practices.[16] Shawn's festival consolidated the divisions between what had now become "modern," "traditional," and "ethnic" dance. Shawn's legacy continues today.

While Shawn had no trouble bringing dancers from non-Western countries in the 1950s, he began to encounter difficulties with Immigration and Naturalization Services and the dancer's union in the 1960s:

> For years I had put in my petitions "to import Aliens with Distinguished Merit" and the petitions had all been approved without question. The union decided three of my artists did not have sufficient distinction to suit them! Having explained that this was all new to me and that I had innocently gone ahead on the many years past experience, and that Jacob's Pillow and the artists involved would be seriously injured if the petition was denied now, we got them all three cleared—but it means a change of procedure from now on in such matters, I will import only through a New York concert management, who will deal with the union and the Immigration Service for me. One lives and learns! (Letter from Ted Shawn to Marjorie Lyons, 1965)

Despite the troubles Shawn encountered, the Pillow went on. It had been Shawn's goal to foster exchanges between dancers in America and Asia. The travels of modern dancers from America to other parts of the world aided these exchanges, in which American dance became synonymous with white modern dance. Martha Graham also visited Rukmini Devi in Kalakshetra. What went on between them is unclear. Also unclear is how Graham may have dealt with the Kalakshetran form and technique amid the "tradition" masking its modernity.

However, a stronger polemic formed between Graham and T. Bala-saraswati, one of the best-known *devadasis*, who lived and traveled extensively in the United States in the late 1950s, 1960s, and 1970s (Meduri 1996; O'Shea 2007).[17] Bala, as she was known, left an enormous legacy incorporating "authentic" Indian dance on her body. In bringing together the heritage of the *devadasi*, she called on the discourse of "authenticity" and American orientalism to secure her place in dance history in India and America. Bala offered a deep critique of the practice that Rukmini Devi had reconfigured; yet, she still danced under its new name, Bharata Natyam. Bala's ability to capitalize on the discourses of modernity, tradition, and authenticity, enabled her to catapult her career, particularly in the United States. Bala also taught in American universities, along with her brothers, leaving an undeniable legacy (Meduri 1996; O'Shea 2007). Bala became the "other" to modern dance choreographers such as Graham. The presence of the *devadasi* on the American landscape served to mark the differences between modern and traditional dance. As immigration policies altered the face of American dance once again, however, this changed. In the United States, numerous white students of Balasaraswati- and Kalakshetra-trained dancers also made a name for themselves as early gurus of Indian dance before the large influx of dancers from India in 1965. Although many were displaced, a few remain gurus and performers, including Luise Scripps, Aggie Brenneman, and Kay Poursine (students of Balasaraswati) and Katherine Kunhiraman (student of Rukmini Devi from Kalakshetra). Medha Yodh, a Gujarati Indian woman who married a white American man, migrated early to the United States and taught Bharata Natyam at UCLA until her retirement. She also maintained the legacy of Balasaraswati for many years until the newer gurus arrived. I explore this transformation of the form from primarily white female bodies to Indian bodies in later chapters.

Modern dance continued to borrow Asian practices in constituting and reconstituting itself, thus perpetuating the discourse of orientalism. Students of Graham, such as Merce Cunningham, who became famous for his "chance method," used Asian practices and philosophies, such as martial arts and Zen. Steve Paxton's contact improvisation, which became popular in the 1970s, used yoga, tai chi, and martial arts as its inspiration. As Yutian Wong (2002, 2010) persuasively argues, these borrowings that operate within the logic of orientalism remain unacknowledged because of the binary between modern dance and its "others." It is also evidence that the discourse of orientalism had changed such that Oriental borrowings were no longer openly acknowledged. Modern dance choreographers can thus continue drawing from "old" Asian practices in forming their American identity through inventing "new" practices. Despite the strong presence of Asians in America from the 1940s onward, their practices remain on the periphery: "alien," "foreign," and "different" from American ones. These fictive divisions have thus established the precedent for how we view what is American dance and what is not, and what constitutes the American-citizen dancer and the foreign dancer.

In this intermission, I have argued so far that what is and is not American and Indian dance practice changes over time. Who gets to be authentically American, modern, or traditional varies from period to period. Modern dance attempted to establish itself as new and original, while denying its Oriental origins. This construction participates in the larger myth of American citizenship as a purely white endeavor. American nationhood was constantly shifting, but in the 1920s and 1930s, it was reestablished on the battleground for citizenship rights. When the Supreme Court ruled that whiteness was the only category in determining authentic citizenship for immigrants, it shifted prior understandings of American identity. Whereas previously dancers openly appropriated Oriental ideas and practices to form American dance, this was no longer possible in the late 1920s and throughout the 1930s. Americanness absorbed Asian practices and then subsequently rejected them as foreign, just as Asian people had been used for their labor and then denaturalized. These major shifts helped mask the crucial connections between American Oriental and modern dance.

The nationalist project in India served the modernist project in America. The American and Indian projects both needed the bodies of performing women to constitute their respective cultures at the turn of the century. In India, the drive toward independence and the urge to find a national identity that could wipe out the history of its colonized heritage enabled a unique link between nationalists and orientalists. So formed a cultural identity and a dance form that denied their modernity and invoked "authentic" tradition.

Thus, the label of tradition is not a simple one created by the colonial orientalist or the white imperialist American alone. Through the performance of Indian dance, Indians themselves contributed to the creation and maintenance of the binary of modernity and tradition on the bodies of their women, in reaction to, and negotiation of, colonialism, nationalism, and orientalism. The form's travel to the American diaspora raises issues of the geographic boundary of national cultural practices, especially as seen in the multiple legacies of orientalism sedimented on the women and girls who practice

Indian dance in America. In this context, both Bharata Natyam and modern dance performance call into question which culture is performed when, and both blur the lines between what constitutes Indianness and Americanness.

Costume Changes?

When the borders reopened for Indian immigrants with the National Origins Act of 1965, the picture changed yet again for Indian dancers in particular. These multiple strands of history, diasporic travels, and nationalist quests for modernity and tradition in the United States and India have led to the current staging of diasporic Indian dance practices. In Chapters 6 and 7, I argue that these histories have had implications for Indian diasporic practices in the United States as well as the political and cultural battles that waged on female bodies through the Bharata Natyam dance practice. Arguably, post-1965 model minority status for Indian communities in the United States has created a completely different environment for Indian dancers as compared with the pre-1923 dancers who visited the United States. While the *nachwalis* of pre-1923 dealt with extreme racism, contradictory terms of citizenship, and deportation, it appears that post-1965 dancers have a different engagement with the terms of citizenship. In the chapters to come, I critically engage this question and track the contradictions that minority citizenship status enables. The intermission has provided time for costume changes, so let the curtain rise and the second half of the show begin.

6

Negotiating Cultural Nationalism and Minority Citizenship

I n writing this chapter, I became increasingly frustrated over my inability
to deconstruct the ethnographic experience in Bharata Natyam dance
classrooms. I wrote. I rewrote. I then deleted what I had written. I stopped
writing for a long time. I tried to write again. I couldn't write. I circumvented,
procrastinated, stared at the computer screen, listened to music, cooked,
looked out the window, and just plain twiddled my thumbs. I did not want to
write this chapter. It was difficult. It was too difficult, perhaps, because I had
to write about the living. This was unlike my other chapters, in which the ethnography (although challenging at times) gave me pleasure in the writing process. I was often moved to tears in thinking about the dead dancers I wrote
about. These dancers negotiated with my body, but I was in control most of
the time. But the living dancers are a different story. I am scared to write about
them. I am afraid of what they will think. I am afraid they will not like what I
am saying about their classrooms. That I am not giving the teaching process
its due credit. That I am not even always respectful of the sacred spaces called
classrooms. This unruly spectator finds it quite difficult to be unruly in these
spaces.

But I realized that my body was trained not to be unruly in these spaces.
It had to follow the rules. My body had to be pliant, quiet, silent, and demure. And even as the ethnographer determined to be unruly, I could not
really become so, not from within the sites of the dance practice and not even
in the writing of it. The Brahminical ideological discourse that is imprinted

in the form and its pedagogy has too much power still. The unruly spectator has to be a pliant body in this site in order for friendships to be maintained and in order for her to return to these spaces that she both fears and
admires. She cares about the gurus and the students that she writes about.
And she wants to be a part of their lives. This dilemma is not very different
from the experiences of insider-outsider, or halfie, ethnographers (those of
two or more cultures) (Visweswaran 1994). But there is yet another part of
the inability to deconstruct the ethnographic experience and this involves
the guru-*sishya* and the *sishya-sakhi* relationship. What happens between the
guru and the student is not just a harsh disciplinary pedagogical experience.
There is love too, the care with which the guru instructs the student day after
day, for weeks, months, and years on end. A relationship develops and there
are secrets to this conflicted relationship between the young girl and the
powerful guru. There is also love and companionship that develops between
the young girl and her friends who share her experiences in class. These
Bharata Natyam spaces are also homosocial spaces offering contradictory
and momentary opportunities to desire, loathe, assist, befriend, compete, and
control (Gopinath 2005). The dance form in diaspora has become a private
space and a homosocial space similar to its pre-twentieth-century past in
India where women interacted with other women. These are women's spaces.
The Indian nationalist reconfiguration of women's spaces to the domestic
sphere is complicated by Bharata Natyam practice because young women's
dancing bodies negotiated both public and private spaces. There are secrets
in the private spaces that are not revealed in the stage performance. While
the stage performance tends to be a polished, costumed, masked, focused,
and controlled bodily performance, the classroom performance is not. Revealing all these secrets does not always make sense to an outsider/reader.
Obviously the unruly spectator has a critique of this process. But this is at
times a private critique that can only be shared between the *sishya* and her
sakhis, her friends who share the classroom space and are also privy to the
relationship with the guru.[1] The private critique, if made completely public,
would be distorted. So this chapter remains frustrating at times. It will not
fully deconstruct the Bharata Natyam classroom; nor will it offer a fully
bared public critique. Rather it will offer dilemmas for the unruly spectator,
who has to make some tricky rhythmic moves even while accounting for her
performance.

Using the frame of a transnational Indian dance practice, Bharata
Natyam, to explore the terms of citizenship for minority Indians post 1965, I
am interested in how this practice stages cultural nationalism as a turn away
from mainstream culture and as a way to understand the terms of minority
citizenship discourse. Attending to the Bharata Natyam dancer and the labor

evidenced through her sweat and body gestures helps us to better understand how today's terms of citizenship are both similar to and different from the terms for pre-1924 Indian immigrants. I attend to the gendering and homogenizing of heterosexual "model" behavior imparted through dance items since it is the female Indian body that is expected to perform "ideal" discourses of nation, tradition, and model minority. I am particularly interested in how power operates in Bharata Natyam dance classrooms in Los Angeles and the pedagogical tools used by "gurus," who are often first-generation-immigrant female teachers, to inscribe specific discourses of "model" cultural identity on Indian American girls.

I argue that the young female Indian dancing body laboring in dance classrooms in the U.S. highlights the inherent contradictions of "minority" citizenship. That is, even though the 1965 act enables Indians to enter the United States with the promise of full citizenship, they still remain minorities at best. I suggest that the drive of cultural nationalism offers an alternative to dominant mainstream citizenship and allows young Indian dancers to access possible alternatives to assimilation, even though it is only temporary.[2]

The discourses of cultural nationalism are power laden and contradictory. The patriarchal, heterosexual, and often orientalist overtones of cultural nationalist discourse, while resisting the strains of U.S. national assimilation, also discipline young second-generation girls' bodies to become the vehicle through which Indian culture is cast in opposition to mainstream white culture, even while maintaining its "model" status. These contradictions come to light when examining bodily labor through the sweat that emerges from the female dancing body as it moves in garages, basements, and suburban homes. I examine how "cultural" and "ethnic" symbols such as the sari are intertwined with the body and the dance practice and are fundamentally connected to the attainment of "ideal" Indian womanhood and, subsequently, to the tenets of Indian cultural nationalism. But this puts the practice somewhere between cultural preservation and assimilation (Sunder Mukhi 2000) or between orientalism and cultural citizenship (Kwan 2011), and practitioners engage this spectrum in their dance.

I use feminist dance and performance ethnography to examine the labor of middle-class Indians in dance classrooms in California. As Johannes Fabian (1983) suggests, ethnography should be written as a response to, not about, the other; on view in the following sections is the performance of ethnography in methodology by including myself as interpretive interlocutor, actively creating meaning in relationship to other subjects who are also actively creating meaning themselves. Thus the ethnographer as unruly spectator surfaces not just as an observer but also as a classroom participant who affects the dynamics in the room by her mere bodily presence.

To explore these complexities in the next sections, I have a "conversation" with one dance guru and examine her journey from India as a dancer to her arrival in California and the start of her career as a dance guru to the birth of her Indian American children. Ramya Harishankar and I have been friends for a long time. Ramya and I met in 1995 when I first arrived in Los Angeles. We have had ongoing conversations about the intersections of her life with the history of Bharata Natyam as it has moved through the diaspora, particularly from the late 1970s and early 1980s. I have collected notes throughout the years on this subject but for this chapter, I asked her to write down her own thoughts about her journey. I interspersed my notes within this narrative and asked her to respond to my notes in writing. This is something Ramya and I had not done before and something I could not do with the *nachwalis* or the many Indian dancers who arrived in the United States long before she did, and who precede her in this book. I use this conversation to demonstrate how her journey is at once typical of and different from that of other female gurus who arrived after 1965. She is not a subaltern in the ways that other Indian dancers have been, but in the processes of negotiating representational control that accompanies ethnographic writing, she can be only partially visible and not fully represented. As the friend, *sakhi*, I do not always narrate what Ramya wants to be narrated. There are disjunctures in the conversation between what I as the ethnographer want to argue and what Ramya actually says; these disjunctures are made evident by the unruly spectator. I then narrate events that occur in different dance classrooms in Northern and Southern California as well as Chicago that exemplify and highlight how the discourses of cultural nationalism and citizenship are negotiated. The unruly spectator does not always sit still and refuses to accept the disciplining that happens in the classroom.

Ramya's Journey

My mother enrolled me in dance class in 1963 under the tutelage of K. Dakshinamoorthy in New Delhi. He was the brother of the legendary guru Dandayuthapani Pillai. My only memories of those classes are that of his sarcasm. I remember watching Srividhya [the famous singer M. L. Vasantha Kumari's daughter] rehearsing at his place. She was completely out of shape but incredibly graceful. Hema Rajagopal and Mythili Kumar were my seniors in that school.

As a young Brahmin woman, Ramya was trained in two different kinds of *devadasi* lineages because Dandayuthapani Pillai came from one lineage of *devadasis* while her next guru came from another. Since *devadasis* were no longer able to dance because of India's National Abolition Act of 1949, many of the men from the *devadasi* families took over as gurus and began teaching dance to young Brahmin girls such as Ramya, Hema, and Mythili.[3]

> *Yes, that is right, I suppose, because I never met any devadasis who were teachers at the time. In 1969, my mother decided to send me to Madras so I could grow under the mentorship and supervision of my grandmother and with a private teacher. Swamimalai Rajaratnam was chosen, as he used to teach Jothi Raghavan [a contemporary of Ramya's who now lives in Boston], [and] her sister and mother who lived on the next street. He was also recommended by family friend Y. G. Doraiswami, mentor to many dancers including Kalanidhi Narayanan. So began my sessions with Vadyar. He was extremely patient, a wonderful singer, and, interestingly, learned choreography entirely through guru kula vasam. He came to Madras to sing for the legendary Kamala and stayed with her guru Vazhavur Ramiah Pillai. In the early 60s, he broke away from Ramiah Pillai and started teaching dance.*

Ramya started classes with Rajaratnam because he was recommended to her by Y. G. Doraiswami, a Brahmin with clout in Madras. Y. G. Doraiswami was a respected impresario who created performance opportunities for dancers in India and students from the West who wished to learn dance. Therefore, his recommendation of Rajaratnam was the gold standard of approval for Ramya's family. Bharata Natyam had gained popularity in India among middle-and upper-class families by the 1960s and 1970s, and therefore, young women who were often upper-caste Brahmins were trained extensively in the dance form. It must be remembered that the *sadir* form practiced by temple dancers, or *devadasis*, was removed from the *vallavar* community (of which the *devadasis* were members) in part because of the anti-nautch campaign that was part of the larger reforms for women under the nationalist agenda. Since the *sadir* practice became ideologically linked to prostitution by the late nineteenth century, it became impossible for *devadasis* to continue their practice legally. By the 1960s and particularly by the 1970s and 1980s, hundreds of thousands of young women were carrying out the agenda of the postcolonial nation-state, both in the nation space and in the diaspora. But the gurus for Brahmin women were the men of the *vallavar* caste. When Ramya says her guru had learned all his choreography through "guru kula vasam" she means that although her guru never danced, he trained in the house of a *devadasi* guru, living there daily and learning from his method of teaching.

I don't know for sure, but I think he did not learn by dancing himself,
only watching, so he must have lived and learned the practices there.
My arangetram was in October 1970. My grandmother was very sup-
portive and organized as many performances as she could all over
India. 1977 winter was my first foreign tour, with performances in
Thailand, Hong Kong, and Malaysia. It was initiated by a German,
Helga Burger, who stayed with us in Chennai during the season of
1976.

Ramya performed her solo debut recital, the *arangetram*, in 1970 and then
began her solo career under the auspices of her grandmother. She also began
learning from a woman Brahmin guru, Kalanidhi Narayanan, who at that
time was just emerging on the dance scene as a teacher of *padams*.[4]

Kalanidhi, or Kanthu Mami, as I called her, returned to the dance scene
in 1973 after an absence of nearly three decades. She had been asked by
YGD to teach abhinaya, as most male gurus were teaching the basic or
sterilized version of it. She insisted that the students should get permis-
sion from their gurus, as they would have to depend on them to conduct
their performances. Mami was a very close family friend, and that was
the reason given to my guru so I could start lessons with her. Otherwise,
it would have been difficult to get my guru to let me start learning items
from someone else. I was actively involved in every aspect of her work,
her growth, and the spread of her style of abhinaya in those early years.
In fact, she was quite upset when I moved to the U.S. Her style of teach-
ing was unique in that she gave a lot but also provided space to create,
to add one's own personality and make it one's own. That is what turned
me on to dance—the ability to personalize my dance.

For the next ten years she performed at various venues in India even while
continuing her education and obtaining a degree in business communications. Her overseas tour was the start of an ideal "solo" career, the penulti-
mate trophy for upcoming dancers of the time.

In the late 1970s, I was just beginning to perform frequently around
India and was possibly at the threshold of a career in performing. As
young newlyweds looking for adventure, we decided to migrate to
the U.S., as we had the opportunity, and with the thought that we
could always return to India. So I traveled to California, perform-
ing en route in Thailand, Malaysia, Hong Kong, and Japan. My
gurus were disappointed. Vadyar had just given me the varnam in his

production Bharathil Bharathi, and we were actively involved with
Mami in popularizing abhinaya and Mami's style. Harish was Secy of
Abhinayasudha.

Ramya says she decided to go to California in 1981, a few years after marrying her husband, Harish, who was secretary of Abhinayasudha (Kalanidhi Narayanan's dance school). But what she does not say is that her husband was sponsored through a family green card process. Having obtained the green card, he felt it would be wasted if they did not use it, and so, even though he did not have a job, they decided to move to California. Arriving in America in the 1970s and early 1980s, with few options to work, many young newly married women who also happened to be Bharata Natyam dancers, prompted by parents with young daughters, opted to perform and begin dance schools operating out of their apartments, homes, garages, and local schools, charging a few dollars that would be given in cash for classes. This is an example of an informal economy at work, which was and is very common for Asian American women who otherwise have few options. As scholars have argued, Asian American women have turned to different kinds of innovative work thus changing their traditional roles as culture bearers within the household into income earners in or out of the home (Espiritu 1996).

Harish did not have a job but he did have a green card. I had graduated
with a degree in business communications, and I could have pursued an
MBA or worked in administration or accounting—scary! Upon arrival
in California in 1981, I found that there were already a handful of parents anxiously awaiting my arrival so their young daughters could learn
dance. I often remember Mami's comment as I left: "Don't you also start
teaching in the U.S.!" And I had never taught and was not keen either.
But soon I realized that the option was to go to work in a corporate
environment, and I chose teaching. Started with six students in April
1982, and it was special because my grandmother/mentor, Babushka,
was there for my first class. And I vividly remember her comment after
that first session: "How far are you going to get teaching these children?"
By the end of the year, I had about twenty-five students and was teaching in Cerritos, Irvine, and Long Beach.

In my research over the years, I encountered only a few gurus who came with green cards. Currently, Ramya has more than one hundred students in any given year. She has conducted more than 120 *arangetrams* and has taught hundreds of girls in her classroom over the years. I wonder what her Babushka would have thought about this development over the last three decades.

The Female Guru

As the unruly and errant *sakhi*, I was paying keen attention to Ramya's ascension to guru status following her arrival to California, more so than to her accounts of her touring and performing career. To me, what is most interesting about Ramya's account of her travels is her subsequent unplanned career transformation from performing dancer to female guru. She makes this transformation seem both accidental and inevitable. After arriving in California, she could not bear the thought of an eight- to ten-hour office job. Rather, dance offered her a path to continue being an artist, albeit functioning simultaneously as a teacher. What is unique about Bharata Natyam pedagogy in the United States is the emergence of powerful women gurus as authority figures. The guru title brings with it a culturally and historically power-laden position. Generally, male gurus dominated the scene for much of the twentieth century and, particularly after the *devadasi* practice had been decimated, it was the men from the *vallavar* caste that continued teaching Brahmin girls. But with Ramya's travels through the diaspora, she chose to become a guru. She was certain she did not want to enter the corporate world, and dance was her life. If she could not dance professionally on a daily basis and enjoy an international touring career, she decided that teaching was the next best thing. This was frowned upon, however, by Mami, Babushka, and her guru Rajarathnam. Perhaps this was because it was quite rare for a Brahmin dancer to become a guru in her own right. That trend did not start until the mid to late eighties in India but there was a precedent being set by the female dancers arriving in the United States in the 1970s and 1980s.

The guru position allows first-generation female gurus to negotiate male dominance in the immigrant Indian community and mainstream patriarchy. But it also forces them to make unexpected bargains. In negotiating male dominance and community pressures, gurus are able to establish economic independence through their schools, which bring them financial security and the respect of the Indian community. Further, they are given the authority to shape the minority community's cultural identity and to perform it onstage from time to time, albeit through the disciplining of young girls. In the practice of Bharata Natyam, first-generation female gurus perform and teach "model" culture as a series of naturalized behaviors that are perceived to be innately Indian, emphasizing discipline and religion (primarily Hinduism), as well as chaste sexual behavior among other things. They instill these tenets to second-generation girls and young women to perpetuate the notions of authentic cultural identity and ideal womanhood. Teachers get paid well and in general have flexible work hours, often teaching after 4:00 P.M. each day (when girls return from school) and on weekends. What the unruly *sakhi* has not reported in detail here is that Ramya often teaches *padams*, a type of dance within the Bharata Natyam repertoire that contradicts the chaste sexual behavior of women. Perhaps the unruly one will change her mind soon and explain further.

Facing increasing pressure to assimilate to mainstream American culture, mothers and fathers who want their daughters to maintain cultural heritage have turned to Bharata Natyam teachers (and teachers of other classical dances as well, including *Kathak* and *Odissi*) in their area and began taking their young daughters to be educated, not just in Indian dance but also in Indian culture. What is interesting to note is that the gurus' establishment of schools in the United States displaced the many white ethnic dancers who had been the primary gurus from the 1950s to the 1970s (Khandelwal 2002). Many had been students of the great *devadasi* Balasaraswati, who had frequently come to the United States to teach. Others, following in the footsteps of ethnic dancers such as La Meri, had gone to India to study dance and return to the United States to impart their teachings to the small Indian communities that were forming in the 1960s and 1970s. By the mid-1970s, these white men and women were no longer needed as gurus by the Indian community, laments an unnamed white woman dancer (Khandelwal 2002, 52–53). Indian communities turned to newly arrived immigrant "authentic" brown bodies from India, signaling a shift away from white male and female gurus.[5] As Madhulika Khandelwal notes (2002, 52), it was not until the late 1960s and early 1970s that Indian artists migrated to the United States as immigrants and not as temporary visitors. When Indian communities were presented with choices about gurus for the first time in the history of the United States, they turned to brown women dancers from India. This was vastly different to the scenario presented to American audiences from the 1880s to the first decade of the twentieth century when white audiences turned away from Indian *nachwalis* and toward white women dancers performing "India." These new choices created a variety of issues and power differentials within the burgeoning Indian community, as "India" became performed on new bodies.

In the next section, I illuminate a few interactions in the dance classrooms from the perspective of the unruly spectator. I have not necessarily chosen to depict all that happens in the rehearsal spaces. After attending hundreds of rehearsals in many classrooms over the decades, I have chosen only a few examples to make a particular argument about power. In this account, my narration is partial, biased, full of half-truths, and at times fictional. The unruly spectator relishes the opportunity to be unruly in telling these stories. She offers narratives in the following section that are a compilation of several months and years of research and participation. The story structures are thus a fictive rendering of a collection of actual events that have been placed together.

Giving the Finger

Tam tata kita naka jam. Takun tari kita taka. Tata kita taka naka jam.
Kukkum tari kita taka . . .

The students and I are in a rehearsal room. The dance floor is wooden. There is a large bronze Nataraja statue in the back of the room. The bodies are many, their histories and social backgrounds varied. The guru, who is in her midforties, sits wearing a cotton sari in the front of the room beating out rhythms and chanting drum syllables, such as "tam tata kita naka jam," with her stick and wooden block. These are rhythmic syllables that have no specific meaning; they merely reflect the sounds that the drum makes to guide the dancers in their movements. I sit next to her dressed in a *salwar* (long shirt and pants), tapping the *tala* (the rhythmic count) with my hand. There are five female dance students aged between fourteen and sixteen, dressed either in *salwars* or saris and wearing *bindis* (ritual mark Indian women wear on forehead). Their mothers, between forty and fifty years old, wear saris, pants, sweaters, or *salwars*, and sit on the side watching the class as it unfolds.

The dance teacher beats out the rhythm and the dancers follow, slapping their feet on the floor, moving their torsos, gesturing with their hands and arms. With the final beat of the rhythmical cycle, the pure dance section changes into a dramatic interpretation of a Telugu (a South Indian language) text that the guru sings: *Rupa mu juchi valachi va achi theeni . . . kopa museya thura, swami inde.* As this dramatic section begins, the guru stops the class and says to the students, "Your faces are not working. You are not moving elegantly like a graceful Indian woman would. You look like *rakshasis*. What is wrong with you girls?" The guru interrupts the students and chastises them for their awkwardness, rebuking them for their *rakshasi*, or demonic, uncouth ways of moving. She admonishes them to maintain a distance from the pressures of mainstream assimilation and to discipline their bodies into ideal Indian women: "You should listen and watch your mothers more often." She turns to me and to the mothers who are sitting on the side watching and comments:

> Girls these days are not like us in our day, ya? We listened to our parents and did what we were told. I don't know what to do with these girls. How can I begin to make them understand the importance of elegance, of devotion, of spirituality that is so essential to our form? I'm sure your guru had similar problems, too, isn't it, Priya?

I half smile and nod. I do not want to join in with this guru and alienate the students. I do not know the guru well; nor do I know the students. But my gut feeling makes me want to tread carefully because, after all, I do not even know what my position is. I am neither a guru with that kind of power nor a student. I notice, with their guru's face turned away, the students roll their eyes upward and signal to each other, half snickering and mocking the teacher. They look at me from time to time to see whether I notice. Again, I half smile and nod. I do not want to take their side either and alienate the guru. Their posture is casual, their legs are spread apart, and their backs are limp. The girls stand still, but their bodies are communicating many complex messages. The guru enforces her power in the classroom on the students; she disciplines these young women's bodies, just as gurus have done for generations. But her students resist in this moment. Abruptly, the guru turns toward them and becomes angry, as if sensing their momentary resistance:

> Excuse me, girls; did I say the class was over? Where is your posture? Did I ask you to look at each other? When I look away, you suddenly have wonderful communicative emotions on your face, and yet when I ask you to do it in the dance, you cannot move your stonelike faces.

The girls' faces are now deadpan. Their feet are together, their backs straight, and they look at the floor in seeming penitence, paying deference to their guru. She commands: "Next *jathi* ready, *dhalanku taka dhiku taka tadhinginatom.*" With a stern voice, the guru thus forces them to pay attention and uses her full authority to make them take notice of her power. She co-opts their resistance back into the disciplinary frame she requires. She is satisfied for the moment and moves on with the next section of the dance. The girls ready themselves and begin the next section. She chants, *Tat kita jam, tata kita jam tatdhiku didiku dhalangu ta.* I almost burst out laughing but control myself in time. The girls, having pretended to be penitent for their actions, are now resisting the guru's authority by inflecting one of their gestures slightly so that it reads very differently. They turn the gesture *kartarimukaha* from a classical, harmless symbolic interpretation of the dance into a rude rebellion. Literally, they are giving their guru the finger! The guru does not notice at first, but gradually she understands. She can do nothing at this point, since they are not blatantly breaking any rules, and she is in the middle of chanting *jathis: Tatdiku didiku ta, dit thalangu taka ta.* She makes a note of it and will undoubtedly discipline them accordingly when they complete this dance, but for the moment, the dancers are very pleased with themselves and beam proudly. The mothers sit on the side, oblivious to these undercurrents and satisfied that the guru is disciplining their daughters into model Indian womanhood. Am I imagining this encounter? Perhaps there is nothing going on here after all and it is only wishful thinking on the part of this unruly spectator. It takes me back to memories of my own rebellion against my guru back in Melbourne, more than a decade earlier. I wish to believe that these students are shrugging off the imperatives of the discourse of cultural nationalism here and now, but maybe it is all in my imagination. I am not quite sure. Just as I begin to look away, one student looks directly at me and smiles triumphantly, giving me the finger too. After all, who am I in that space but another body of power they can give the finger to? As the unruly spectator, I smile back, acknowledging silently that I, too, have been in their place and understand why they are doing what they are doing. But they have already moved on and do not see me smile.

The anecdote of the sweating saris in the Preface ties into the current anecdote. If you remember, the saris were slipping off many of the young women's bodies for a variety of reasons. Students in these two classrooms on these particular instances rebelled against the authority of their guru and the discourses of power she attempted to sediment on their bodies. What this example demonstrates is that students are not always passive subjects who let discourses of power write over them. In the U.S. context, second-generation Indian American girls have access to another world: TV, media, and, of course, high school, where different models of femininity are possible. The model behavior expected in Indian mythologies is not the only alternative. I am not suggesting, however, that mainstream American models of femininity are more empowering than Indian ones. There are models of femininity in Indian mythology that belie the quiet, demure figures of the goddess Sita or Saraswati (the goddess of knowledge who rides a swan), like Kali, the black, naked goddess who sticks her tongue out as she holds the severed heads of demons. While wearing a garland of skulls, she stands astride the inert body of her husband Siva. Then there is Durga, the warrior goddess. Riding a lion, she carries a trident in one hand as she pierces the demon-bull, Mahisha. It is the eye of the unruly spectator that sees the ways young dancers do not readily accept the guru's authority. My bodily presence and my knowledge as unruly dancer and spectator enable this reading, which would otherwise be missed. *Tat kita jam, tata kita jam. Takita dikita dhalangu ta. Kirkirtakatom.* Twisting and turning, jumping and stamping, a whirl and a flourish of fingers at the end. This body moves in rhythms. Differently syncopated, mixed up, discoursed polyrhythms.

What the students may not realize is the predicament the guru finds herself in. On the one hand, the community awards gurus for doing their work in teaching model Indian womanhood to young girls and thereby invests the teachers with power. On the other hand, the community also forces them to abide by their codes, which is part of the bargain they make. To have power within the community, female gurus have to perform Indian patriarchal expectations of model Indian womanhood, such as maintaining a marriage to an Indian man, accepting its heterosexual contract, and reproducing Indian children. Gurus encourage this contract in their pedagogy by reinforcing many patriarchal expectations including encouraging endogamy (marriage to other ethnic Indians), perpetuating the hallmarks of ideal Indian woman-hood (including restricting dating practices), and encouraging the practice of Hinduism. While practicing Hinduism in and of itself is not a problem, what can become problematic is the insidious links to the religious, fundamen-talist, and right-wing Hindutva movement that has spread to the diaspora. Gurus may not always be aware of the claims that the Hindutva movement makes on the diaspora and unwittingly participate in many of its fundamen-talist tenets. The costs of this subservience to Indian patriarchy, particularly as it relates to model minority discourses, remain hidden.[6]

In addition, parents encourage their female children to take dance lessons like Bharata Natyam but curb their dating activities and forbid them to wear "sexy" clothes—norms that are perceived to be essentially American. However, they do not put such pressures on their male children. This is not to say that second-generation Indian girls actually listen to their parents, or that other mod-els of femininity outside the dance studio do not influence them. The unruly spectator interrupts. Some gurus support their students' choices over the wishes of parents—in secret, of course. Not all female gurus ascribe to the patriarchal expectations of the Indian community, and some even take the young girls' sides when it comes to rebelling against the parents. They function as confidantes, as "parents away from parents," and as mentors, but often in secret.

As discourses sediment and shift on moving bodies, they continue to be negotiated, constantly changing and being modified as they interact on the bodies they encounter. For example, the dancer in the Bharata Natyam rehearsal room does not neatly perform the effects of colonialism, nationalism, transnationalism, orientalism, or model minority. Instead, the dancer and the teacher negotiate with the multiple discourses moving on their bodies even as they themselves move to different rhythms and songs. The relationships between the dancer and the music, the dancers in relation to each other, the camaraderie of the group of female dancers, their relationship to the guru, the guru's relationship to them and their mothers, and the bodies in relation to different discourses of power, to multiple histories and communities are all interactions that occur simultaneously. A virtuosic dancing body cannot be understood on its own. To locate the artistry on the singular body misses all the other relations. Power cannot be understood as neatly parceled packages but rather as shifting, negotiating practices conducted by bodies in relation to one another. Thus, who gives the finger to whom depends on the context.

The unruly spectator, feeling sorry that she has not quite translated the message of the gurus, plans to intervene now. In the next section, I demonstrate how the study of the *padam* contradicts the relationship between the guru and students outlined above. What I will show is that power is played out differently in different classrooms; when the *padam* form is being taught in California classrooms, it ruptures the ideals of the Indian community's sense of cultural nationalism in the United States. Because it is one of the only remaining fragments of *devadasi* practice and because of its overtly sexual and sensual textual contents, the *padam* places alternate models of female sexuality front and center when young girls begin learning and practicing the form (P. Srinivasan 1997).

The *padam* practice seems to have redeveloped on the bodies of Brahmin women in India after the 1980s, owing in large part to the work of Kalanidhi Narayanan, the woman credited with reviving the *padams* in India during the 1970s. However, in the United States, there are clear issues surrounding the *padam* within the diasporic Indian community and between gurus themselves who are often hesitant to teach the form. In the next section, I focus on my role as a student of the *padam* form in Ramya's classroom and as an observer when she teaches the same piece to other students. I combine these experiences to narrate the conflicts that emerge in the practice of this aspect of the Bharata Natyam form.

Netrandhil Neyrathiley (Yesterday at Dusk)

One of the reasons I became such good friends with Ramya the guru is because of her specialty in performing and teaching *padams* that she learned from Kalanidhi Narayanan. As I mention in the first chapter of this book, I met Ramya because of my interest in the *padam* form and because I wanted to learn from Kalanidhi Narayanan, who was visiting Los Angeles in the summer of 1995, just as I arrived in Los Angeles to begin my master's program.

The performance of a *padam* involves the visual interpretation of poems sung by a vocalist, which in the classroom is the guru herself. The movement involved in this section is minimal and not vigorous. The emphasis is on the facial expression and the use of specific hand gestures. This theme revolves around the dancer's relationship to her lover, be it angry, sarcastic, sad, or some emotion that lies in between. For the communication of the message to occur, the dancer must be able to "feel" the character at an intense level so as to then emote her feelings. An important feature of the *padam* is that it allows a great deal of creativity for the dancer, unlike most other structures in the Bharata Natyam repertoire. The dance itself is explicated in several levels of meaning. It is very nuanced and requires a high level of sophisticated training to understand, internalize, emote, and communicate its message to the audience in performance through the interpretation of the text.

This was Ramya's specialty. Having learned from Kalanidhi Narayanan, Ramya was an expert. Although it was not my intention, I began learning *padams* from Ramya a month after our first meeting. After taking the workshop Kalanidhi Narayanan had offered in Ramya's home in October 1995, I began developing my *padam* training with Ramya. I told her right at the beginning that I would not consider her my guru and she should not expect me to behave as a "typical" student; if she accepted this condition, I would really like to learn from her. She understood and said that she had enough students and was happy for us to work together to develop the interpretation of *padams* as a collaborative effort. After the workshop with Narayanan (Mami, as we called her), I realized Ramya's style also hinged on analysis of the poem text and the subsequent immersion in the main emotion (*sthayi bhava*) by the dancer.

We began with the *padam Netrandhil Neyrathiley*. The *padam* itself is about a woman addressing her lover, the god Murugan, telling him that she has seen him with another woman but that ultimately she is willing to forgive him if he comes back to her. We know this information only by examining the entire *padam* and not its exclusive parts.

Section 1—*Pallavi*
Netrandhil neyrathiley neeraadum karaidhanile
neringi ummai jaadai kati azhaithaval yaro swami

Yesterday at dusk time by the river bank,
there was a girl who approached you, making overt signs, calling to
    you, who was she?

Section 2—*Anupallavi*
vetri mamayil yerum kanda neer avallum yedhir muzhiyai
nirkayilley shorkayilley pakkathiley yerundhen swami

victoriously sitting on the peacock, you and she faced each other
while standing in this infatuated state, I was near there my Lord,
    witnessing this event

Section 3—*Charanam*
munnaalil yennidathil sondham poll kittey vandha
muthu muthai sarasamaadi moha madhanai thanda

in those days you behaved with such familiarity toward me, coming
   near
you made love to me so beautifully and gave me such joy

mannava un ninaiva konda annam kandoru madham undu
vaarum ayya yen doraiye theerum yen kavalayai

my King, lost in thoughts of you, I have not seen food in more than
   a month
please come my Lord and do away with my sorrows

The *padam* has a complex set of often-contradictory emotions and is open to interpretation. Ramya explained that if we take the first section, the *pallavi*, we have some text that states that the heroine has seen her lover, the god Murugan, with someone else. She is also accusatory. If we go by that single line, we can say that she is angry. But does that mean she dislikes Murugan and does not want to be with him? Why is she saying what she is saying? What is the purpose of this sentence? What is her personality? We cannot know until we have examined the rest of the text. It is only in the *charanam*, the third and final section of the song, that we become aware of who the protagonist is. Although she is angrily accusing Murugan, the heroine will take him back. The fact that she is still very much in love with him contextualizes the second section, the *anupallavi*. She is very hurt by what has happened. She is vulnerable, but at the same time, she wants him back and will forgive him. So throughout the rendering of the piece, we must keep in mind the overarching personality of the woman, referred to as the *sthayi bhava*. Whatever she utters or thinks is influenced by her state of mind and personality. In this particular piece, the *sthayi bhava* is the woman's hurt feelings. She would not be so hurt if she did not care for him so deeply.

Ramya believes, in her interpretation, that the woman cares so deeply that she is willing to overlook his "affair" with the other woman. I was not sure I agreed with this interpretation but I kept silent. To construct even one plausible interpretation of the text, an in-depth psychological exploration is required. There are no hard and fast rules. However, we have to read the text for the nuances of a particular interpretation, and at the same time, we are not bound by a single vision. In other words, there is a structure but there is room within it for different interpretations.

While interpreting the text, I attempted to render a specific line and its elaboration. For example with the first line, although the text does not change, the interpretation does. The first line literally repeated through singing is "Yesterday at dusk time by the river, there was a girl who approached you, making overt signs, calling to you, who was she?" One interpretation I used was "As I was walking toward the river, I heard the rustle of leaves, I looked and it was you with the other woman, who was she?" Ramya said she thought that interpretation would work. Another interpretation Ramya suggested was "I was collecting water and I heard voices and it was the two of you talking to each other, who was she?" An interpretation laying the blame wholly on the other woman, which I did not like as much, was "As I headed back from the river, when the sun was setting, I saw her making eyes at you who was she?"

In our sessions, just as she did with her students, she would ask me to try it my own way, but most of all, to feel what I was doing. She wanted me to feel the part of the *nayika*, feel all her emotions and then think of how to make that evident to an audience. She said: "Don't look at the mudras your hands are making, focus on the characters, concentrate on the main feelings and everything else will fall into place. Speak to yourself in order to make your ideas clearer. If you want to, make up sentences in your mind." She wanted me to visualize the characters with whom I was speaking, to understand them and make her and the audience "see" them too. In the beginning I was not sure of anything and could "see" no one. I believed that I had to reproduce her interpretation before I could put my mark on it. I did not know how to communicate my feeling outwardly. Ramya was usually quite respectful to all her students, never yelling or screaming at them, but she was especially so to her senior students. Even her tone and quality was friendlier, perhaps because they were older and did not require as much instruction as the younger ones. This seemed to create a more relaxed atmosphere—a shared space of creativity, if you will—or maybe it was the *padam* form itself that allowed multiple collaborations to exist. In this place, power between guru and student seemed much more in balance, or perhaps it was just wishful thinking on my part.

In trying to get into the *padams*, I "felt" the character within. I immersed myself in becoming this *nayika* and embodying her emotions. However, no matter how hard I tried, I was not able to sustain the oneness with the character. Sometimes I would find myself looking at my hands and the mudras they were making instead of maintaining the emotion. At other times, I could not always maintain the visualization of the other characters to whom I was speaking. I would "see" the friend or lover with whom I was supposed to be conversing; her or his face would be clear in front of me. Then, if I blinked or just lost focus for a second, she or he would vanish. What was most frustrating was that all my life I had struggled to become a good dancer, and just when I felt that I was finally becoming proficient after eighteen years of training, suddenly I was like a child again, unable to do even the basics.

Perhaps, it was not just about practice but also about relaxing and enjoying the character portrayals, Ramya suggested. As I worked on this idea, the *padam* form became easier to master and perform.

After a few months of classes, when we became more familiar with each other, Ramya and I began discussing how different heroines would be classed, that is, the theoretical ways of classifying the *nayika*. Ramya explained the levels were many and complex. For instance, we discussed the idea of the *ashtanayikas*. Although the literal translation of the word suggests eight different heroines, these are psychological states of being. A *nayika* is a *Vasakasajja*, when she is dressed up to receive her lover; a *Virahotkanthita*, when she is distressed at his absence; a *Svadhinapatika*, if she is confident of her love and her lover who is under her subjection; a *Kalahantarita*, when she, having repulsed her lover out of indignation, suffers remorse; a *Khandita*, when she is afflicted with agony (anger) on account of the absence of her lover, who has gone to meet another woman; a *Vipralabdha*, when she does not find him at the appointed place and/or feels cheated; a *Prositabhartrka*, when her lover is away for an indefinite period; and a *Abhisarika*, when she, lovesick and having renounced all modesty and bashfulness, goes to meet her lover. I began questioning Ramya about this history and what she thought about the *devadasi* practice because, after all, the *padam* form exemplified their lifestyle. These *padams* were, in essence, the characteristic item in their repertoire that most comprehensively represented the *devadasi* lifestyle because they were erotic spiritual texts that spoke of the lover as the human manifestation of the Divine God. The *devadasis* were married to God, and thus any *padam* pieces they performed would be the finest symbol of their relationship to their lover, who was actually God.

Dating back to the seventh century, *devadasis* had a history of performing within temples, dedicating their dance to God. These women lived in a liminal place, mediating between God and humans, because they were married to the deity of the temple in which they served and simultaneously could take on human lovers.[7] The devotion to God, Bhakti, as practiced by Hindus and *devadasis*, was not something unusual in Hindu culture. Bhakti itself could be seen on many levels. An important aspect of Bhakti included the worship of God as a human lover known as *madhurya* or *shringara*—erotic spirituality. The *devadasis*, being married to God, were themselves the exemplary embodiment of *shringara*.[8] The insertion of *devadasis* in the temples can be correlated to the Bhakti movement that also began around the seventh century in South India. Thus, the *devadasis* were reflecting aspects of the Bhakti movement through their very existence and especially through their dance practices within and outside the temple.

Poets such as Ksetrayya, whose texts were performed as *padams*, lived among *devadasis* in the sixteenth century. Ksetrayya, the poet and composer, was involved with the court, the *devadasis*, and their courtesan lifestyle, which is reflected in his writing (P. Srinivasan 1997). One could argue that Ksetrayya's *padams* are a historical archive of his relationship with a *devadasi*.[9] The *devadasi* lifestyle was embedded within the *padam*. For instance, the *padam Andagadav auduvu lera* describes implicitly the courtesan lifestyle. The text is erotic and sexual. The mention of the Lord God Adivaraha takes it to the liminal place of erotic spirituality. Is it any wonder that the *devadasis* would identify so keenly with the *shringara padams*? After all, these *padams* reflected their day-to-day existence and their unique relationship to God, to the core. In fact, it could be said that the *devadasi* was the personification of *shringara* and therefore of the *padam* as well.

But my point to Ramya was that middle-class, and often Brahmin, Indian women, such as she and I, especially in twentieth-century India or America, did not live in such liminal spaces. So how could we truly understand and perform *padams*? She gave me the standard answer then that I came to expect from many of the first-generation gurus. That is that the *devadasis* had fallen into ill repute and had let their art forms go. Their practice was not the "high art" that Bharata Natyam was today, and if it had not been for Rukmini Devi and the male gurus of the *devadasis*, we would not have any art today at all. I explained to her that there was a more complex history that had removed the *devadasi* from her dance. Puffed up with my newly gained historical knowledge of the *devadasis*, and as the unruly spectator, I told her that during the "nationalist revival," coupled with the reform came the need to "revive" the dance without the *devadasi*. The dance was seen as primary, separate from the *devadasi*, because of its capacity to easily encapsulate large artistic traditions through the use of symbols. *Sadir* became Bharata Natyam in the 1920s but with marked differences. The repertoire was changed with an overriding impetus to remove *shringara* from the dance. The reason that *shringara* was removed from the new construction was part of the "purification" process of the form, enabling "respectable" women to do "respectable" dances. In other words, the "shameful" dancer's body was transferred to a respectable woman's body; the dance went from the *devadasi* to the Brahmin woman who had no previous connection with the dance form (A. Srinivasan 1988). But the *padam* form still contained within it the bodily traces of the *devadasi* practice. The *devadasi* was still haunting the *padam*.

So that the resurgence of *padams* by Brahmin women meant that the *devadasi* could not simply be excised from it. The "revival" of the *padam* in the

1970s and 1980s spearheaded by Y. G. Doraiswamy, the gentleman Ramya herself had mentioned earlier, was responsible for her learning from Kalanidhi Narayanan. What connoisseurs such as Doraiswamy and others were discussing in the 1970s was the lack of "feeling" evident in many Bharata Natyam performances, and the mechanization of the form, which could be seen in the repertoire items that focused on *nritta* and rhythmical parts to the exclusion of emotion and *abhinya*. Ironically, it was hoped that with the return of the *padam*, the expressive, imaginative, and improvisatory section of the Bharata Natyam repertoire would also return through its structures. This paved the way for the Brahmin middle-class woman Kalanidhi Narayanan's reentrance to the field as she began teaching *padams* in the 1970s in India. The erotically charged, sexually explicit *padam* texts could therefore be controlled, if mediated, through the Brahmin female body, and Narayanan became the perfect solution. Subsequently, it was also what enabled Ramya to teach *padams* in the present moment. What was not being accounted for was the haunting presence of the *devadasi* in the practice and what it would mean to middle-class Indians in America. Ramya had often lamented to me that many gurus did not teach *padams* to their students, sometimes because they themselves had not learned the forms but more often because the erotic texts would disrupt middle-class Indian sensibility. Ramya felt that she was one of a few gurus in the United States who persisted in teaching these *padams*.

While I lauded Ramya for teaching *padams*, I pressed further; I told her that I felt our dance form was ahistorical and that it had no contemporary relevance, especially if it did not account for the *devadasi* history and everyday themes that people could connect with. I told her that unless we embraced the presence of the *devadasi* in the *padam* without restraint and explore the violence done to the *devadasis*, we would be continuing an injustice to the *devadasi* women, their forms, and their practices. She was silent and did not respond. Had I pressed too heavily? Was I now betraying her by writing about this encounter? Was I being unruly or just foolish?

Conveniently, the phone rang. Usually she did not answer the phone when we were in the middle of class. Today she did. A few minutes later, after completing her phone call, she changed the subject as if she did not remember that I had asked her a question. She asked me what I thought about the fetish that many dancers had for enacting dramatic roles at elaborate length, role-playing rather than focusing on emotional content, while bringing out a particular character. I told her I thought role-playing and dramatic elaboration had its usefulness. I was restrained in my response, trying not to judge her for changing the subject. I realized also that she was probably chastising me because she knew that I was having a difficult time sustaining the *sthayi bhava* of the *nayika*. She remembered, too, that my guru's style had focused more on role-playing and dramatic elaboration than her own. This was her way of not only changing a difficult conversation but perhaps also marking her authority in the classroom. Although I was irritated by the turn of events and the gist of the conversation, I had no choice but to enter into this discussion about the choreographic choice exercised by gurus in imprinting their "style" on their students.

Then, in November 2006, she had a large class of students to whom she began teaching a very sexually explicit *padam*. I asked Ramya while we had a cup of tea and before she began the class whether the parents would be all right with her teaching this *padam* because it was very erotic. She just smiled at me and said nothing. She gestured with her hand that I would have to be patient but that I would find out soon enough. I was curious because of a recent article written by another dance guru condemning the teaching of the *padam* to young girls in the diaspora, arguing that the form would corrupt them.[10] In essence, her outrage was that the *devadasi* practices of illicit relationships and bed hopping would pollute middle-class sensibilities. Shock and horror! The *devadasi* had returned to middle Indian America. Forget Madonna, Shakira, Pamela Anderson, countless Bollywood actresses, and the images of sexually active, strong women entering middle Indian America's living rooms each day through television, film, and other media. We had to worry about the haunting of the *devadasi* in five-hundred-year-old texts. What would happen next?

There were five students ranging in age from about fourteen to twenty-seven years; I was curious about what the parents of the younger girls would say and thought it was bold of Ramya to teach this particular piece. In any other context, the texts would hardly be shocking. They were, after all, texts based on heterosexual desire. But in middle-class Indian America, they become something else. Among sexually explicit lines in the text of the *padam*, the *nayika* in this *padam* is young and single and is having a relationship that is made public. Rather than shrinking away from the gossip, she confronts her accusers and openly admits her affair. This *nayika* was bold in the fifteenth century, but in contemporary Indian America, as a young girl, she would be quite foolhardy to make her sexual exploits known.

Ramya turned to me and quickly raised her eyebrow before looking at the few mothers sitting next to me, watching in the classroom, and addressed them directly. She said, "I want you all to understand that these four- or five-hundred-year-old texts are not going to corrupt your daughters. They already know everything from their schools, the TV, and the movies. Right girls? Who or what is a *devadasi* in twenty-first-century India and America is complicated, and the lines are fast getting blurred. We need to remember that these were dances practiced by the *devadasis* in the temples, dedicated toward God, and we are now doing them in our classrooms in very different contexts in order to learn about love, emotion, and life. The *devadasis* are dead and gone, but perhaps a little bit of them still remains in these *padams*. It's a way for us to understand their lives." She did not really wait for a response from the mothers. She focused on the younger girls in the class and began asking them to imagine themselves in the place of the *nayika*, who was writhing in pain, exquisite torture, and longing. I smiled. This unruly spectator was ready, willing, and obedient enough to translate this message verbatim, if possible. Had our conversations over the years changed her thinking about the *devadasis*, or was this thought just arrogance on my part? Perhaps she had come to these conclusions herself. We were still far from confronting the violence done to the *devadasis* in the form, but we had come a long way. The construction of the model minority Indian female as chaste and "ideal" was being disrupted in these particular teachings. The *devadasi* had returned to haunt a seamless construction of Indian womanhood in the United States through the very middle-class bodies that had erased her in the past.

Conclusion

Bharata Natyam practice as taught in twenty-first-century American classrooms is complicated and contradictory. While power plays itself out between gurus and students in bodily exchanges through the dance practice, history continues to form and reform as the discourse of "model" middle-class Indians proliferates. Vastly different in class to previous dancers coming from India in the late nineteenth and early twentieth centuries, the dancers arriving in the United States after 1965 held new kinds of power positions, unavailable to earlier dancers. The position of guru, for example, enabled female dancers coming from India to create new, economically viable positions of power for themselves. Indian American communities not willing to accept the tenets of American assimilation attempt to counter its effect by putting their daughters in primarily female-run dance schools to teach them how to be "ideal" Indian women and accept the tenets of cultural nationalism. As I have demonstrated in this chapter, power is not just handed down through extreme physical and bodily conditioning in Indian dance classrooms, it is also negotiated by young girls, and not simply accepted as given. Through bodily labor, Indian American girls resist and subvert the power of the guru and also the expectations of cultural nationalism. They do not just become the bearers of multiple discourses of nation, immigration, diaspora, and citizenship. They negotiate it, even if it is only by "giving the finger." But as this last study shows, gurus are not simply the guardians of the Indian American community's expectations of cultural nationalism; they too negotiate with those expectations, and change over time. The *padam* form, with all its eroticism and "un-ideal" womanhood, is embedded in the Bharata Natyam practice, revealing that the *devadasi* still haunts the form and its middle-class practitioners in diasporic America, even a century after her disappearance. The discourse of cultural nationalism and its ideal expectations of middle-class Indian women are contradicted by both gurus and students. Bharata Natyam practice in America is not just a static practice with a top-down approach to power, history, and community that is meant to inculcate ideal minority cultural values to young Indian American women. It is also a changing, dynamic form that, when mined for bodily labor, reveals itself in negotiation of cultural nationalism and citizenship.

Just as I am about to step out of the classroom in order to beat traffic, I hear Ramya say, "*Yarakaheelum bhayama* . . . Who am I afraid of? This *padam* is called *Yarakaheelum bhayama*, in the raga, *begada*, *tala: misra chapu*, the seven-beat cycle. Can you beat out the rhythm, girls? It is written in the Tamil language by an unknown poet. The *nayika* is an *abhisarika*, one who goes bravely looking for her beloved. She is indifferent, bold, proud, and arrogant. She is having a relationship with her male lover and she is unmarried and young. But she doesn't care about what society says about her: *Yarakaheelum bhayama chumma sollattum yidha yenna rahasiyama* (Why would I be scared of anybody? Let them say whatever they want. Is my relationship with you a secret?). There are several elaborations that can be done on the text. One interpretation can be more confident than the next. So people are pointing. Am I scared? Let them say what they will. There is no secret to be covered up. Obviously, my parents will say what they have to—it is their duty—but I can't listen to it. My relationship with him is out of the closet, so there! My friends are gossiping. Should I be scared? What a joke. They're stupid anyway. In any case, I am going to broadcast my relationship with him to everyone. Who am I scared of? Let them talk; this is no secret."

One student in particular catches my eye. She is a beautiful dancer, and she's about sixteen years old. She did not want me to mention her name. I know why she is so affected by this *padam*. She has an African American boyfriend that only her friends know about. It is not unusual for young Indian American girls to express cross-racial desire and date at the age of sixteen, but what is common is the secretive nature of the relationship. She has immediately understood what the essence of this *nayika* is. Her hands move from her waist to make a gesture using the *pataka* mudra. Her hand circles in front. She looks around haughtily at the parents sitting in the classroom. Her eyes flick over to her side. Her eyebrows narrow downward. She interprets the line as "People are pointing. Am I scared? Let them say what they will. There is no secret to be covered up." She is walking backward this time. Another gesture is formed with her hand, and this time the *shikhara* mudra is used to question. Her eyebrows narrow downward. She jumps to the side. Her hands are close to her chest. Then she smiles. She flicks her hands outward. Her eyes look directly ahead. She shakes her head from side to side. *Yarakaheelum Bhayama?* No I am not.

7

The Manufacturing of the Indian Dancer through Offshore Labor

To the beat of the *mridangam* and the sound of the *carnatic* vocalist's *alapana* in the haunting *raga* of *Nattai*, Madhavi walked to the front of the stage, positioning herself right in the middle.[1] The audience went wild cheering her onstage. Perhaps it was the sight of her in a mango yellow sari with a dark purple *zari* border, with her ankles adorned by a pair of leather and metal dancing bells. Or her body bedecked in jewels shimmering against the backdrop of the sari. For the largely diasporic first- and second-generation Indian American audience, Madhavi perhaps transported them magically back home to India, just for a few hours, on that stage. This was the fifteen-year-old girl's solo debut recital, the *arangetram*, the culmination of years of dance training, and now it was all going to be worth it because she was going to give back to the community. She would allow their immigrant nostalgia to transport the audience to an ahistorical, mythical space. Only the world of the gods and demons existed and the dancer herself became a goddess onstage. For the smattering of non-Indians in the audience, she allowed them an orientalist spectacle ready for consumption, symptomatic of U.S. multiculturalism at its best. She is thus the example of an ideal ethnic minority body both within U.S. models of multicultural diversity celebrations and for cultural nationalists and racialized Asian/American immigrant subjects who attempt to resist cultural assimilation.

The aerobic quality to the dancing, with the emphasis on the rhythmic footwork and leaps and bounds, had the girl laboring well. Although her face from time to time belied this bodily labor with a sweet smile, which was quite inappropriate for the nature of the piece, her body could not be cheated out of demonstrating its labor and began leaving its mark on her clothing. Although Madhavi was by no means sweating profusely or even obviously, the telltale marks were beginning to show, as dark patches appeared under her arms. Every time she lifted her arms, there were the patches for all of us to see. Beads of sweat had turned into thin rivulets and began flowing from her neck and back, imprinting dark marks on the silk sari. I am sure other audience members saw it too, but why was I the only one getting so upset? Why were they pretending not to see any of the dancer's bodily labor?

I argue in this chapter that Bharata Natyam, primarily a solo dance form, deserves consideration as the labor of many bodies, techniques, and material objects that produce the body onstage. I pay attention to the dancer's bodily labor, evidenced in sweat, muscular exertion, and cultural work, and to the material objects that construct the Bharata Natyam dancer's body on U.S stages—material objects that are viewed as "asides" or pretty paraphernalia and costuming. By paying attention to the labor that produces these "asides" such as the silk sari,[2] jewelry, bells, flower ornamentations, as well as the body onstage, I argue for a reconsideration of the solo dancing body as a product of multiple and often messy laboring bodies.

This chapter again picks up the question of how examining the Indian (American) dancing woman as laborer allows us to see her negotiations with the terms of U.S. citizenship. I suggest that Indian American dancers are dealing with at least two "master" discourses of citizenship. The first is the cultural nationalism of South Asian communities in the United States; the second is the U.S. multicultural discourse, which seeks to divide minority communities, even as it celebrates their "national" ethnic forms as the "other" of mainstream practices. Embedded in these is the model minority citizenship discussed previously that shapes both kinds of discourses of citizenship for Asian American minority communities. As I have argued, U.S. multicultural discourse in the form of the problematic model minority citizenship label given to Asian Americans seeks to divide minority communities even as it celebrates their "national" ethnic forms as model but nonetheless "other" to mainstream cultural practices. In this chapter, I further develop this argument to think through the terms of cultural citizenship.[3] I do this by focusing on the *arangetram*.

The *arangetram* is the graduation ceremony and debut recital for Bharata Natyam dancers, in which they present a full repertoire of solo dance performances onstage for the first time. The *arangetram* performs a dual function in the United States. On the one hand, it is *the* performance of Indian nationalism and defines the terms of its cultural citizenship. It embodies an alternative to U.S. mainstream assimilation pressures, one that extinguishes the threat of exogamy by teaching primarily young Indian American girls to become ideal Indian women cultural citizens.[4] The *arangetram* functions as the performance of that alternative cultural citizenship. The female dancer onstage conjures up the gods, demons, temples, and India itself for the Indian diasporic community audience, seated, in this instance, in a darkened California theater. On the other hand, the *arangetram* also serves the U.S. multicultural discourse wherein Indian ethnicity, through the function of model minority, can be traded and, as I argue, the female dancer as the ethnic minority woman is a commodity.[5] She functions to iterate and maintain "difference" to mainstream communities. The *arangetram* serves that function much like other multicultural dance festivals in which a variety of cultural dance forms are displayed for consumption like a cultural buffet. Here, there is only the performance of Indian difference, the minority whose "model" culture can never be assimilated into the mainstream and whose brown, racially different body can never be fully American. The young Indian American dancer's bodily performance is thus a commodity being traded for the service of dual cultural citizenships, but as the contradictions of her danced bodily labor reveals, she is not simply a commodity.

The *arangetram* is the graduation ceremony for Bharata Natyam dancers, but it also functions as a cultural performance of citizenship for the Indian community at large which comes and witnesses the young girl modeling Indian cultural citizenship onstage as she performs mythological stories, ideal female characters, and summons Indian gods to American stages. This includes partaking in food and drink (usually nonalcoholic), wearing traditional clothes and jewelry (primarily for women), socializing, and merrymaking. All of this at the expense of the young girl's parents, who foot the bill for the entire evening. *Arangetrams* these days can run into the tens of thousands of dollars, depending on the guru and her expectations, as well as the parents' desire to demonstrate their wealth and success to the Indian community. What is often the subject of conversations at the *arangetram* is the young performer's visual appearance, particularly her costume and *aharya* (material layers) that cover the dancing body—be it the sari, jewelry, makeup, hair ornamentation, or bells.

In this emphasis on the *aharya*, Indian communities focus on similar objects as the writers who describe Bharata Natyam dance performances in Euro American contexts.[6] For Indian diasporic communities, it is the buying and wearing of *aharya* that makes the young female dancer "authentic." The seeming binary created between the body and the *aharya* that covers it also serves to hide the labor that goes into the performance. I argue in this chapter that it is important to value and evaluate the labor that produces the dancing body instead of veiling it. In the labor of dance, the dancing body as a commodity cannot be separated from its means of production. Yet somehow the objects that construct this body seem to have a fetishized life of their own. I attempt to trace these objects not as fetishes but as tangibles that have material lives and are embedded in human labor. In what follows, this unruly spectator views these layers of clothing differently and approaches these bodily encumbrances as actually constituting the Bharata Natyam body, wherein the sari, jewels, objects, technique, body, and discourses cannot be separated in performance, and the myth of their "authenticity" in constructing the diasporic subject needs to be destabilized.

In the process of destabilizing, I am concerned with making visible the class encounters that help construct the classical female Indian Bharata Natyam dancing body.[7] Middle-class and upper-caste women in post-independence India have dominated the Bharata Natyam practice. Scholarship on the foremothers of Bharata Natyam in the form of *sadir* as practiced by *devadasis* has proliferated since the 1980s and helps us account for caste differences.[8] What has not often been dealt with are the class differences in relation to global capital that currently create and stabilize the practice of Bharata Natyam in India and its diaspora. For example, there are few critical analyses of the flow of global capital between India and the United States generated by Bharata Natyam. This chapter highlights these issues and offers perspectives on the intersections between the labor, capital, objects, individual bodies, and collective bodies that create the Bharata Natyam performer.

This is where a focus on the dancing body's labor offers insights that trouble the homogenization of global cultures in the "cultural citizenship" discourses, which swing from utopic (i.e., cultural practices as pure resistance) to dystopic (cultural practices are purely commodities to be traded). These homogenizations often fail to address dominant, residual, and emergent global trends as well as messy intersections of and friction between these categories of thought, as Aihwa Ong (2004) and Anna Tsing note (2004). I argue in this chapter that the Indian American dancing body, although a minority body, experiences, inhabits, and differently articulates universalizing modes of multiculturalism and mainstream cultural assimilation. In the process of resisting cultural assimilation and critiquing the U.S. state through the realm of cultural capital, Indian American communities, albeit minority communities, end up colluding with the U.S. state in terms of economic capital. Power thus does not flow in a simple top-down direction, and cultural citizenship does not simply resist hegemonic structures of U.S. citizenship. Therefore, although I use social anthropologist Lok Siu's (2001) argument for diasporic cultural citizenship in which diasporic communities have dual loyalties to homeland and land of residence, I make the case that both these ties to citizenship are superseded by the pull of capital. I am influenced by Ong's (1999, 2004) persuasive line of reasoning that cultural citizenship is an adaptive process and Lisa Lowe's (1996) feminist, class analysis that complicates the argument of cultural citizenship and frames it as a multilayered process. I suggest that when it comes to dance practices and laboring dance bodies, the adaptive process exceeds the terms of U.S. and Indian citizenships. So it is not that Indian Americans simply have allegiances to Indian citizenship as an alternative to American citizenship—in fact, they demonstrate an allegiance to neither and end up colluding with the terms of capital, which supersedes national borders. This process sets up a messy dynamic but one that demonstrates how culture is contested, shaped, and remade by many bodies (Tsing 2004). I demonstrate this by exploring the young Indian dancer during the ultimate performance of cultural citizenship, her *arangetram*.

To pose this argument, I borrow from the structure of the *varnam*, often the central item in a Bharata Natyam *arangetram*. The *varnam* transports the dancer and the audience imaginatively to different places, in order to experience different bodily subjectivities, often through a series of interruptions in the dance structure. It interrupts abstract rhythmic dance sections with mimetic textual sections. The dancer begins by executing a complex rhythmic section known as the *jathi*, and then interrupts this by interpreting a line of text sung to music that is repeated numerous times through *abhinaya* (mime, gesture, and expressive emotions). Although the text repeats, the dancer improvises multiple scenarios for understanding the text by taking on different character positions, evoking an emotional quality, or by describing a scene or event. The audience is thus transported to many places in short amounts of time. Once she has explored the single line of text to her satisfaction, she quickly moves into two *jathi* sections. She then returns to another line of text that again shifts the spectator into focusing on her mimetic improvisation. She repeats this pattern another three times and then begins the second half of the piece with a faster rhythm and quicker overall pace. A *varnam* can take more than an hour to execute, depending on the dancer. To some audience members, the shift from the slow moving, descriptive *abhinaya* to the fast-paced *jathi* can seem abrupt. To others, the movement seems to flow, allowing them to seamlessly make the imaginary voyage from place, scene, or subject. I make a conscious effort through my writing to account for these movements in the actual execution of the dance, through the device of interruption and transportation.

I examine the Bharata Natyam body onstage from the view of the unruly spectator, building from previous chapters as one who takes pleasure in critically examining what is not supposed to be seen in an "ideal" performance. The *rasika* of the twenty-first century operates within the economy of desire and consumption of the Bharata Natyam dancing body, girded by the frame-work of capital. This twenty-first-century national or global viewer in the nation-state and diaspora consumes the female Indian dancing body onstage, exercising a patriarchal, heterosexual gaze, while "his" body is rendered inac-tive, or at least suspended in the state of spectatorship, by these discourses of power. Meanwhile, the dancer actively labors on the global stage to mask the nationalist rewriting of dance history and makes numerous sacrifices with her body to achieve this. Simultaneously, she attempts to efface the labor of the multitudes of bodies and their histories, which helped create her performance. The unruly spectator is thus placed in a subject position that demands a call to action. "She" moves between different positions, discourses, and gazes to revel in, critique, historicize, deconstruct, and participate in the performance. The unruly spectator's movement is not spectacular; rather, it is minimal, sometimes unconscious, and at times tactical, but it leaves her with corporeal marks on her body and transforms her.

The Sweating Sari

I am in an auditorium in Orange County, California, that seats about five hundred people. The largely Indian crowd is buzzing with activity and noise. Most of the boys and men are wearing Western pants and suits, while a few are dressed in traditional *kurtas*. There are young girls, middle-aged women, and older women dressed in traditional clothes of *salwars* and saris.[9] A range of color and material dazzles my eyes and nicely matches the chunks of gold, silver, platinum, and stone jewelry displayed around feminine necks and ears. Wanting to blend in with the crowd, I wear an olive-green *kanjeevaram* sari with a *zari* border and a simple gold chain with earrings. Despite feeling like I have dressed appropriately for the occasion, I still look underdressed com-pared with many in the audience. Although the auditorium is air conditioned, the dry heat from outside combines with the layers of fabric draping my body and I feel quite hot. As I chat with a few of the young girls and their mothers about the weather, complimenting them on the colors and fabrics they are wearing, I hear others talking about the costs of putting this evening together. One mother says, loudly, that she heard the parents have spent well over $25,000, while another says it was at least $35,000 to $40,000, with the musi-cians and expensive saris included. One father is chatting with another about the latest Lakers game, saying he was sorry to be missing tonight's match but that he has TiVoed it. He wonders if anyone has the current score. My friend taps me on the shoulder, arriving late as usual, and sits down next to me just as the lights go down and the curtains rise to begin the *arangetram*. I smile at her and whisper that she has arrived on Indian Standard Time and that her timing could not be more perfect. She takes out a packet of sour Mentos and offers me a sour-apple piece just as the music begins. Spotlighting the musicians and guru onstage, the initial musical piece invokes Ganesha, the elephant-headed god and remover of all obstacles. As a second piece begins, the dancer enters the stage.

Raising her arms above her head, Madhavi Manoranjan (a pseudonym) salutes the audience with her palms folded together and begins her performance. She, too, begins with a piece dedicated to Lord Ganesha to remove any obstacles in her path so that her *arangetram* will go smoothly. The audience erupts in cheers, hoots, and screams. My friend too starts screaming along with the crowd, chanting the girl's name. I just look at my friend and grin at her "enthusiasm." She raises an eyebrow, signaling with one hand in mudra form, as if to say, "So what? Might as well get into this performance!" Many in the audience are familiar with the *Ganesha Kavuttuvam,* and I can feel and hear them as they tap their feet, slap their hands on their thighs, and even hum along. This popular *kavuttuvam* often opens dance performances and is a crowd-pleasing favorite for *arangetrams.* The dancer smiles a broad smile and jumps to and fro extolling the virtues of Ganesha. She shows us his large elephant ears flapping to and fro, his divine birthright as son of Lord Siva, his ability to remove obstacles, his potbelly, which was probably the result of his constant desire for *modakams* (sweet dumplings) and food in general, his intelligence, and the way he rides elegantly on his mouse. Hail to Ganapati (another name for Ganesha)! Interspersed between descriptions of the deity are light rhythmic sections that do not puncture but flow in-between the lyrical movement, offering rhythmic and gestural interpretations of the piece. Madhavi ends the piece quickly and disappears offstage to catch her breath and ready herself for the next item. I am quite happy watching this piece, perhaps because it is short in length, the melody is infectious, the dancer smiled in all the right places and evinced the right facial gestures at the appropriate moments, and her spritely figure held my attention. My friend elbowed me as I was tapping along to the rhythm of the piece, as if to say, "You are enjoying yourself after all!" I make a mental note that this was a good choice to begin this girl's *arangetram.*

The precise slapping of her feet in perfect rhythm, the beautifully formed mudras, the clear arm and body lines, as well as the decision to perform only *nritta* to *sahityam,* all make the second piece spectacular, too.[10] Instead of translating the vocalist's text through dramatic expression to describe the various qualities of Lord Siva, she chooses to depict the text through *nritta* (rhythmic dance) to point to the temple where this Siva was located. At chest level, her right hand forms the *shikhara* mudra depicting the phallic *Siva lingam,* with four fingers closed tightly inward like a fist but with the thumb raised up, and her left hand resting beneath in a simple *pataka*, with four fingers stretching outward and the bent thumb tucked neatly on its side. This gesture is not a sufficient clue as to the location of the temple. It is when she depicts the peacock with the *mayura* gesture, that it becomes clear that the particular temple space she is referring to is the Kapaleeswarar Temple in Mylapore, Chennai.[11] As an audience, we are transported to the site. Imagining ourselves in the temple, we can see the dancer propitiate herself to the Siva lingam.

But I am getting restless and distracted. My friend glares at me because she can sense me drifting away and wants me to be more engaged. However, I am a miserable failure as a fan, and after the first five or six minutes of the piece I find my mind wandering. I had allowed her choreography to transport me mentally to the temple site of the deity, but my mind/body do not want to stay there. For quite a few years, I have found myself unable to concentrate in dance concerts, particularly in solo Bharata Natyam shows. The thoughts range widely, but this evening I find myself thinking about the sweat marks on Madhavi's sari and other things normally unaccounted for when looking at the "ideal" Bharata Natyam dancer. Perhaps I notice it because my own body has begun sweating in odd places. Even though the auditorium is air conditioned, I can feel the heat traveling down my body causing small beads of sweat to form, and I am not even moving that much. Madhavi, on the other hand, is moving all over the stage, so I am curious about the sweat that appears on her blouse and sari.

She wears a beautiful *kancheevaram* silk that probably cost her anywhere from eight thousand to ten thousand rupees (approximately US$160–$200). How will she get the sweat marks off? Will it leave stains? I suppose it can be dry-cleaned. Yet her dancing body is leaving telltale traces of its labor. No amount of dry-cleaning could remove all the bodily juices. What a price to pay! This is obviously a costly sari and a unique one, too. I wonder where she purchased it. Although it could have been at almost any of the large sari shops in Chennai, I decide it was probably from RASI (Radha Silk Emporium) on North Mada Street, Mylapore. This decision is probably influenced by the fact that I had been to the shop just a week earlier, during my annual visit to the Chennai Music and Dance Festival. I was shopping for a friend of mine, and RASI often carries unique sari pieces that attract well-to-do dancers.[12]

The bells of the Kapaleeswarar *kovil* on North Mada Street had been ringing auspiciously as I arrived via "auto," a three-wheeled taxi, landing at the doors of the temple at 10:00 A.M. The temple forms the base structure of the urban sprawl in that area. The water tank, an ancillary but crucial appendage of the temple, stands right next to it, forming the usual square shape. Various bazaars, shops, and homes line the square. On the other side of the temple is the sari store RASI.

Although I had asked to be dropped at the RASI store, for some reason the driver had deposited me on the temple steps. Deciding it was fate, or perhaps because RASI was not yet open, I went to have a brief *darshan* before commencing my shopping. I paid the auto driver handsomely for getting me there in record time and stepped out of the vehicle, taking care not to trip over the ends of my deep purple *pochampally*[13] sari. I quickly bought flowers as offerings for the deity, rushing to pay an old woman twenty rupees (about 45 US cents) who was competing with at least a dozen other vendors for the sale. The smell of jasmine and tuberoses made me heady as I headed into the sanctum just as the priest was performing the last rituals of the morning. The priest sang his ritual chants to Lord Kapaleeswarar (Siva), here instated in the form of the lingam (phallus), and his raga haunted and distracted me at once.

I was leaning against one of the pockmarked black stone squares that make up the inner sanctum and found myself searching for the melodies of the voices and bodily traces of the *devadasis* who had danced here for two hundred and fifty years.[14] As mentioned previously, the nationalization of Bharata Natyam had effectively stripped the ritual *devadasi* workers from their role of performing in specific cultural contexts and replaced them with new upper-caste bodies. Replication of laboring bodies is the imperative of capital. Capital, colonialism, and subsequently nationalism went hand in hand.

Trying not to think too far back in time, I focused on the early twentieth century, attempting in my mind's eye to locate the *devadasis*, the women dancers who had been consecrated at this temple before they had been removed from their god-husband's home. Had a *devadasi* leaned against this wall much as I was doing? I had my palm pressed against the wall to support myself, and I wondered if a *devadasi*'s hand had been there, too. Could her sweat marks have mingled with mine on the temple wall? I was wondering how a *devadasi*'s ritual performances to propitiate her god-husband through music and dance might have differed from that of the male priest standing before me.[15] In particular, what struck me about *devadasi* ritual practice was how the dancing woman used her human, fleshy, female body to protect her god-husband when he ventured out in the temple procession. The *devadasi*'s body was always in between the eye[16] of the devotee and the bronze idol as it traveled in procession around the temple. The *devadasi* woman used her entire body as a ritual offering, completely surrendering to her god-husband through dance and movement. She had sacrificed her body many times over for her god-husband. She was a truly consecrated devotee, the special one, marked for her undivided labor to the lord. The male priest here made sure his body was not in between the devotee and the deity. Instead, he stood to one side, ensuring that we could clearly see Lord Kapaleeswarar. I remembered Kersenboom's detailed account of the intricacies of *devadasi* culture, yet I still could not help myself from playing with the corporeal possibility of sweat mingling and imprinting itself in this ritual sacred space. The coldness of the stone harkened back to the reality that there seemed to be nothing left of any *devadasi* women's bodies, save the spaces they had moved in. The deity Siva lingam stood mute, as if dumbfounded at the loss of its human wives, even as rivulets of milk, butter, and water flowed over it in propitiation or perhaps to compensate for the diminished power of the divine phallus.

While waiting for the propitiations of the male priest to end, I spied a small statue of Thirugnana Sambanthar along with many of the other *nayan-mars*[17] on one side of the temple and thought to myself that perhaps I should pray to this great saint to restore the *devadasis* back to life now, just as he had brought a woman back from the dead. I was thus reminded of an important and constitutive legend associated with the temple. Story has it that Thirugnana Sambanthar, a great Saivite Saint from the eighth century C.E., revived the daughter of a devotee of Lord Siva named Sivanesa Chettiar from the dead within the temple grounds. One day the young woman was bitten by a cobra and died. After the cremation of his daughter's body, the Chettiar collected her ashes and kept them in an urn. When Thirugnana Sambanthar visited this temple during his pilgrimage of the area, he asked the Chettiar to bring the urn of his daughter's ashes to him. When the saint sprinkled some water from the temple tank onto the urn, the daughter came alive and walked into the temple. After her miraculous restoration, this young woman volunteered herself into the service of Lord Siva and became a *devadasi* in the temple. What kind of prayers would I have to do to restore the *devadasis*? What sacrifice could I make to bring them back? Was there even a sacrifice I could make, and what would it achieve? As I was about to give up my nostalgic, ahistorical, and perhaps orientalist quest, I was rewarded (maybe because I had propitiated the temple deity appropriately?) with a reminder of the famed *devadasi* Mylapore Gowri Ammal, whose title "Mylapore" came from her dedication to this temple.

Mylapore Gowri Ammal's claim to dance fame came when Rukmini Devi Arundale sought her out in 1936 to guide her reconstruction of the *sadir* form into Bharata Natyam. Rukmini Devi had come to the Kapaleeswarar Temple asking the great *devadasi* to come with her to Kalakshetra, fifteen kilometers away in Besant Nagar, in order to teach her the finer points of *abhinaya*. What had ensued in the temple? How had Rukmini Devi convinced Gowri Ammal to impart her knowledge? By 1947, Gowri Ammal and other *devada-sis* dedicated to temples all over India were declared divorcees or widows, ripped from the temples and their god-husbands.[18] Yet, in Chennai, despite the absence of *devadasi* bodies, the cultural, ritual, and urban spaces they had inhabited were now filled by other bodies. Middle-class or often upper-caste Brahmin women had taken over the forms of the *devadasis*, replacing their local cost-effective silk saris with the costly urban kanjeevarams meted out by silk houses such as RASI, Nalli, and Kumaran.[19] A sari house such as RASI thus thrived next to the temple.[20] The priest handed me some *vibhudhi*, *kumkum*, *chandanam*, and jasmine flowers as I was being rushed out with the crowds. I placed the red *kumkum* on my forehead beneath my *bindi*, the white *vibhudhi* ash on top of the *bindi*, rubbed the fragrant yellow san-dalwood paste on my neck, and placed the jasmine flowers in my hair. The traces of the temple and the gifts from the deity were now ritually marked on my body. Consecrated, "blessed," and ready to make my purchase at the sari store, I made my departure after resting for the prescribed few minutes on the temple doorstep.

Choreographies of the Thumb[21]

Walking approximately thirty steps—actually, it was thirty-five steps because I had to avoid a large pile of cow dung—I arrived at RASI. I was greeted with a burst of cool air as the air conditioners and fans were on full blast. Normally, this store would provide a wonderful respite from the Chennai heat, but it was cool today and I found the hair on my arms and various other body parts standing on end from the cold. I braved the conditions and took a step forward into the heart of sari shopping territory. I was greeted warmly by the owner and various salesmen who recognized me from my years of dance shopping. I was given "special treatment" accorded only to the rich and/or famous. Sipping a cup of hot tea and seated comfortably, I secretly thanked my dance guru in Australia, who had enabled me this special status because of our collective spending for all his dance students. I remember one year, we purchased seventy-five saris totaling lakhs of rupees and thou-sands of dollars!

Feeling caffeinated and refreshed, I sat near the *kanjeevaram* section. Mani, one of the RASI salesmen, spied me and started laying out saris for me to examine. I had not opened my mouth to make my requests known, yet with the flip of his wrist and a turn of his thumb, he deftly and quickly displayed a stunning array of *kanjeevarams* in brilliant aquas and deep oranges, *venkata-giris* in mustard yellows, *ikat* greens and black prints from Orissa, *jamdhani* blues shot through with purple, pink interlaced with blue tie-dye *bandhnis* from Gujarat, deep red Mysore silks, *mangalagiri* burgundy laced with cream, black *benaras* with elegant *zardosi* borders, all layered one over the other so

I could see the full range of possibilities. Mani was clearly an expert in displaying saris; he must have recalled some of my earlier purchasing days and thought he could meet my needs before I said anything. His performance had been superb, and I was dazzled into silence. All I could do for quite a while was touch the saris in awe and experience the thrill of feeling the texture of the materials.

A half hour or so later I was forced to emerge from my reverie as I felt the sting of a mosquito on my left calf. My first instinct was to scratch the itch, and I was just about to do so when I realized I was holding a beautiful, expensive, blue, *jamdhani* in my hand. It would not look good for me to reach down in an ungainly fashion to scratch my calf. Where was my mosquito repellant when I needed it? Though mosquito bites are quite intense in Chennai, I stoically composed my face, even smiled, controlled my bodily urge to itch, and instead went about the task of examining *kanjeevarams* as a good customer should. Eventually, I had to tell Mani that, sadly, I had come to buy one sari, and he was to show me saris only within the range of four thousand to six thousand rupees, in the colors that had been requested by the young girl. I explained that it was for an NRI[22] *arangetram*, and he immediately understood. He smiled wryly and commented about my buying power, or lack thereof, these days. Yet he went to a corner of the display area and brought out some beautiful and unique pieces. Carefully and slowly, Mani layered one or two pieces with exquisite characteristics such as unique borders, body designs, or colors. Although his dark hands seemed manicured, his thumbs nails were exceptionally long. I could not tear my gaze from those irregular thumbs. They teased open sari borders, ripped out staples that bound the packaging of the sari, darted in between the elegant silk cloth panels and then out to smooth the material. Those thumbs were doing a lot of work at an even rhythmic pace. While it is true that the other fingers helped enhance this performance, they were merely framing devices acting as weights to control the material. The thumbs were the principal performers. In particular the thumbnails played an important role in allowing Mani to gauge the layers and thickness of the sari material, often inserting themselves between the folds to move layers of material apart. A duet would unfold before my eyes when Mani would run his right thumb quickly down one yard of the gold *zari* border of the sari to show me the exquisite work that had gone into making the design, and the nail would make a slight rasping noise in accompaniment. The other thumb with the assistance of the forefinger would hold the remaining five yards of the sari. The dark finger would be highlighted and frozen against the brilliant hues of blues, greens, and red silk material until the next sari was displayed.

As I was viewing Mani's thumb in isolation, its movement sharply recalled a vision of severed thumbs. I remembered the Indian weavers in the mid-nineteenth century whose thumbs were cut off so that the East India Company could monopolize trade with Indian textile merchants in the region.[23] This violent act, along with the deliberate destruction of native Indian factories, damaged the technology of weavers and was accompanied by the forced trade for cheaper but inferior British textiles, which ultimately led to the collapse of the Indian economy and the colonization of India. This colonization, accompanied by an array of complex discourses, led to the destruction of the *devadasi* and her cultural practices. When M. K. Gandhi began his famous "Quit India Movement" to rid the Indian subcontinent of British colonizers, he encouraged Indians to weave their own cloth by hand using their spinning wheels and boycott the inferior British cloth imported from factories in Birmingham and Manchester. A deeply political, "materialist" move, this agenda had the desired effect and severely impaired the British export infrastructure. Post-independence, the Indian flag still sports the symbolic wheel (which can be read in multiple ways) at its center. Thus, the Indian nationalization of women and their inclusion as Indian citizens involved covering the female body in layers of discourse through layers of cloth. Rukmini Devi followed Gandhi's grand design and further enhanced it by not only setting up local weaving centers in the confines of the Adyar dance compound that produced saris and various cloth but also emphasizing other local technologies that supported dance performance and production. Bharata Natyam practice in the United States also places an emphasis on using specific national cultural symbols such as the sari in Indian dance classrooms. The histories of cloth, saris, independence, nation, women, diaspora, and dance are intertwined.

Blood "Memories"

A beautiful deep pink sari with a purple border caught my attention. It was quite unique, but its memory vanished as I was suddenly interrupted and transported back to Madhavi's performance in California. I think I see her glancing my way, so I make a pact with myself that I will focus on her dance completely. She has moved on to the main piece of the night: the *varnam*.

She has me focused for almost six minutes when I become distracted by a small bell that has detached itself from the rows of bells adorning her ankles. I cannot help noticing it. Why is no one else concerned with the danger this bell poses to Madhavi? It strays a little from center stage and moves stage right, lingering tantalizingly on the side. I am sure Madhavi has seen it and will avoid it to complete this dance piece. However, springing to and fro as the deer, she does not see the stray bell and lands on it with her right foot after one very high jump. Landing on the sharp metal with such weight must surely have been painful, yet Madhavi shows no signs of injury on her face. She has been coached by her guru well. Her foot, however, reveals otherwise! A telltale trickle of blood flows from underneath her foot. The blood follows her movement, and she begins creating patterns on the floor marked with her own juices. Unlike *devadasi* performers who actually used their feet to create powdered colored artistic masterpieces of peacocks and palaces,[24] Madhavi has just created a Picassoesque abstract. I think this unintentional abstract is getting quite interesting, but to my dismay, she abruptly stops and sits down right in the middle of her own blood floor-painting to portray the *nayika* dressing and decorating herself, waiting for her lord to come. This destroys any further interpretation of her artistic creation, and furthermore, her pink sari is now stained with her own deep red blood. What will the dry cleaner say? More than that, what can we do about this stray bell that is still firmly ensconced right beside her onstage. Perhaps Madhavi's body resisted being weighed down with the layers of sari, jewelry, and heavy ankle bells. Maybe her body has willfully and violently attempted to rid itself of the bell. Or, as Avanthi Meduri (1996) suggests, the *devadasi* foremother is haunting the contemporary Bharata Natyam dancer, and in this particular performance, the ghost was exceptionally angry at being written out of history. Is the bell the trace of the ghost of the *devadasi*? Or is it that whoever had sewn this belt of bells together had not done a good job? Maybe it is a combination of these factors.

Having finished my purchases at RASI, I began walking toward the opposite side of the water tank where Radha Gold Jewelers stood. I needed one temple jewelry necklace to complete my list. The street perpendicular to North Mada Street was quite narrow, and I had to walk through this dusty road to get to the other side. As I walked, a number of street vendors caught my eye. In particular, the bell-weavers sparked my interest. The women who wove the bells together into one belt had tough hands. One woman in particular stood out. She was wearing a cream-colored cotton sari with a dark pink border that was fading either because of exposure to the sun or as a result of constant wear. She used the *pallu* to wipe the sweat away from her face and also as a polishing cloth for the belt and bells she held in her left hand. Her sweat mingled with the metal on her sari cloth. Her dark right hand was wrapped around the white and pink *pallu* because she was engaged in cleaning and polishing a bell, so I could see only her fingers and thumb. Her thumb, forefinger, and middle fingers were the principal performers, engorged with fat and fluid on the inner sides, which lightened the skin there. Clearly, they had labored intensely for her over the years. Ironically, she had worked for the middle-class Brahmin woman dancer's performance but had most likely never even seen the dance. She let go of the sari, and I saw her inner palm for the flash of a second. It was scarred deeply with wrinkles, but the skin looked tough with calluses.

Hers was an arduous performance, very different in quality and flow from both Madhavi's and Mani's performances. This performance had sweat, strength, and ritual elements to it, and although it was not dazzling, it had depth in terms of corporeal labor. She had to ensure all the bells were tightly woven together. Taking one large needle and extremely strong string, she battled to thread the string through the tough leather belt and finally string one bell through. She tightened it and knotted it carefully and bit off the remaining thread with her teeth. The process then began all over again with a second bell. I was taken aback when she actually looked up at me quizzically, wondering why I was looking at her. Her performance moved me deeply, but I was uncomfortable that she was looking back at me. Our locked gaze was broken when my body jerked rather violently as a result of a bicycle that knocked my elbow and then grazed my ribs. It was enough to throw me sideways, but luckily I jumped and grabbed onto a pole nearby to steady myself. I was breathing heavily and sweating profusely in what had now turned into a hot morning, but my mind would not stop racing.

The street was even busier than it had been fifteen minutes earlier. Had it been this crowded when Rukmini Devi had arrived here to meet Gowri Ammal? The dance business and industry took off only in the mid- to late 1950s, accompanying the popularity and growth of RASI and other sari stores. This street had been filled with bodies that primarily catered to the temple, which was the physical and spiritual center of Mylapore. The new economy around the water tank was recent and an offshoot of nationalist reconfigurings of the dance practice that led to its boom in the 1970s. It was Rukmini Devi's inventions at Kalakshetra that set this process in motion. She had prioritized the hand weaving of cotton saris (giving rise to the famous Kalakshetra cotton sari) and had carefully selected the costuming and grooming of the "ideal" Bharata Natyam dancer. For her, it had been about respectability and a set of aesthetics alternative to the *devadasi* women. Hers was an aesthetic that was internationally developed, informed by a global vision of theater and performance. Now, there were numerous vendors working for the dance economy. The division of labor was such that the poor working-class women and men who created dance accoutrements from raw materials never encountered the shopkeepers who sold them at marked-up prices to middle-class and upper-caste female dancers. I was told there were large factories, too, where these products were being made, but the detailed labor still had to be done, and this was evidenced in the work of the bell weaver.

I heard a thunderous applause since the dance item was over and the audience was cheering wildly. Perhaps the sight of blood had driven the "natives" wild. They thought Madhavi had sacrificed some of her blood onstage for them. The propitiations had been deemed appropriate and so the applause was overwhelming. Madhavi clearly had to change out of the sari and wear a new one. The musicians took charge and began an interlude that lasted a good ten minutes. Would she appear in a green, blue, mustard, or black number? I, too, was intrigued.

Intermission

It is a peacock blue sari with a deep burgundy border. On the edge connecting the sari to its *zari* border are embroidered peacocks that intensify the peacock blue color and the richness of the sari. The beauty of the sari enhances the dancer's tall stature and slim form. It is not the sari I had bought for her. She has already worn that one in the first half of the performance for the *varnam*. This sari will have to last the entire second half of the performance, including the speeches and the *mangalam*. The audience is hooting and cheering as she enters the stage again in her new sari. She is, after all, transporting them back to an India over three thousand miles away and a hundred or perhaps even a thousand years back in time. The exact date does not matter because the India that Madhavi's body conjures up is timeless. Madhavi's body is the vehicle for the immigrant diasporic community's vision of a precolonial, authentic India. Her sari, costume, and jewels clothe the perfect and iconic Indian woman's body. Time and space could stand still, and the immigrant community could feel free to project their nostalgic desires of home and an "ideal woman" onto her. I, too, am feeling nostalgic, thinking of the delicious food that had been served during intermission. The *samosas* and *chana batura* had left an indelible impression, not to mention the warm tea afterward. It could not have been a more perfect prelude to an afternoon nap. But that was not meant to be. I am not sure I have the patience to sit through to the end. It has been hard enough watching the first half of this performance, and there are still four or five items left, not to mention the tiresome speeches. But I know the dancing in the second half will go relatively quickly. The pieces will be short and quite lively, except perhaps the *padam*, and I know I will have to maintain focus and not get distracted as much as I did in the first half. My body is aching already from sitting in the auditorium for two hours, and I know there is still an hour and a half to go. I am also jetlagged and exhausted from the flight. I find my eyes closing on several occasions and am fighting to keep myself from literally falling off my chair. I arrived from India only yesterday and have not adjusted to Pacific Standard Time. But I have no choice. I have to be here today. After all, I brought one of the saris for her *arangetram*, along with a pair of bells and some jewelry. My suitcase was heavy, and my back is aching from lifting it on and off the baggage claim and carts. My right thumb is particularly sore from dragging the suitcase. It did not help that I was not allowed to go through the green channel even though I said I had nothing to declare. I had been fingerprinted and made to wait. My baggage was thoroughly searched, and I was made to explain to three separate officers that the pickles my grandmother had sent were drug-free edibles and that the jewelry was fake and not worth more than a hundred dollars. Finally, without any help from any of the officers, I had to clean up the mess they had made, repack the suitcase, and hoist it back onto the baggage cart. I think that was when my right thumb folded itself between the metal of the baggage cart and the hard fabric of the suitcase. My thumb could not move after that. It was silenced.

The audience cheers wildly when she appears in the new sari. Ironically, although it is Madhavi's first solo in the United States, it will also most likely be her last. She will leave for Princeton shortly to begin a career in the sciences, engineering, or computing, and her dance practice will end, unlike those of the *devadasis*, for whom the *arangetram* signaled so many new beginnings. Madhavi could sever herself from dancing completely in ways the *devadasi* women never could. In this first piece following the intermission, Madhavi is describing a *nayika* playing the veena, a stringed instrument. The *nayika* in this instance is an imaginary character/heroine loosely based on the life of an actual *devadasi*. Madhavi begins the piece center stage in a spotlight. She is balancing, with only slight wobbling on her right leg, with the left ankle placed over her right knee. Madhavi is gesturing toward holding the veena on an angle with the heavy part resting on her left ankle. She makes a pretty picture, especially once she gets her balance. I see some photographers capturing the still image of her quickly and quietly. This pose deserves a photo frame in her dorm room! It is perhaps the glitter of the large gold anklet she wears above the bells that gets me thinking. It seems like the anklet is about to slip off. I am worried for the girl. It might cause her serious injury if it falls off in the middle of her dancing. I am taken back to another image of Madhavi, a *devadasi* who emerges from a Tamil literary text.

Madhavi, the thirteen-year-old *devadasi*, presented herself to the Chola[25] King Karikalan, performing on "stage" with her veena and other instruments for the first time before the king, his queen, artists, scholars, learned men, connoisseurs, and courtiers. The grand Tamil literary marvel of *Cilappatikaram*, in which Madhavi is featured, dates to around the fifth century C.E.[26] Credited to Prince Ilango Adigal, the brother of the Cheran king, Senkuttuvan, the story, it is said, was based on an earlier legend of a goddess woman named Kannagi. The *Cilappatikaram* text, though fictional, contains within it one of the earliest, most detailed accounts of *devadasi* performance practices. It is this text among others that has been used to secure an uninterrupted history for the contemporary performance of Bharata Natyam, devoid of colonial contact. Nirmala Ramachandran's essay "Bharata Natyam: Culture and Dance of the Ancient Tamils" (1966) is a classic example of nationalist and orientalist revising of Tamil history, in which the contemporary framework of the dance form from Sanskrit dramatic treatises is collapsed with Ilango Adigal's description of Madhavi's dances. Ilango Adigal's fictional account of Madhavi is believed to be indicative of his contemporary experiences with *devadasis* during the fifth century C.E. Whatever the case, his writing is indeed captivating and convincing, especially for a doubly colonized Tamil people searching for ways to rid themselves of colonial histories. As a Tamil and a dancer, I, too, have been seduced by the story of the ancient Tamil dancing woman, Madhavi, as a noble *devadasi* who could redeem herself.

At the age of seventeen, I performed Madhavi's *arangetram* at the Victorian Arts Center in Melbourne, Australia. Our dance company was putting on a season of the "Epic of the Anklet" for sixteen consecutive performances. My bodily memory of performing Madhavi's *arangetram* resonates far more clearly than performing my own *arangetram* two years earlier. I know Madhavi, the precolonial *devadasi*, only through my own orientalist imaginings of performing her and not just through Ilango Adigal's textualization of her. Ilango Adigal describes Madhavi's transition from a novice to a professional through her debut performance in court. Entering the stage wearing a peacock blue sari with a deep burgundy border, I moved downstage right and bowed before King Karikalan and his queen. The King handed me his *Thalaikkol*, the royal staff of approval. I placed the staff in the ground and bowed before it. I then had the ritual power of authority to commence my, or rather, Madhavi's, *arangetram*. There was no one in the audience that day—only a video camera recording the event and a photographer. Looking into the video camera, I realized instantly that I was wearing the wrong sari. The photographer would take a photo of me in the wrong sari, and my mistake would be memorialized forever. As Madhavi, I was supposed to wear the mustard yellow sari for the *arangetram* and the peacock blue for the seashore scene. The musicians were already beginning the next section, and I had to dance. My feet began moving in time, and my body mechanically performed the moves, but my mind was elsewhere. I spied my guru out of the corner of my eye, and his stern look sent waves of panic through my body. It was the wrong sari! But I could not think about that anymore. I had to focus on my dancing because the rhythms were too difficult to allow my mind to drift. I would worry about the sari later. Although Ilango Adigal details the many varieties of dances that Madhavi performed for her *arangetram*, which lasted several hours, including the songs she sang in various ragas and her ability to play different instruments such as the *yal* and the *isai*, I did it in seven and a half minutes in the form of a *jathiswaram*. The *jathiswaram* was invented as a structure in the late nineteenth century by the Tanjore Quartet, and my dance guru, and choreographer, used it to demonstrate all of Madhavi's fifth-century accomplishments in symbolic form. I pretended to play the *yal* (the precursor to the modern veena) and *isai* for ten seconds, demonstrated my ability to sing in various ragas in five seconds, and displayed my dancing skills in what we would today term "folk" and "classical" forms in thirty seconds. At the end of the piece, I bowed to the King accepting his *margosa* leaf garland and gold coins as a token of my achievement and graduation to professional status. As I started to walk away, the haunting raga of *Huseini* was enveloping my body. That was not right. It was supposed to be the raga *Behag* to which I exited. But I was hearing *Huseini*.

I felt goose bumps rise on my arms and the back of my neck and a current of energy travel through my body and to the top of my head. It was the raga *Huseini* enveloping my body. Even before I saw the vocalist and Madhavi Manoranjan onstage, I heard and felt the notes of the raga emerging from his full-throated singing. I started to hum the raga quietly, sometimes preempting where the vocalist would take his *alapana* improvisation and elaborations. I felt my eyes well up with tears at the emotion this raga carried with it. I was ready now to watch Madhavi's performance of the *padam, Netrandhil Neyrathiley*. She was by a body of water and saw her lover in an embrace with another woman. Madhavi as the main character, the *nayika*, was confused. Had her lover not promised that he was faithful only to her? Yet here he was behind the bushes with this other woman. I wondered why the mythical *devadasi* was so important to contemporary Bharata Natyam performances. The mythical *devadasi* who predates the colonial encounter is indeed a beautiful, unsullied, and desired creature. She can be imagined as each dancer chooses, through the interpretation of the *padam* text, where the *devadasi* is fictitiously housed. *Padams* are perhaps the only structure in the Bharata Natyam recital that have the ability to hold my interest. I am curious about how each dancer will perform a known text with her own interpretations, and these are not even her own interpretations. Although the item has been choreographed by her guru, her performance holds the possibility of seeing Madhavi's ideas in the dance.

I have to admit that Madhavi Manoranjan is doing a nice job of this *padam*. She is also sweating much less than in the first half of the *arangetram*, perhaps because the *padams* do not involve much aerobic activity and focus instead on the dancer's facial and bodily expression. The male vocalist is singing the first line of the poem repeatedly in the Tamil language, *Netrandhil neyrathiley neeraadum karaidhanile neringi ummai jaadai kati azhaithaval yaro swami?* I am surprised that Madhavi holds my attention throughout the *padam* performance. Although she is a young dancer, she seems to be really getting into this *nayika's* role. What is it about the *nayika* in this *padam* that captivates Madhavi and resonates with her? Why does the *padam* format allow her to project her own emotions into the text? Or is it so easy to imagine this *nayika* because she is such an ahistorical and mythical figure that it allows Madhavi to portray her unproblematically? Are those the very reasons I am able to focus on Madhavi's performance without distraction or is it simply the music itself that holds me in thrall?

The pace of the evening has picked up. Even though the *padam* was slow the fact is that she had already completed several pieces in quick succession. These pieces did not require the sustained energy and focus of the *varnam*, for example, which came before intermission. I reach down into my handbag to take out my book so I can take some quick notes in the dark when suddenly the house lights come on. I realize Madhavi has to do her obligatory thank-you speech, which has become part and parcel of diaspora *arangetrams*. It is sometimes jarring to see the silent dancing girl come onstage with a microphone and break out in a thick American accent, but there it is. Her voice is loud and her posture garish. She has her feet spread out and her back is hunched but she seems confident. She begins by thanking "aunty," meaning her guru, who is sitting onstage right with the musicians, explaining that it was "aunty" who taught her about Indian culture and tradition. Now that she knows the ancient history of the dance she practices, she will cherish it forever. She knows she was dancing for the Gods and that this is a divine form she has been given. Like dancers of two thousand years ago in India, she is continuing to practice Hinduism in her own small way. Madhavi has made many sacrifices to get to today, and yet she is thankful and would not have had it any other way.

I am struck that unlike other *arangetrams* speeches, this girl is calling on the fictive history of the Bharata Natyam form with such conviction. The religious reference is a common one, but turning to the history of the *devadasis*—that is interesting. What is the investment in this fictive authenticity, in drawing a particular history from the nation into the diaspora? It disturbs me to think of this constant pull of authenticity, whether it is the need for "authentic" objects such as the sari from India or merely "authentic" discourses whose falsified histories seem to plague Bharata Natyam practice. It is particularly interesting to me as waves of jetlag shoot through my body and my thumb aches from the pain of traveling between India and the United States to think about the many forgotten Indian dancers who came to the United States just one hundred and twenty years ago. I ask myself why, along with so many other girls who have done their *arangetram*, I, too, participated in the myth of the *devadasi* of two thousand years, fifteen hundred years, or three hundred years. Why is no one thinking about the actual *devadasis*, *nachwalis*, and dancing girls who arrived in the United States in the nineteenth century?[27] Why is nobody performing these early dancer's stories? I remind myself wryly that this is perhaps because few people know anything about these early dancers, and I am asking too much. Anyway, most Indians have collective amnesia about things that happened in the United States before 1965, since that was the year the National Origins Immigration Act was instituted to enable a large number of Asians and Indians to emigrate to the United States. As previously mentioned, before this time, there had been many racist anti-Asian immigration policies that prevented Indians from consolidating in any great number. It was only after 1965 that droves of different Indian dancing women started landing on American shores.

Oomdah, Bhoori, and Saheb were seasick. They had never traveled on a ship before, and certainly never one this large. The company of dancers and musicians that had come with them were sitting below deck. But these three were bold and had gone above deck. The rough, choppy waters of the Atlantic Ocean were more than they could bear. They had been traveling for a month already and had almost reached the shores of New York, but this last leg of the journey seemed the worst. It was November and perhaps the winter had begun early. Whatever the case, the three were happy to reach the shores of New York and disembark. They were met by theater impresario Augustin Daly himself. He wanted to make sure his prize possessions arrived in one piece. His show would begin in just over a month and he wanted his troupe ready for their big debut. They were the talk of the town. A reporter was on hand, eager to capture the first images of them. Oomdah, Bhoori, and Saheb agreed to go to his photo studio a few days after arriving. Although it was freezing, they refused to wear anything but their saris and a few shawls. They could hardly understand anything anyone was saying. It was a good thing their manager could translate a little for them. The photographer asked the women to do several dance poses, but he finally he settled on a simple image. One of them sat down in front while the other two stood behind her. They touched each other and looked back at the camera boldly. The shot was taken. It was printed in the *New York Clipper* the next day ("The Nautch Dancers," January 22, 1881, 345), and they became overnight celebrities. Each day, they cooked in large pots to make their own food and to keep warm by the fire. Reporters came in to watch them as they lived their daily lives. Everything they did was noted. They were equally excited by Augustin Daly's stage: the bright lights, the wooden floor of the stage, and the multitude of white cast members. They huddled in a corner whispering to each other about the strange costumes of the women actors, until called to rehearse their own material.

Soon it was time to perform onstage before an audience. It was cold onstage, and even the bright lights gave them no warmth. No sweat emerged from their bodies. But their feet cracked in many different places. Although their feet were trained to withstand heat, weight, pressure, and pain, dancing barefoot on a cold New York stage was difficult. Oomdah winced in pain as her foot thwacked on the ground creating rhythmic patterns. She hid it well, focusing on audience members' white faces and pale blue, and even some dark brown, eyes.

Although the first performance seemed to go well, soon, their fame turned to infamy. After their first few performances, the New York audiences did not want to see them perform. Ala Bundi died of a strange sickness that was probably made worse by the cold weather. Oomdah gave birth to a child, but it, too, died on American soil. Some of the troupe returned home, but some stayed. Although there were several groups of Indian dancers who came to and left the United States, they disappeared after 1907 and little was heard from the great subcontinent until after 1965, when droves of them started landing on American shores, this time not on ships but airplanes. Madhavi had been born in Santa Ana, California, at the Irvine Medical Center. Her father was a medical doctor who had come to the United States in 1984 for further studies. He stayed on after his residency and had an arranged marriage to her mother in Chennai, India, in 1989. Madhavi was born a year later. Madhavi's guru had arrived in California in 1981 with her husband, who came as a professional in search of a job. The guru's school was well established by the time Madhavi started classes there in 1996 at the age of six.

Madhavi finishes her speech and bows to her guru who is sitting onstage, next to the musicians. She gives the musicians and her guru a bouquet of flowers. She then turns to the audience and makes a deep bow with her hands folded and to cheerful applause. The musicians in turn smile, stand up, take a bow, and sit back down. Most of them are male.

She looks up, grinning at the audience. The sweat stains under her arms have dried up temporarily during the speech. This is not the dainty *nayika* she had performed earlier; it is Madhavi in all her bodily form. The full-toothed grin says it all. She is rather proud of herself and so is the audience. She has fulfilled their nostalgic desire. But did the audience see the many performances that were undertaken to make this one solo performance happen? Madhavi's body and all the objects and discourses that constituted her Bharata Natyam dancing body, including the jewels, bells, sari, and the various histories of transnational labor, were performing also. Madhavi, Mani, the bell weaver, unnameable imaginary and real *devadasis*, Oomdah, Bhoori, her own guru, her guru's guru, all were performing, laboring alongside Madhavi. The transnational bodily labor that is unaccounted for in watching Bharata Natyam dancing in the United States is performing itself through Madhavi's body. These many performances are happening simultaneously and we do not know how many of them are being seen. Many sacrifices were undertaken to enable this performance to happen. The biggest denial comes from the audience who pretends to not see these many sacrifices laid bare before them. What would it take for these sacrifices to be acknowledged?

In a global economy, the labor that is in plain sight and yet not always visible is that of variously classed Indian bodies in India. As Lisa Lowe (1996) and Aihwa Ong (2004) point out, and as I develop in this chapter, there are discrepancies between the wars waged through the cultural and the economic (neither of which are outside the political). An attention to many laboring bodies onstage highlights the negotiation of discourses of globalization that privilege some laboring bodies over others. In viewing performances of middle-class dancers in Chennai, the labor needed for cultural nationalism is just as unacknowledged as the "offshore" labor needed for Indian American diasporic production in California. A materialist analysis brings to light the sweat stains, the falling bell, the blood, and the dangling flowers as some of the telling signs of bodily labor that point to "other stories" of global capital's contradictions, excesses, and ruptures (Hong 2006).[28] The sweat stains, the falling bell, and other missteps are the telltale signs of contradictions and ruptures in response to the pressures of multicultural discourse and strains of cultural nationalism, especially in considering the hidden costs of offshore labor.

When pressured, Indian American communities battle U.S. agendas at the cultural level, even while colluding at the economic level. The labor in plain sight and yet not always visible is that of Asian bodies in Asia, they are the offshore labor needed for Indian American diasporic production. Indeed, this dancer onstage demonstrates the vigilance with which we need to watch and understand Asian American diasporic labor as it masks transnational Asian labor within the logics of late capitalism and globalization. Here is where the attention to dancing bodies as laboring bodies offers insights into the discourse of cultural citizenship. In other words, to stage cultural citizenship, diasporic middle-class Indian American (minority) communities in California resist mainstream acculturation by creating cultural performances of citizenship such as the *arangetram*, but in the end, they still end up colluding with mainstream discourses of capital. Cultural citizenship is thus differentially experienced neither fully as a practice of resistance nor in an assimilationist fashion, and it is the attention to female Indian American dancing laboring bodies that enables such an analysis.

Unlike the oppositional viewpoints of cultural citizenship discourses that position minorities as either resisting cultural assimilation or succumbing to it, I suggest that Indian American cultural performances participate in the very hegemonic structures of United States–Asia relations and the highly differentiated forms of flexible labor (i.e., offshore labor) that are based on unequal divisions of labor. This performance is vastly different from the performances of the *nachwalis* of the late nineteenth and early twentieth centuries, separated not only by time but also by class differences. The dancing body onstage performs these discrepant wars at cultural and economic levels and makes visible aesthetic cultural forms from India, while occluding the many laboring bodies from India who create her performance. It is in paying attention to the performance of dance labor that contradictions to global capital become visible.

Madhavi's sari fan is flying behind her as she rushes offstage. She disappears into the wings and is getting ready for the *thillana*. I think this would be a good time for me to leave in the dark before I get caught. I spring out of my seat just as I spy a bell that has rolled off Madhavi's ankle and is sitting on the stage where she will enter. Will she step on it? I cannot stay to discover the next series of performances that will unfold. I make it to the exit door just as she enters for the *thillana*.

Epilogue

I turned on the TV in January 2009 and was shocked to see an Indian woman dancing on the screen. It was not a documentary about Indian dance in India but a prime time show on NBC called *Superstars of Dance*.[1] She was dressed in a blue gauzy *salwar kameez*, with bells on her ankles, her eyes and face fully made up, and a smile on her face. Her feet were shuffling and striking the floor from time to time, and she was doing a number of *chakkars*, spinning around and whirling herself so that her dress would fly out around her. She was Amrapali Ambegaokar, a girl I had watched grow into a woman in Los Angeles, and daughter of renowned Kathak dance teacher, Anjani Ambegaokar.[2] The image of her spinning on TV with that particular costume reminded me not only of Ruth St. Denis's *Radha* and *Nautch* but also of the numerous *nachwalis*, including Oomdah, Bhoori, and Saheb, who had visited and performed a version of this Kathak form 129 years earlier on a New York stage. This time, instead of a few hundred spectators, there were about six million American viewers who tuned in to see Amrapali and others dance each week.

Amrapali was one of several contestants performing different styles of "world dance," and although she was competing in the solo category, there were others in duet and group categories representing a range of countries.[3] It soon became clear that the performers from Australia were professional dancers from the Australian Dance Theatre Company who had traveled to Los Angeles for this show. It was also evident that performers of the Shao Lin group had come from China, that dancers from South Africa had flown in from Johannesburg, and a majority of the Irish step dancers hailed from Ireland. But Amrapali and several other Indian dancers were not brought in from India. They were born and raised in California. As the unruly spectator once again, I knew this because, through years of ethnography and community interaction in the Southern California region, I knew most of the Indian dancers performing on the show. I not only knew Amrapali but also other young women who performed traditional Bharata Natyam numbers in the competition, including Mythili Prakash (daughter of Viji Prakash, a renowned Bharata Natyam guru based in Los Angeles) and Nakul Dev Mahajan (team coach), who choreographed the group's Bollywood numbers.[4] So, although it appeared to the TV audience that these bodies were outsourced, they were in fact American citizens laboring onstage and performing as if they were foreigners (Indians from India). They were thus both American and Indian, but their Americanness was being hidden.

Even though interviews with Amrapali, Mythili, or Nakul before or after each performance would reveal broad American accents, Michael Flatley, the host of the show, introduced them as dancers from India revealing the mysteries of "their" culture. The judges followed suit, and most of their responses reflected a naiveté about Indian dance forms. The Irish judge went as far as to say, "I'm sure in your country, what you do is very technical and amazing." What he did not say was, "But I have no idea how to judge you, especially in comparison to hip-hop, modern, or ballet performers." Essentially, he and the other judges (except perhaps the South African judge) rendered all the Indian dance and dancers alien and foreign to Western sensibilities of dance, despite the fact that the dancers were all Californian and American citizens.

As solo dancers on the TV stage, Amrapali and Mythili had no live musicians accompanying them. It was just their singular bodies laboring onstage as artists performing their citizenship. But that citizenship still remained ambiguous, even in 2009. Despite this, and unlike Bhoori, Oomdah, and Saheb, who were removed from center stage after their first few performances on the New York stage in 1881, Amrapali and Mythili remained on center stage in 2009. Although Mythili lost in the semifinals, Amrapali reached the finals and scored a second-place win, with the first place going to a Russian ballerina and third to a popping dancer labeled as American. The irony is that despite being American citizens performing diasporic Indian culture, Amrapali and Mythili continue to be viewed as foreign performers. But from another perspective, Amrapali and Mythili were straddling multiple citizenships. Using the cultural capital of Indian classical dance, they performed as Indians from India, something they could easily do, given the complex and continuous waves of Indian immigration to the United States after 1965. Costuming and makeup played a big part in their ability to shift citizenship.

Given that their costumed labor came primarily from India, they could easily play the role of authentic Indian dancers. But there were plenty of clues to their dual ties of citizenship. Amrapali and Mythili performed to digitized hybrid music created by musicians in Southern California, which had a base in Indian Hindustani and Carnatic music structures. The choreography of their dances had a distinctly Southern Californian use of space, design, and interaction with the audience, something quite different from how performers in India might dance. Finally, the interviews before and after their performances also revealed their distinctly Southern Californian English accents, which could not easily be acquired in India (although I am aware there are many schools training Indian workers to speak in perfect American accents for outsourcing purposes). This straddling of two citizenships enables performers like Amrapali and Mythili to grapple with power, media, and capital in ways that other Indian dancers from the late nineteenth and early twentieth centuries were not able to do. But it is their middle-class privilege and global sensibilities that enable them to do so.

This was not unlike Madhavi Manoranjan's performance in Southern California a few years earlier, in which the largely diasporic Indian audience also believed that Madhavi was performing Indian nationalist culture in a way that had nothing to do with anything American. Madhavi Manoranjan had performed with live musicians on stage for her *arangetram*; these musicians sat on the side of the stage watching her perform. They had been brought from India, and it was their foreign labor on American soil that helped construct diasporic Indian identity in the United States. Similarly, when Ruth St. Denis performed *Radha* in 1906, the Indian men onstage, acting as her "priests," not only aided but authenticated her performance and helped establish her as an "Indian" dancer. The *devadasis* who had been absorbed by middle-class Brahmin dancers and the *nachwalis* whose practices had been assimilated by Ruth St. Denis were not clearly visible in the dances of Amrapali and Mythili; yet, they had not disappeared. Their labor remained in the kinesthetic traces, particularly evident in Amrapali's turns and whirls and Mythili's *abhinaya* and facial expressions.

Dance is embodied and passes from body to body whether we like it or not. The bodily interactions of the many dancers who traveled between India and the United States were present yet not necessarily recognized as such by most of those watching the show each week. These historical bodies were moving and dancing between layers of visibility and invisibility. Paying attention to them allows us to rethink how citizenship, too, is a moving discourse.

Sweating Saris illuminates how performance, choreography, and questions of "staging" make visible the changing gender, race, and class formations of Indians in the United States as they intersect with discourses of citizenship. I have demonstrated how studying dance offers unique insights into the terms of labor and citizenship, including contract work, the working visa (H-1B), alien status, permanent residency, naturalized citizenship, and denaturalized alien status, at different stages for Asian Americans. I have offered the idea that because the terms of citizenship are in constant motion, turning to dance as an unrecognized form of labor critiques the discourses through which citizenship has been constructed. Ultimately, although I critique the dance form of Bharata Natyam as it is often taught in a political and historical vacuum, I still hold out hope for its emergence as a critical practice that acknowledges its complex and intertwined histories with dance in America and its violent extraction from *devadasi* bodies.

In *Sweating Saris*, I have illuminated the possibilities of thinking through the terms of citizenship in the United States from the perspective of the unruly spectator. This unruly spectator has considered how the Indian dancer as transnational laborer offers intriguing insights into the discourse of citizenship within the United States. I suggest that considering the Indian dancer as transnational laborer offers a nondualistic approach in thinking about the binaries of self-other, migrant-citizen, foreigner-native, and transnational-national from an embodied racialized, gendered perspective. From this point of view, I make evident the labor of multiple invisible bodies that produce the singular citizen body on "center stage." Such a framing tells us that it is the labor of transnational sweating bodies that creates possibilities for citizenship in the United States, and for Indians (like other immigrants of color) it has been difficult, changing, and unpredictable.

My attention in this book to Indian dancers through their danced labor demonstrates that race and class change for Indians in the United States. Attending to women dancers in the nineteenth century reveals that immigration law was playing out on performance stages well before the laws themselves were enacted. Examining the movement of *nachwalis* in the early twentieth century highlights the importance of kinesthetic traces and the exchanges between differently raced bodies. Even though *nachwalis* disappeared from the North American landscape, their bodily impact was left on the bodies of white American women dancers, who then contested their terms of U.S. citizenship. Examining feminized male Indian performers and their failures in obtaining citizenship during the first three decades of the twentieth century reveals the "twinkling" of their presence in the archives. As the class composition of diasporic Indians changes in the United States, so too does their relationship to citizenship. A study of Indian dancing bodies post-1965 highlights how multiple citizenship possibilities are played out on- and offstage. Paying close attention to Indian dance on U.S. stages tell us that the terms of citizenship are not always about race. Instead, the terms of U.S.

citizenship for Asians are about who benefits from U.S. capital formation. Indian dancers as transnational laborers tell us that citizenship is not just lived but also performed and negotiated on a daily basis. Ultimately, this book seeks to make visible how many invisible laboring bodies have collectively created the singular citizen we see on stages. Highlighting the labor of dance moves the process of citizenship in the United States away from binaries and toward nondualism.

A Meditation on Nondualism, Liveness, and the Moving Body

> *Brahma satyaṃ jagat mithyā, jāvo brahmaiva nāparah*—Brahman is the only truth, the world is illusion, and there is ultimately no difference between Brahman and individual self. (Adi Shankara, 788–820 C.E.)[5]

As this quotation suggests, *advaita* is about nondualism, recognizing the illusion of the self and the Other. At heart, this book is about nondualism and how to understand that nondualism through bodily practices. We are often forced to think about ourselves in relation to others. The binaries of self-other, insider-outsider, laborer-consumer, dancer-nondancer, alien-citizen, margin-center, colored-white, and minority-mainstream have consumed us historically as they do today. When we focus on the question of material bodies, what are the possibilities of these dualities becoming nondualities? That is the central, if utopian, question of this book.

In answer to that question, the material dualism of alien/citizen would be compromised, in particular, and we would have to reconsider nationalist understandings of our cultural practices and ourselves. The body has always been a slippery subject to deal with. I embrace several understandings of the body that inform my work: a body is spiritual, sexual, semiotic, fluid; it moves and transforms. With such understandings, I do not reject the textual body in favor of the phenomenological body. Nor do I dismiss the written text in relation to bodily texts. I consider them all in dialogic relation.

I am interested in the body that is always already in discourse, but also moving and not locatable. I advocate an approach that requires recognizing the materiality of the body in all its interactions and understanding that the body is produced within discourse. It is a sign, it is unstable, it is porous, it cannot be fixed, and it demonstrates its temporary existence—its "liveness"—through movement. This liveness allows us to understand how the discourses of race, gender, and ethnicity are lived and that the dancing body, through movement and embodiment, makes visible the labor that goes into performance. Whether we are examining the past or present, an attention to liveness highlights the racialized material body of Indian women dancers, and it is the haptic, sensorial relation between the audience and the dancers that shifts their reception.

Indian philosophers have indeed developed their own unique theories of the body. *Shareera*, "the physical body," as it is referred to in Indian philosophical contexts, is a transitory body that is full of holes and fluid and is easily dissolvable. Indeed, our bodies are full of holes; we are composed of building-block atoms that are more empty than full.[6] We are brimming with space, yet our dissected cadavers demonstrate a thickness, a fullness of entities like muscles, ligaments, bones, organs, blood vessels, and tissues, all jostling for space under our skins. In life, our bodies are seamless entities covered by skin, albeit containing pores that allow a little bit of our inside juices to seep outside in sweat and tears. When we dance, our fluids work overtime and sometimes escape to the surface, becoming visible. The unruly spectator makes due note of this and asks us to reconsider how fluids expose the labor of the dancer onstage and therefore the dancer as laborer. The unruly spectator reworks the bargain that audiences make to not "see" dancers' labor and instead highlights this danced labor in the viewing of sweat, tears, and blood. The unruly spectator smiles and celebrates the ways that dance exposes *shareera* as liquid labor.

Glossary

Abhinaya: art of portraying emotions or ideas using various hand, facial, and body gestures

Abhisarika: heroine who goes to meet her lover with pride

Adavus: basic units of movement in the technical aspect of Bharata Natyam

Adhama: a "low-class" person

Adi: an eight-beat cycle

Aharya: costuming and ornamentation

Akam: inside/private, of the home

Alapadma: the open-handed gesture of the flower

Alapana: unmetred improvisation of the raga, a prelude to a song

Alarippu: the first rhythmic piece of the dance repertoire

Anga suddha: bodily perfection

Anupallavi: the second section of a song or composition, composed of one or more lines of text in Carnatic (South Indian) music

Araimandi: half-seated position

Arangetram: the solo debut performance of a dancer

Ashtanayikas: eight states of the heroine

Bandhnis: tie-dye cloth

Behag: a raga or melodic scale

Benaras: A holy city in North India, also home to a kind of silk sari

Bindi: a ritual dot or ornamental mark on the forehead that women wear

Bowli: a type of raga or melodic scale in Carnatic music

Carnatic: refers to the southern region of India and also to the classical musical style from that region

Chana batura: a north Indian dish of chickpeas and fried bread

Chandanam: the ritual mark of sandalwood fragrant paste on the forehead or neck

Charanam: the third section of a song, or composition, composed of one or more lines of text

Corvei: a phrase of dance steps strung together

Darshan: to be in the presence of divinity; to simultaneously see and be seen

Devadasi: temple dancer

Dharmavaram: a type of cotton or silk sari, usually of muted colors, named after Dharmavaram, a place in Andhra Pradesh, India, famous for making such saris

Dola: a mudra that involves the relaxed hanging of the hand elegantly to the side

Ganesha: the elder son of the god Siva, Ganesha is the elephant-headed god, the remover of obstacles, who rides on a mouse

Ghat: steps leading down to a body of water

Huseini: a particular type of raga

Ikat: style of weaving that is similar to tie-dye

Isai: music

Jamdhani: hand loom–woven, fine cotton muslin of Bengali origin

Jathi: a series of steps strung together

Jathiswaram: an item in the Bharata Natyam repertoire using rhythmical dance movement

Kalahantarita: heroine who is repentant

Kanjeevaram: silk sari made in the town of Kanjeevaram in South India

Kartarimukaha: scissorlike hand gesture

Katakamukaha: deerlike hand gesture

Kavuttuvam: a rhythmical/lyrical dance piece in the Bharata Natyam repertoire

Keertana: an item in the Carnatic music repertoire

Khandita: heroine who is angry

Kolhapuri: cotton sari made in Kolhapur in the state of Maharashtra

Kovil: temple

Kumkum: red powder used for ritual purposes to mark the forehead

Kundalini: the latent potential energy of the feminine principle of creation

Kurtas: North Indian style of clothing traditionally worn by men like a long shirt

Lingam: phallic stone of worship symbolizing the god Shiva

Madhyama: a "middle-class" person

Mangalagiri: a sari with a heavy gold border from the state of Andhra Pradesh

Mangalam: the last "thank-you" and benediction piece in the Bharata Natyam performance

Maya: illusion

Mayil: peacock

Mayura: hand gesture depicting peacock

Modakam: a sweet that is offered to Ganesha, the elephant-headed god

Moksha: liberation

Mridangam: double-headed barrel drum

Mudras: special hand gestures that symbolically express various ideas

Nataraja: the celestial dancer, another name for god Siva

Nattadavus: basic dance steps that help build larger dance patterns

Nattai: a Carnatic raga

Natya: dance

Nayakan: the hero

Nayanmars: saints who are Shiva devotees

Nayika: the heroine

Neti: not this

Nritta: rhythmical abstract dance movements that are not intended to convey specific meaning

Nritya: rhythmical and lyrical/textual-based dance movements that convey meaning

Padam: an expressive genre within the Bharata Natyam repertoire structure

Pallavi: the first section of a song or composition, composed of one or more lines of text

Pallu: the end of the sari that is draped over the shoulder, usually filled with complicated designs

Pataka: a mudra that involves the displaying of the palm of one's hand

Prositabhartrka: heroine whose lover is away for an indefinite period

Pochampally: cotton and silk sari from the town of Pochampally, Andhra Pradesh

Raga: a complex melodic idea set in a modal system

Rakshasis: demonesses

Rasika: ideal audience

Sabdam: item in the Bharata Natyam repertoire combining interpretation of text and some rhythmical interludes

Sadir: a temple dance genre of the *devadasis* that later evolved into Bharata Natyam

Sahityam: lyrical text of Carnatic music compositions

Sakhi: friend

Salwar: long pants and long shirtlike dress from North India

Sari: traditional cloth worn by Indian women

Shikhara: hand gesture often used to depict the Shiva lingam or a spire on a Hindu temple

Shringara: erotic spirituality

Shringaraprabandam: collection of songs written around the fifteenth century dealing with the notion of erotic love toward God

Sthayi: main; permanent or unchanging

Svadhinapatika: heroine who is confident of her lover's devotion

Tala: meter occurring in cyclical patterns

Tattadavus: basic footsteps

Thillana: the last main item of the Bharata Natyam repertoire involving fast, interlaced rhythms

Tolkappiyam: earliest known work of Tamil literature dealing with grammar in the Tamil language

Uttama: a "high-class" person

Varnam: the main item of the Bharata Natyam repertoire composed of both rhythmical abstract dance and lyrical, textual, and dramatic components

Vallavar: poet singers

Vasakasajja: heroine who is dressed up to receive her lover

Veena: a wooden stringed instrument

Ventakatagiris: cotton colorful saris from the town of Venkatagiri in Andhra Pradesh

Veshti: white cotton cloth worn by men mainly in South India

Vipralabdha: heroine who feels cheated or abandoned

Vibhudhi: white ash ritual mark on the forehead

Yal: an ancient wooden stringed instrument (the precursor of the modern-day veena)

Yogi: a master of yoga (one who had renounced worldly pleasures)

Zardosi: a sari with heavy metal embroidery work

Notes

INTRODUCTION

1. *Nachwalis* were traditional or hereditary dancers (as they are now known) from northern India. They lived in matrilineal societies and often inherited dance practices, economic capital, and land from their mothers. The British mistakenly called these dancers "Nautch," not differentiating between dancers dedicated to temples, courts, or streets. *Devadasis* from South India had a very different history from *maharis* of Orissa (East India) and the *nachwalis* from the north. The nautch dancers mentioned in this book were not primarily linked to temples, and any existing patronage from kings had already dissipated by the 1880s. (A glossary of Indian terms is provided at the back of the book.)

2. During the colonial period, national boundaries did not differentiate between the regions we know today as Pakistan, India, Bangladesh, Iran, Afghanistan, and Sri Lanka, to name a few examples. Much of the region was called "India."

3. One of Michel Foucault's (1984) seminal arguments based on Nietschze's work is that genealogy deconstructs truth. Foucault argues that truth is often discovered by chance; it is subjective and backed by structures of power.

4. Bourdieu (1985) has discussed embodied cultural capital as both consciously and passively acquired properties through socialization over time.

5. I adopt Michel Foucault's call for a critique of history through an analysis of "subjugated knowledges." First, I look behind the dominant histories to find dancers who have been hidden for a number of reasons. In India, it is because of the converging discourses of colonialism, orientalism, and nationalism that the transnational Indian dancers I examine have been left out of Indian dance histories. Post-independence Indian scholars have focused on "star" figures as key to the revival of Indian dance and ignored the travels of many "unnamed" transnational performers. I explore this history in more detail in Chapter 4.

6. This is important to note because dancers as purely aesthetic beings can be separated from the historical political economy that they operate in. The focus on their bodies as laboring bodies forces a simultaneous attention to the aesthetic and the politico-historical. The history of Indian dance in India in the twentieth century attempts to divorce the politico-historical from the aesthetic aspects of the form.

7. Mudras are hand gestures in dance performance that function as signs.

8. See Espiritu 1996; Hong 2006; Kang 2002; Lowe 1996; and Yung 1995, for example.

9. As a methodological approach, transnational feminism is generally attentive to intersections among nationhood, race, gender, sexuality, and economic exploitation on a global level.

10. As Tracy Davis (1991) persuasively argues, actresses as performers can be understood from an economic perspective as wage earners and working women even in the nineteenth century. Although my book does not discuss in great detail the wages earned by each dancer I describe, I focus on the framework of the dancer as wage earner, worker, and laborer.

11. The exceptions are the female *nattuvanars* and gurus that emerged under the training of Rukmini Devi in Kalakshetra, who herself became one of the first female gurus of the Bharata Natyam form.

12. Further, transnational and postcolonial feminists who are critical of Western forms of feminism—notably radical and liberal feminists contributing to theories on the universalization of female experience, such as Kumari Jeyawardana, Angela Davis, Chandra Mohanty, and Sarojini Sahoo—see Western feminism as ethnocentric, suggesting that it does not take into account the unique experiences of women from third world countries or the existence of feminisms indigenous to third world countries.

13. I am informed by these scholars in rethinking how the physical female dancing body can be conceived as a material, laboring body and why that matters. I turn to both cultural and economic capital to think through this argument.

14. I frame my project on immigration policies pertaining to Asians in the United States using Lisa Lowe's work (1996).

15. In 1918, the court in *United States v. Ozawa* ruled that only Caucasians could be naturalized. Indians believed this meant they would be granted citizenship, since they considered themselves Caucasian (Chan 1991, 93–94; Takaki 1990, 298). However, in 1923 the landmark *United States v. Bhagat Singh Thind* decided to revoke all citizenships granted to Indians (Chan 1991, 93–94; Takaki 1990, 299). Although the court considered Indians to be Caucasian in a "scientific" sense, they did not qualify as white. The racial classifications set out by the "Founding Fathers" had to be reinterpreted to account for this anomaly.

16. Sunaina Maira (2008) argues that while legal citizenship does not guarantee protection for South Asian American youth post-9/11, cultural practices of citizenship offer ways of negotiation through the notion of flexible citizenship.

17. Diana Taylor (2003) suggests that the archive is often positioned in opposition to the repertoire (defined as live performance). Calling for new ways of historicizing the repertoire, Taylor argues that the archive does not seem able to capture the live event. I expand this notion by suggesting that the repertoire is its own archive.

18. But the absence of the body has been a potent focus of study in performance studies for many decades. Peggy Phelan's remarkable book *Unmarked* (1996) is a classic example of this genre.

19. See, for example, Grewal and Kaplan 1994; de Lauretis 1987; hooks 1992; Gopinath 2005; Halberstam 2001; and Staiger 2000.

20. These include Ananya Chatterjea (2004), Ann Daly (2002), Jane Desmond (1991), Susan Foster (1995), Avanthi Meduri (1996), Susan Manning (2006), and Janet O'Shea (2007), to mention a few.

CHAPTER 1

1. The divine should not be misunderstood in terms of a Christian divinity. The divine in Vedanta can be understood as the ultimate collective consciousness, the Brahman, which can paradoxically at once represent a personal god and a godless consciousness. According to Adi Shankara, the human subject is always united with the ultimate consciousness, but the human subject believes he or she is separate from this ultimate consciousness. The human subject thus lives in maya (illusion) until he or she accepts the nondual nature of existence. To attain *moksha* (liberation) from ignorance, or the removal of illusion, one must meditate wisely. Both great yogis and average people can achieve this but through extremely different paths.

2. Beaudrillard argues that the world is a simulacra. Everything is a copy of something else. There is no pure origin. The body itself is an illusion. Similarly, in the philosophical tradition of Vedanta, there is also no body; the body is only maya, an illusion, formed in our minds.

3. In this section, I shift between my experiences as a dancer in training and general descriptions of how dance techniques are imparted in the classroom. In describing Bharata Natyam training, I draw on my experience as a dancer and teacher, as well as on the methods of several dance teachers, to create a scenario that might unfold in the classroom.

4. I recognize that the context of learning dance is quite different in Australia and the United States, but Indian dance teachers working in the diaspora face common struggles. Commonalities include economic backgrounds (although Indian immigrants arrived in Australia mainly in the 1970s, they were also professionals like those who came to America after 1965), struggles against racism, and Indian community pressures to maintain an ethnic immigrant identity in the face of mainstream assimilation. I apply my experience in this section because my own training was unique. I had learned from a female teacher in Calcutta, S. Rajalakshmi. When we migrated to Australia, I learned from a guru who was not only a man but also a Malaysian Muslim (nonpracticing) and first-generation immigrant. He had arrived in Melbourne to earn his Ph.D. in anthropology, having been trained in Bharata Natyam from a very young age and continued with his training in Chennai, India, under Adyar K. Lakshman. His credentials as a dancer and teacher were impeccable. In later years I wondered if he was such a strict disciplinarian because, in donning the mantle of the guru, he then had to perform authentic Indianness in Australia. Aside from Indian community pressure to perform a Hindu Indian identity, perhaps his adherence to and emphasis on tradition in teaching young Indian girls in Australia was a compensation for the fact that he was not Indian by birth. My experience learning from a male guru in Australia

offers new approaches to arguments I make about girls learning from female Indian gurus in America.

5. The complex history of the *devadasi* is explained in later chapters.

6. The Bharatam Dance Company did not perform only Indian classical dance. In fact, as a premier experimental Asian dance company, we performed a range of themes and stories—from Rudyard Kipling's *The Jungle Book* to Euripdes's tragedy *Medea* and more postmodern shows, such as *Bodhisattva*, that involved gender-bending, mask-wearing, speaking, and even singing roles that were often the antithesis of the ideal Indian woman dancer.

7. This is not to say that other immigrant groups were not persecuted at different historical moments, but this book focuses on U.S. immigration laws as they pertain to Asians.

8. Although, as Mari Yoshihara notes in her recent book *Musicians from a Different Shore* (2007), the study of Western music in Asian countries is not necessarily a Western practice and can be read as a nationalist Asian practice as well.

CHAPTER 2

1. This is the first mention of Indian women dancers in the United States in newspapers. Anandbhai Joshi, the first Indian woman doctor who came to the United States, in 1886, was also publicly cited in later years.

2. There are several articles, advertisements, and some description of nautch dancers when they first arrived in New York in 1880: J. Daly 1917, 338–341; Felheim 1956, 178; Odell 1939, 233; "The Nautch Dancers," *New York Sunday News*, November 21, 1880, 19; *New York Times*, November 21, 1880, 2; "The Plays and Shows," *Brooklyn Daily Eagle*, December 5, 1880, 3; *Brooklyn Daily Eagle*, December 12, 1880, 3.

3. An exciting body of scholarship linking the dancing/performing body to discourses of culture, citizenship, and labor has emerged (T. Davis 1991; Franko 2002; Graff 1997; Joseph 1999; J. Lee 1998; R. Lee 1999; R. Martin 1998; Shimakawa 2002; Tchen 2001; Yoshihara 2002). Working from this body of literature, I suggest that it is important to place immigration and labor questions in dialogue with Indian women dancers who traveled to the U.S. in the late nineteenth and early twentieth centuries to understand how their labor and citizenship played out. Furthermore, in U.S. narratives, the Asian/Asian American body is always already conflated with the laborer/immigrant body, although historically this body is associated more with men (Lowe 1996). But it is not a far stretch to think about female Indian dancers as immigrant laborers without conflating them as only laborers.

4. Following Edward Said (1979), initial discussions of orientalism focused primarily on literature. However, the excellent work of Asian American theater and performance scholars such as Josephine Lee (1998), Shimakawa (2002), San San Kwan (2011), Burns (forthcoming), Esther Kim Lee (2006), Yutian Wong (2010), Theodore Gonzalves (2009), and Sean Metzger (2004) analyze U.S. orientalism in films, theater plays, popular performances, and other performances both on- and offstage. I enter this conversation with an argument centered on corporeal discourses. While several excellent studies have emerged that consider women and orientalism (Ceylik 1996, Yegenoglu 1998, and Lewis 2004), most of these consider women in the Middle East

or Turkey. Apart from Mari Yoshihara (2002), few studies have focused on women and orientalism in the U.S. and in relation to performance practices.

5. Immigration law prevented Indian men from bringing their wives, since bosses thought they were more efficient as a workforce without family distractions, and the law did not permit women to enter the United States on their own as laborers (Espiritu 1996, 16).

6. I am informed by Michael Omi and Howard Winant's (1994, 61) work in thinking through the racialization process of minorities, particularly Asians and Indians in the United States. As they point out, racial formation is determined by social, economic, and political processes that shape the structure of racial categories and racial meanings.

7. The words "jan" and "bai" or "bhai" are suffixes used after proper names as titles for dancers. Hereafter I do not use these to refer to the dancers. Also, it appears that Saheb and Oomdah were known as Sundar and Fatima, respectively, in different places, but for the sake of consistency, I refer to them by the former rather than the latter.

8. Several newspapers reported that some of the dancers were married and traveling with their husbands and that one had even given birth to a baby in New York ("Oomdah's New Year's Gift," *The Sun*, January 3, 1881; "Another Hindoo Arrival," *The Herald*, January 3, 1881).

9. Augustin Daly's scrapbook collection (Locke 1870–1920) and other sources reveal the complex negotiations that were undertaken to bring the performers to New York and to house them there, as well as the subsequent performance reviews. See "A Nautch Dance," *Daly's Theatre Programme*, November 10, 1880; "Mr.Daly's Nautch Girls," *Truth*, November 22, 1880, 19; "Nautch Girls and Jugglers," *The World*, November 21, 1880, 19; "Introductory," *New York Clipper*, January 3, 1881, 334; "Advertisement for Zanina," *New York Clipper*, January 8, 1881, 334; "Amusements," *New York Times*, January 12, 1881, 7; "Stage Sensations," *Brooklyn Daily Eagle*, January 16, 1881, 3; "Advertisement for Zanina and Nautch Dancers," *New York Mirror*, January 22, 1881, 9; "The Nautch Dancers," *New York Clipper*, January 22, 1881, 345; "A Week of Novelties and Disappointments," *New York Mirror*, January 22, 1881, 6–7; *Brooklyn Daily Eagle*, February 13, 1881, 1; "The New York Drama," *Brooklyn Daily Eagle*, January 23, 1881; "Amusements," *New York Times*, January 23, 1881, 11; "Introductory," *New York Clipper*, January 24, 1881, 358; "Nuna: A Hindoostanee Story," *New York Clipper*, January 29, 1881, 356; "Untitled Article on Nautch Dancers," *New York Times*, February 2, 1881, 4; "Advertisement for Nautch Dance," *Brooklyn Daily Eagle*, February 13, 1881, 1; "Untitled Review on Zanina," *Brooklyn Daily Eagle*, February 15, 1881, 3; "A Nautch Girl's Wake," *National Police Gazette*, February 19, 1881, 4; "Contagious Foreigners," *New York Times*, May 16, 1881, 4.

10. *Patrician orientalism*, as argued by John Tchen, refers to the social, conferring status provided to elite Americans who possess Chinese things and ideas. It also refers to the transplantation of European orientalisms into the American context in the early nineteenth century. *Commercial orientalism* developed in the 1870s and 1880s and involved the consumption of Asian imports by a wide range of people. Whereas previously only elites had been able to purchase Asian goods and products, this popular orientalism matched the growth of consumer culture and the desire for

Asian goods, cultural spectacles, and theater. Tchen argues that *political orientalism* was the discourse that manifested at the end of the nineteenth century on the question of who could and should be an American citizen. Tchen suggests that this question was primarily focused on the polemic debate over Chinese labor, people, and things. He suggests that those aspects of patrician orientalism that had created a culture of distinction served to aggravate conflicts between labor and capital. The anxieties of these conflicts were vented toward Chinese laborers through racist immigration acts.

11. As Tchen (2001, xxiii) argues, political orientalism was the tool through which discourses of racism, exclusion, and segregation were effected on Chinese bodies.

12. Mari Yoshihara (2003) points out that in the case of white women, Asian products were being consumed not only by the elite but by middle- and working-class women in the late nineteenth and early twentieth centuries.

13. Avanthi Meduri and Jeffery L. Spear (2004) briefly mention the presence of the *devadasis* in London in 1838.

14. I thank Justine Lemos for sharing this information with me.

15. See http://www.balletmet.org/Notes/Petipa.html for more details on this subject.

16. By and large, Asian laborers were not afforded the same rights as migrants from Europe, but naturalization laws treated Asian subgroups differently in various time periods. See Chan (1991) for detailed accounts of immigration and naturalization law. In 1878, the U.S. government denied Chinese already in the United States naturalized citizenship, in contrast to their German and Irish counterparts. By 1882, the Chinese Exclusion Act, which prevented the entry of Chinese laborers into the United States, was fully implemented (Chan 1991, 37).

17. From 1907 until 1917, when Congress prohibited immigration from India, 6,400 Asian Indians, mostly Sikhs and farmers from Punjab, came to America's West Coast, and less than 1 percent of them were women (Chan 1991, 18–23; Takaki 1990, 294).

18. Some exceptions to this include the mentions of early Indian women coming to the United States in the works of Joan Jensen (1988) and Karen Leonard (1992).

19. *Devadasis* of South India had a very different history from *maharis* of Orissa (East India) and from the nautch dancers of the North. Nautch dancers were not primarily linked to temples, and any existing patronage from kings had dissipated by the 1880s.

20. It was even reported that *Zanina* was just the vehicle to promote the actresses Laura Joyce, Ada Rehan, May Fielding, and Maggie Harold on Daly's stage. Joyce played the title role, while Rehan, Fielding, and Harold played the roles of "Muttra," "Nuna," and "Nauchida," respectively (Odell 1939, 233).

21. In 1917, the anti-Asian Indian Immigration Law was enacted to exclude Asian Indians from entering the United States because their racial or ethnic status was unclear, which prevented Asian Indian males from bringing their wives to the United States (Lowe 1996). Further, antimiscegenation laws were enacted, and Asian Indian men were denied the right to marry white women. So Asian Indian men frequently married Mexican women as a way to continue their lives in America and live like other free men.

22. What I mean by "brownface" here is that white women, like white men (doing blackface and yellowface minstrelsy), painted themselves brown. They did not just paint their faces but their whole bodies to look like Indian women onstage. Although

blackface and yellowface minstrelsy was about denigrating black and Asian people, and brownface was not always about denigrating, nevertheless, this representation of Indians on U.S. stages is deeply problematic.

23. Anti-Asian sentiment had reached the boiling point by 1875 when the Page Law barred entry to Chinese, Japanese, and "Mongolian" prostitutes, felons, and contract laborers. See Chan (1991, 105) for detailed accounts of immigration and naturalization law. The government also prohibited Asian women from immigrating to the United States during this time period, and it often labeled those who had come prostitutes, outlawing them by 1878. Chinese women in particular were hypereroticized; hence, all were deemed prostitutes.

24. This report contradictorily suggests that two of the dancers, Sunder and Bhoori, were dedicated temple dancers, but there is no clear evidence of this.

25. New York Times, March 9, 1884, 11; "Barnum's Great Parade," New York Times, March 11, 1884, 2; "Curiosities Showing Off: Nautch Girls, Nubians, and Zulus Put through Their Paces," New York Times, March 17, 1884, 8; New York Times, April 10, 1884, 7; New York Times, April 13, 1884, 15; New York Times, April 19, 1884, 7; "New Coney Dazzles Its Record Multitude," New York Times, May 15, 1904, 3; "The Gorgeous Delhi Durbar," New York Dramatic Mirror, April 16, 1904, 19. See also Janet Davis (1993) for detailed information and imagery of P. T. Barnum's shows.

26. National boundaries during the colonial period did not differentiate between what we know today as Pakistan, India, Bangladesh, Iran, Afghanistan, and Sri Lanka, to name a few.

27. As Adria Imada (2004, 113) points out, although hula circuits forced performers to exoticize and exhibit themselves in various U.S. cities at the turn of the century, Hawaiian dancers found economic and cultural opportunities to sustain themselves.

28. As Marxist scholars have noted, the separation between the worker and her labor is what creates the process of alienation. But in the case of dance, the worker's body is the product, and alienation becomes much more complicated. The added element of racialization in which white bodies take on brown Indian dance forms further separates the dancer from her labor.

29. Mari Yoshihara (2003) details a similar phenomenon with Japanese-themed performances and "yellowface" by white women in the early twentieth century.

30. As Julia Kristeva argues in Powers of Horror (1982), the "abject" is radically excluded from the object of desire and its meaning collapses (2). There is thus neither subject nor object. The corpse in particular exemplifies Kristeva's concept since it literally is the breakdown of the distinction between subject and object. The viewing of a human corpse is thus the utmost of abjection (4).

31. Kristeva argues that the live human subject knows its condition of living on the border, and it is the subject's own body that provides that border. Kristeva thus employs symbolic identity and semiotic rejection to explain the experience of difference.

32. St. Denis had an important encounter with nautch dancers on Coney Island in 1904, yet this is dismissed in most accounts of U.S. dance history as being an insignificant moment in her career. I have argued elsewhere that far from being insignificant, St. Denis's encounter with the Indian nautch dancers was a constitutive moment for U.S. modern dance (P. Srinivasan 2007). St. Denis was particularly effective in emerging as an independent artist because unlike previous white Oriental shows that cast

large numbers of people, her show cast her as the sole white female, who absorbed all kinds of Asian otherness for the American modernist cultural project.

33. See, for example, the Library of Congress archives for photographs at Ellis Island of brown dancers being deported at the shipyards for overstaying their visa.

34. Ironically, it was the Chinese Exclusion Act of 1882 that enabled Indian male laborers to enter the United States. Since there was a labor shortage because of the 1882 Act, which prevented Chinese laborers from entering the United States, Indians were brought in to fill the void (Takaki 1990, 294). Furthermore, since Indians were at this point not classified in the same racial category as Chinese, it made it easier for them to enter the United States. That is, East and South East Asians were considered to be Mongoloid in race, and South Asians were Caucasian. It was this very issue that South Asians used later to contest racist American laws that prevented Asians from having full rights of citizenship.

35. The 1885 Alien Contract Labor Law prohibited any company or individual from bringing foreigners into the United States under contract to perform labor. The only exceptions were those immigrants brought to perform domestic service and skilled workmen needed to help establish a new trade or industry in the United States.

36. It must be noted that Harry French, the man who brought the performers to New York, had to obtain government permission before bringing them to the United States. What this entailed is not mentioned, but we can assume that since this was the first time Indian performers had come to the United States, French's actions set a precedent for all performers who followed, perhaps making it easier for others to travel (Daly 1917, 338).

CHAPTER 3

1. This was the famous 1941 recording of St. Denis performing her signature piece, *Radha*, which launched her solo career.

2. On the notion of ambivalence and troubling the archive of the colonizer to locate the colonized, see Homi Bhabha's influential essay "Of Mimicry and Man: The Ambivalence of Colonial Discourse" (1994).

3. I have researched newspapers extensively between 1903 and 1905, yet there appears to be only one photograph of female dancers from the *Durbar of Delhi* show at Coney Island (Snow 1984, 91). This photograph seems to depict the Sri Lankan men and women who were part of the *Durbar* pageant. Drawings and etchings from newspaper reports also fail to provide any clear images of the nautch dancers. Investigation of the extensive photograph archives in the Library of Congress reveals many photographs of Coney Island, even a few of the *Durbar of Delhi* in Delhi itself in 1903, but none of the nautch dancers in the *Durbar* of 1904. The Keystone Mast Collection, housed at the California Museum of Photography, contains photographs of Indian jugglers, Sri Lankan warriors, Native American performers, Little Egypt, Japanese performers, and four photographs of three female Sri Lankan dancers being deported from Ellis Island around 1904–1906. The caption of one of the latter reads, "Singalese [sic] women on board a steamer in Brooklyn waiting to be deported by U.S. Immigration Authorities after the expiration of their contract with Western Theatrical Troupe. N.Y. City" (print no. X97779). There are several etchings of South Indian temple dancers from 1884 and 1894 in the Wisconsin Circus Museum

archives (for more detail on South Asian performance in the American circus during this time period, see Janet Davis 1993). The P. T. Barnum and Bailey collection at Princeton University contains several photographs of female Indian dancers in New York; the dancers seemed to have been photographed around 1904, about the time of Barnum's *Durbar of Delhi* show. Thus, the photographic evidence of nautch dancers does not clarify whether divisions between Indian and Sri Lankan dancers and northern and southern Indian dance traditions were understood at the time. The labeling of what was nautch and what was not and which kinds of dancers were performing in 1904 at Coney Island with P. T. Barnum and at the St. Louis World Exposition is unclear.

4. I am informed by both Raymond Williams's (1983) and Pierre Bourdieu's (1985) notion of "cultural capital," which I develop further in this chapter to reflect the ways in which white middle-class American dancing women used Asian women's philosophies, products, ideas, performance techniques, costumes, and labor to combat male dominance and create a new space for themselves in the early twentieth century.

5. There is considerable evidence that nautch dancers performed extensively at Coney Island (*New York Times*, May 15, 1904; *New York Dramatic Mirror*, July 9, 1904). It was reported that nautch dancers performed amid a larger pageant, known as the *Durbar of Delhi*, premiering in Luna Park.

6. The anti-nautch campaign was well under way in India at this time. Avanthi Meduri (1996) also points out that the anti-nautch movement was part of a larger nationalist social reform movement "that was staunchly opposed to the dedication of young girls as brides to temple gods and also to the continued practice of the dance both inside and outside the temple" (56). Indian national debates in the late nineteenth century used the *devadasi*, nautch, and dancing girl symbolically in the anti-nautch movement to address larger reforms for women, including the ban on *sati* (widow immolation), female infanticide, and the encouragement of widow remarriage (A. Srinivasan 1983, 73–99). Western patriarchy set itself against Oriental patriarchy and framed Indian men as barbaric and primitive and Indian women as needing to be rescued from their men, thus reaffirming white man's authority and identity (Tharu and Lalita 1991, 53). Colonial writings condemned Indian character as "irrational, deceitful, and sexually perverse," declaring that India—herself needing "rescue" by the British government—was a "white man's burden" (Tharu and Lalita 1991, 9). As part of the social reform movement, embarrassed nationalists addressed the accusations of the colonizers to prove Indians could be "civilized" and rule themselves. The "women's question" became an important issue for nationalists because of colonial texts that condemned Indian men for their barbarism toward their women. According to Partha Chatterjee (1986), Indian nationalists attempted to resolve the stigma of colonization and the "women's question" by demarcating the public sphere as a male agenda and relegating women's practices to the private sphere. Nautch dancers were "public" and therefore did not fit the nationalist agenda of ideal and moral Indian womanhood. Women reformers such as Dr. Muthulakshmi Reddy, alongside other male nationalist reformers, vehemently opposed nautch practices, condemning their link to prostitution. As Tharu and Lalita (1991) note, the social reform movement in India was also about class and caste struggles; in the effort to create ideal middle-class and upper-caste Indian women who emulated Victorian mores of morality, the movement scapegoated nautch women (11).

7. I refer here to the extremely important work by dance scholars Brenda Dixon Gottschild (1996), Thomas DeFrantz (2002), and Susan Manning (2006), who argue that American modern dance must be examined in dialogic relation to African American dance practices that have not only shaped what we know today as American concert dance but are also constitutive of it. The works of Yutian Wong (2002) and Jacqueline Shea Murphy (2007) highlight the importance of examining Asian American and Native American dance practices, respectively, as constitutive elements in modern American dance.

8. Linda Tomko (1999) states, regarding St. Denis among a variety of dancers, "Through appropriation of 'other' dance cultures they attempted to alter American perceptions of dance as a native endeavor" (135).

9. Exceptions include John Tchen (2001), Robert Lee (1999), and Mari Yoshihara (2003), but none focus on corporeal discourses as the center of their argument; instead, they examine literature, film, theater plays, circus, or popular forms of performance.

10. Diana Taylor (2003) suggests that the archive is often positioned in opposition to the repertoire (or live performance). Calling for new ways to historicize the repertoire, Taylor argues that the archive seems unable to capture the live event. I expand on this notion in this chapter by suggesting that the repertoire is also an archive, its contents found in traces of live bodily interactions, its records captured in muscle memory and through bodily labor and kinesthetic contact.

11. Kinesthetic research, or the study of ways of moving as ways of knowing, was a key method used in the contemporary dance ethnographies of Sally Ness (1992) and Deirdre Sklar (2001). I build on their work in approaching archival kinesthetic contact as a way of knowing.

12. Spivak has revised her argument in numerous different ways since these first formations. However, these early theorizations on the subaltern still have valence in historiographical analyses.

13. The literature on women's history and dance employs frameworks of fiction in reconstructing the past. I pieced together evidence from the lives of performers traveling at the time by reading the autobiography, biography, and dance articles on St. Denis, as well as newspaper reports on Coney Island, advertisements in various newspapers of the time, and film recordings. Newspapers include the *Brooklyn Daily Eagle, New York American and Journal, New York Clipper, New York Daily News, New York Dramatic Mirror, New York Evening Post, New York Herald,* and *New York Times* from 1903 to 1905. The main film recording of St. Denis's *Radha* is a reconstruction performed at Jacob's Pillow in 1941. I acknowledge that there are historical gaps between her 1904 encounter with nautch women, the 1906 performance of *Radha*, her tour of the Orient from 1925 to 1926, her autobiography published in 1939, the 1941 film of *Radha*, and Shelton's biography in 1981. The multiple fabrications of history that take place in between must be acknowledged, and thus any search for an objective truth is impossible. On the evidence of photographs, newspaper accounts from 1906 to 1911, and St. Denis's diary, I argue that kinesthetic encounters took place between St. Denis and the nautch dancers, which must have left traces in St. Denis's body. See my essay "The Bodies beneath the Smoke or What's behind the Cigarette Poster," in *Discourses in Dance* (2007), for a more detailed and performative discussion from the nautch women's perspective.

14. I am borrowing the concept of "Plumette" from Marta Savigliano, whose story about the tango emerges from a marginal place and is constructed through a historical fictional narrative (1995, 106–108).

15. I draw on the work of Pallabi Chakraborty (2000) and Sumanta Banerjee (2000) to imagine nautch women's backgrounds in Calcutta before they left for the United States in 1904.

16. I want to make it clear that in this chapter I am not arguing for another fountainhead moment for Oriental or modern dance by privileging the 1904 encounter. Rather, I am providing an analysis of transnational circulations that rupture such origin myths. It is also important to note that the term *classical* was significant in Indian dance reconstruction post-1930, and particularly postindependence. The careful systematization of the repertoire in the reconstruction process, its transition from the temple to the theater, and the changes in costuming, lighting, and structure were implemented by Rukmini Devi Arundale, who as Avanthi Meduri (2005) argues, was a global, transnational, and cosmopolitan subject in her own right. In this chapter, I point to the transnational movements of Indian dancers prior to Rukmini Devi, Anna Pavlova, and St. Denis, whose practices came before classical/folk categories.

17. There is another possible explanation as to why the Indian dancers have been left out of dance discourses. Since the *Durbar of Delhi* was a multidisciplinary performance, it defied labeling. Also, because Indian dance itself is a complex amalgam of music, movement, and drama, it would have been difficult to define the performance of Indian women as dancers in the Western sense.

18. I elaborate on this in greater detail in "Bodies beneath the Smoke or What's behind the Cigarette Poster" (2007), where I offer a performative view of this encounter from the *nachwalis'* perspective.

19. It is interesting that St. Denis believed she was witnessing a "real East Indian village," particularly because advertisements and newspaper reports note that the *Durbar of Delhi* was only a "representation" of the *Durbar in Delhi* that had taken place in India (*New York Herald*, March 27, 1904).

20. I suggest that the nautch dancers might have been performing such items based on the work of Pallabi Chakravorty (2000, 44–45), who notes the kinds of dances nautch women could have been performing at the time. Also, I mention that nautch dances at this time displayed aspects of folk dance because the differentiation between the terms *classical* and *folk* did not exist in India at this time.

21. When St. Denis went to India two decades later, she was astonished to see an old nautch dancer perform a dance with just facial expressions. St. Denis had perhaps witnessed the more rhythmic aspects of the nautch repertoire during her visit to Coney Island and had not been exposed to the dramatic components of it. Alternately, she might have seen the dramatic components in Coney Island and just forgotten about it two decades later. It is possible that the nautch dancers at Coney Island were instructed or decided to perform eye-catching, audience-pleasing numbers minus the expressional aspects of their repertoire. It is also possible that they may not have been as well trained as the dancer St. Denis met in India years later.

22. Francois Delsarte, a French musician in the early nineteenth century, developed a system known as the Delsarte method in which performers explored the expressiveness of their bodies. It is possible that St. Denis was trained in this technique by her teacher Genevieve Stebbins.

23. While we do not know what became of the nautch dancers, we know that some of the jugglers and snake charmers continued their work. One such performer encountered St. Denis on her trip to India on March 10, 1928, in Kanpur and reminded her that he was one of the performers she had seen in Coney Island in 1904 (Shelton 1981, 200). St. Denis herself admits her astonishment in seeing him: "To our amazement, he says he was in the old Thompson and Dundy performances at Coney Island! He must, then, have been part of that troupe of jugglers and snake charmers who started me off on this wild career of Indian dancing" (1939, 289). It is interesting that by 1928, there is no mention of the nautch dancers who started her off, but the story is full of their absence.

24. St. Denis notes that one reviewer wrote, "It was the Hindu Temple dance that fulfilled all expectations, artistic—and otherwise. What matter if the baser minds put their programmes before their eyes and announced that the brown legs of the dancer blended into the tints above the ankles too realistically for the legs to be clad in tights" (1939, 71).

25. La Meri brought Varalakshmi and Bhanumati to the United States to perform in New York in 1942, thirty-eight years after their nautch sisters had performed in Coney Island (La Meri Collection, 1912–1954, New York Public Library; Abrahams 1974, 125–145).

26. Balasaraswati, a dancer from a traditional *devadasi* family (and perhaps the most famous *devadasi* of the twentieth century), first arrived in 1954 under the auspices of the Asia Society and went on to tour and perform extensively in the United States, even teaching at universities including Wesleyan, the University of California–Los Angeles, and the University of Southern California (Abrahams 1974).

27. Amy Koritz (1997), in her article on Maud Allan's performance of *Salome* in early-twentieth-century England, points out that Allan's success was because of her Western, white female body, which safely mediated the threat of the Oriental female "other" in her performance.

28. Robert Lee (1999) discusses the idea of Asian bodies as pollutants on the North American landscape as a rationale for racist immigration policies and an impetus for "yellowface" performances denigrating Asians.

CHAPTER 4

1. I thank Anthea Kraut for pointing out this caption from the *New York Times*.

2. Yutian Wong (2002) is the first dance scholar to note that Indian men were present onstage with St. Denis and calls attention to the dancer's so-called solo performances. She makes the important argument that the anonymous men who aid St. Denis must be acknowledged as collaborators; otherwise, they will remain unrecognized.

3. For a more complex discussion of South Asian men's legal negotiations, see Nayan Shah's (2005) work in which he examines legal regulation and the curtailing of South Asian men's sexuality and subjectivity, as well as social and racial dynamics in the United States. Shah studies legal cases against South Asian migrants who have been found guilty before they are tried and argues that the intense policing and criminalizing of migrant bodies underscores the instability of American normality and masculinity.

4. Vivek Bald (2006) suggests, however, that South Asian men did indeed align themselves with African American and Puerto Rican men and women, even marrying many of them and settling down in U.S. cities. The Indian men who worked with St. Denis, however, seem to have aligned themselves with white women (e.g., Mogul Khan's marriage to Mary the maid) and distanced themselves from being placed in the same categories as African American men onstage.

5. St. Denis was always moving between vaudeville and high society in her performances—from the Hudson Theatre, New York Theater, and Proctor's Theatre to the salons of upper-class women (Shelton 1981, 53–57).

6. Wong (2002) astutely argues that St. Denis continues to be seen as a soloist despite the fact that numerous "hindoos" were onstage with her.

7. See photograph II, Ruth St. Denis and Hindu assistants, "In an Early Production of *Radha*, 1906" (Schlundt 1962, 14).

8. As Linda Tomko pointed out to me, the ballet also surrounded its solo artists with a chorus of bodies, and the relationship between the soloist and chorus was often a classed one. It could be argued here that following in ballet tradition, St. Denis was creating a solo with a chorus of bodies in a racialized relationship that rendered them invisible.

9. St. Denis (1939, 56) and Shelton (1981, 52) admit that the presence of Indian men aided St. Denis greatly in constructing her ideas for *Radha* in 1906. Perhaps the nautch women had left Coney Island by 1906, but there is no account that shows St. Denis was interested in collaborating or working with the nautch dancing women.

10. As Wong (2002) suggests, it is only the white woman masquerading as the "real" Asian that sets the stage for all future performances by actual Asian women, determining the dominant frameworks through which they will be viewed in the United States.

11. A great deal of orientalist scholarship had emerged by this time, including Edwin Arnold's *The Light of Asia* and Max Müller's fifty edited volumes *The Sacred Books of the East*, which incorporated the sacred texts of Hinduism, Islam, and Buddhism, for example. This scholarship framed Indian culture as ancient and "high culture," comparing it to Greek and Roman civilizations of the past.

12. David Krasner (1997, 87) discusses the problematic nature of minstrelsy until the 1890s. He argues that until African Americans began performing on their own, it was easy for white performers to control the representation of African Americans.

13. Jane Desmond (1991) argues that St. Denis as a "colored" white woman (since hers was not a caricature of the minstrel-show variety) also evokes an ambiguous response. The argument here is that St. Denis was not doing a minstrel show because it was not denigrating or caricaturing Indian women performers. I argue that the violence of seizing representation, whatever its context, either adulatory or denigrating, is equally problematic.

14. The "Cult of Authenticity" toward the end of the nineteenth and beginning of the twentieth centuries can be viewed as the discourse through which African American and Native American performers were beginning to contest the minstrel representations of themselves onstage. Unlike some African American and Native American women performers, such as Aida Overton Walker (Krasner 1998), the Whitman Sisters (George 2000), and Gowongo Mohawk (Hall 2001), who were beginning to break through racist traditions and perform in nonminstrel shows from

the 1890s through the 1910s, Indian dancers were not even present to provide viewing alternatives for their dance for several decades. Of course, African American
and Native American performers were still subject to deeply racist attacks, as they
contested discourses of primitivism and struggled for the control of their representation. At least until the 1940s, minstrelsy was an ongoing form, even as African
American performers contested the racist stereotyping typical of minstrel shows. As
Brenda Dixon Gottschild (1996), Susan Manning (2006), and others have argued,
metaphorical minstrelsy of African Americans continued with many modern dance
choreographers who took ideas from African American dancers and dance forms without giving due credit. But the visibility and presence of African American performers
enabled new and contesting modes of performance to be created and exist simultaneously with old racist modes. This provided alternative and oppositional ways of seeing
African American bodies, even as some African American actors and performers
participated in depicting Asian characters, as the case of the performance of the 1939
musical *The Hot Mikado* demonstrates (Steen 2010). But this didn't happen with
Indian dancers. Anti-Asian immigration law enabled St. Denis to represent Indian and
Asian dances without question, to market authenticity and stage a career on the bodies
of absent nautch women and a minimal presence of Indian men.

15. As Robert Lee (1999), Josephine Lee (1998), David Eng (2001), and others
have argued, Chinese and other Asian men were racially castrated in numerous ways.
They were feminized men whose "lack" stood in direct opposition to African American
men's hypermasculinization and overt sexualization. Indian men, I argue, oscillated
between being feminized onstage by St. Denis and hypermasculinized in public places,
such as trains. As Eng (2001) argues, in the case of Chinese men, it was the threat
of their sexualized racialized bodies in the everyday world that perhaps led to their
feminization and domestication onstage.

16. These included cities such as Chicago, Boston, Springfield, Salt Lake City,
Baltimore, Cincinnati, Columbus, Pittsburgh, Cleveland, Buffalo, Milwaukee, Daven-
port, Des Moines, Kansas City, Topeka, St. Louis, Pueblo, Colorado Springs, Denver,
San Jose, Fresno, Bakersfield, Oakland, Los Angeles, San Diego, Santa Barbara,
Sacramento, Chico, and Riverside (Schlundt 1962, 14–16; Shelton 1981, 95–104).

17. Meyda Yegenoglu (1998, 15) suggests that the Orient is feminine and can only
be known as an artifice—an "ideological supplement"—and not anything resembling
the "real" or material.

18. Anti-Asian laws were just one aspect of the gendered and racialized economy
of the time. The different kinds of epistemic violence perpetrated on the bodies of people of color lead to different kinds of histories and performative enactments of power.
The violence of slavery on African Americans, the decimation of Native Americans,
and the indentured labor and selective immigration policies aimed at Hispanics and
Asians are constructed always in relation to specific labor issues and lead to different
kinds of performances. However, as several dance scholars argue, American modern
dance histories reflect how the gendered and racialized economy became constitutive
of American identity (Dixon Gottschild 1996; Manning 2006; Shea Murphy 2007;
Y. Wong 2002).

19. Partly because white bourgeois women were trying to find their own place
within the American state and fighting for equal rights as citizens, they operated in an
economy that forced them to make choices between their gender and their race. Asian

American historian Gary Okihiro (2001, 62) astutely notes that, in the American context, although white women were afforded some privilege, they were situated between
white men and peoples of color and were thus competing with the latter. Like women
in other nations, white women in America were torn between loyalty to their race
and to their gender. Studies of American women's labor history have discussed this in
connection to the suffrage movement; that is, often white women prioritized gender
rights and fought for them in isolation from racial issues (Kraditor 1970). As a result,
suffragists did not align with women of color in seeking the vote (Mohanty, Russo,
and Torres 1991, 10). As Cynthia Enloe points out, "Some suffragists in the United
States and Europe argued that their service to the empire was proof of their reliability
as voters" (1990, 47). As Mohanty et al. note, "Historically, [white] feminist movements
in the West have rarely engaged questions of immigration and nationality" (1991, 23).
Historic divisions within feminist movements fracture possibilities for united coali-
tions across the color line even today. It is not possible to understand current politics
without a history that acknowledges how upper- and middle-class white women, in
obtaining their own suffrage, sold out their sisters of color. Siding with the state on
anti-Asian immigration policies, however, did not prevent white middle-class American
women from being enamored with Asian cultures, philosophies, or practices. In fact,
there had already been an exchange—albeit one-sided—of Asian goods, products, services, and ideas that had transformed American sensibilities. Thus, Asia and America
were already entwined by commodification and consumer culture, and the American
desire for Asian goods fed a desire for Asian practices as well. While St. Denis was no
activist, she was increasingly marketing herself as "an unfettered new woman" (Shelton
1981, 22). She even performed for the National Women's Suffrage Association and cul-
tivated publicity as a daring woman. At the same time, interest in Indian philosophies
and culture abounded, as evidenced by Kalidasa's *Sakuntala* (a famous Sanskrit play
from India), which was performed by sixty young, presumably white girls in June 1904
(*New York Herald*, June 19, 1904, 14).

   20. Evidence from newspaper articles of the period reveal racist underpinnings as
well as a categorization of and fixation on Indian female bodies (*New York American
and Journal*, June 17, 1904; August 21, 1904; August 28, 1904).

   21. Karen Leonard (1992) notes that a large number of Indian men married
Mexican women and established families in northern California, near San Francisco
in Yuba City, and to the south in Imperial Valley. They did so partly to curb the effects
of racist policies that prevented Indian women from migrating and partly to establish citizenship rights. Others resisted by fighting legal battles to retain the rights of
American citizenship in 1918, 1922, 1923, and 1924—all to no avail (Takaki 1990,
298–302).

   22. Asian laborers were often pitted against one another in American efforts
to find cheap labor. Indians were seen as a solution to the Chinese and Japanese
problems because they were cheaper and initially were viewed as cousins of "white
folks," since they were of Aryan descent. This changed, however, as race became an
issue of color.

   23. Tagore was denied entry into the United States. He cancelled his tour and
returned to India, where he commented caustically, "Jesus could not get into America
because, first of all, He would not have the necessary money, and secondly, He would
be an Asiatic" (Takaki 1990, 299).

24. The statistics and information in this section are taken from Schlundt 1962, Shelton 1981, and Takaki 1990.

25. Shelton (1981, 123) mentions that St. Denis's company had grown to five, to include Ruth, Ted, Hilda, Alice, and her brother.

CHAPTER 5

1. See Agnes De Mille (1956, 68, 76) and Selma Jeanne Cohen (1972, 70–81) for more detail on Graham and Humphrey's break from Denishawn.

2. Several Asian American scholars argue that American identity has constantly been reconfigured to reflect whiteness and Eurocentrism, rather than accounting for the Asian influences that helped form its core (R. Lee 1999, 2–9; Lowe 1996, 5–7; Okihiro 2001, 27; Palumbo-Liu 1999, 17–29).

3. The belief that only Asian bodies could be seen as authentic performers of Asian dances manifested itself in rendering white Oriental dancers inauthentic in favor of dancers such as Uday Shankar, who were perceived to be authentic in the 1930s.

4. Until St. Denis and Graham, American dancers did not begin warm-up exercises seated on the floor, as yoga training does. Rukmini Devi also placed an emphasis on starting practice at the ground level when training dancers in Bharata Natyam at Kalakshetra.

5. When I interviewed dancer-choreographer Parijat Desai, who has trained in Bharata Natyam, yoga, and Graham technique, she suggested some similarities between the forms. First, she explained that Graham technique, emphasizing work on the floor, including sitting, kneeling, and lying down, allows the dancer to investigate the mechanics of the spine and hips. While the specific positions held may be different, yoga practice, too, involves using floor work to understand the mechanics of the spine, hips, and other joints in a manner that cannot be done while standing. Second, attention to movement possibilities of the spine in Graham technique is also an important aspect of some Indian dance forms and yoga. Third, working on breathing and examining the effect of air traveling through the body and on posture are common to both yoga and Graham technique (interview by author, December 8, 2002). I do not suggest here that Graham technique is a simple derivation of yoga. I point out that modern dance scholarship has not paid close attention to these connections. It is true that Graham eventually evolved her form in very different ways, but there are clear commonalities between her technique and other forms she came in contact with, particularly in the basic starting positions and in some of the kinesthetic principles she worked with.

6. This is very similar to the argument that Mari Yoshihara (2003) makes in her first book, in which she discusses how white women performers wore Asian goods and products as they were using Asian performance techniques.

7. The turn away from orientalism was not as abrupt as Graham made it seem. Although denying her connections to orientalist practices in Denishawn, she turned to yoga, Joseph Campbell's sense of universal spirituality, Jungian philosophy, and Japanese art to rediscover herself and her dance practices (De Mille 1956, 251, 277–278).

8. It must be noted that both Graham and Humphrey lived hand-to-mouth for many of their choreographic years. Graham emerged from poverty only in her late fifties because of her sponsor, Bethsabee Rothschild (De Mille 1956, 306).

9. Uday Shankar performed with Anna Pavlova at the Manhattan Opera House on October 9, 1923, and toured the United States with her until 1924 (Lazzarini and Lazzarini 1980, 185). The dance was entitled *Oriental Impressions* and consisted of *A Hindu Wedding* and *Krishna and Radha*. They performed the dances in "authentic Indian costumes"; Shankar arranged the dances to the music of Comolata Banerji. However, it was not until 1932 that Sal Hurok invited Shankar to perform with his own company in the United States, rather than merely accompanying Pavlova (Erdman 1996, 90). I argue that Shankar's presence was not fully felt in the United States until he toured with his company from 1932 to 1933 and again in 1934 and 1937.

10. Between 1938 and 1939 what we see is a burst of ethnic dance articles in the *Dance Observer*. Between the "serious" modern dance articles on Graham, Humphrey, and others, we see a number of articles on Burmese, Javanese, Balinese, and Indian dances that mystify, exoticize, and elevate the forms from these countries to the position of "high art."

11. See the program notes in "La Meri Papers" 1912–1954 for further detail.

12. "Negro dance," which later became "black concert dance" around 1970 and "African-American concert dance" in the 1990s, as Manning argues, was seen in opposition to modern dance, especially by the 1940s (2006, 14). So while Oriental and ethnic dance became "other" to modern dance by the 1930s and 1940s, "Negro dance" was also set in opposition to modern. Although both Negro and ethnic dance were set in binary opposition to modern dance, I suggest that a triangulated frame between white, black, and Asian would provide a more complex reading of the interrelationships of these forms. I argue that even as modern dance was rejecting its connections to Negro dance and denigrating the latter's form as "primitive" and inauthentic "low art," it was accepting ethnic and traditional dance as ancient and authentic "high art."

13. It is not my intent to provide a detailed biography of Rukmini Devi or her role in nationalist politics and the revival of *sadir*. Rather, I focus on Rukmini Devi's imbrications within the changing definitions of modernity and tradition within the Indian context. For a more detailed analysis, see the dissertations by Meduri (1996) and O'Shea (2001) and a selection of Kalakshetra souvenirs and program notes in Sarada (1985) and "A Brief Report," Kalakshetra Program Brochure, n.d., Kalakshetra Library, Chennai, India.

14. See also http://www.streetswing.com/histmai2/d2lameri.htm.

15. There were other white women, too, such as Ragini Devi, Roshanara, Ratan Devi, Lilavati, and Madame Menaka, who lived in India practicing traditional dances (Khokar 1961, 210). They were not a significant presence in the American landscape, however, save Ragini Devi, who became a renowned figure in the dance world, especially through her daughter, dancer Indrani Rahman.

16. Ram Gopal, the famed Indian dancer, performed Bharata Natyam at the Pillow in 1953, along with La Meri, Peter de Falco, and Karoun Tootikian, who performed ethnic dances. Myra Kinch and José Limón were performing modern dance numbers, and Sahomi Tachibana was doing "traditional" Japanese dances. La Meri was a member of the Pillow's board of directors, so it was to be expected that she often performed there during the festival. She also trained dancers such as Matteo and Hadassah to perform at the Pillow doing ethnic dances. Matteo started performing at the Pillow in 1955. Initially, he performed flamenco and then became renowned for his Indian dances. Hadassah, who had also trained with La Meri, first performed

at the Pillow in 1954 and was also a recurring performer. She incorporated Jewish, Indian, and other ethnic dances in her repertoire ("Jacob's Pillow Souvenir Programs," 1954, Margerie Lyon Collection, UCLA Library, box 1478). In 1954, Hadassah, Ram Gopal, Pearl Lang (a member of Martha Graham's company), Charles Weidman and his company, and Ernestis (a Native American dancer), all performed under separate billing at the Pillow. Nala Najan, an Italian American, performed Indian dances and his own choreography and made a particular splash at the festival in 1965 and again in 1966 ("Jacob's Pillow Souvenir Programs," 1954, Margerie Lyon Collection, UCLA Library, box 1478).

17. For biographical details and particulars regarding Balasaraswati's career, see Meduri 1996 and O'Shea 2007.

CHAPTER 6

1. I thank Marta Savigliano for pointing this out to me.

2. I say "temporary" because as I argue more fully in the Chapter 7, most young girls who pursue dance do so for only a short period of time. After their debut recitals, or *arangetrams*, they stop dancing and return to full-fledged "professional," acceptable "model minority" careers as engineers, doctors, lawyers, or computer professionals, for example.

3. Hema Rajagopalan and Mythili Kumar are now established gurus in Chicago and San Jose respectively.

4. In my master's thesis, I explore in great detail Kalanidhi Narayanan's impact on the dance scene, especially in terms of her contribution as an *abhinaya* guru and exponent (1997).

5. Ironically, current Indian gurus lament that this pattern has not changed in the sense that Indian communities in the United States continually seek more "authentic" teachers from India and think that the gurus who have established schools are increasingly inauthentic, having lived and taught in the United States for twenty to thirty-five years.

6. Activist Ananya Bhattacharjee links model minority expectations to gender implications, suggesting that it has many undertones (1992, 1997). Bhattacharjee suggests that model minority identity is uniquely gendered. Using her experience as executive director and a counselor for Sakhi, an organization supporting South Asian survivors of domestic violence in New York, Bhattacharjee argues that the South Asian community discourages women who are dealing with domestic violence from speaking out against their husbands by persuading them not to mar the community's model minority status in America. The argument is, since women are the authentic bearers of culture and tradition, a report of domestic abuse would shame not only their husbands but also the Indian community, thereby destroying their performance of a model community. This suggests that in American contexts Indian female bodies also bear the expectations of the Indian American model minority community. Nationalist ideologies continue to work their way insidiously into issues of women's rights, such as domestic violence and physical and sexual abuse.

7. As Saskia Kersenboom (1987) explains, the *devadasi* system as a cultural entity could survive only with art patronage, and who better than the Indian kings to support it? This seemed to work between the tenth and nineteenth centuries, albeit with many

periods of fluctuation in between. Although love poetry and the *shringara* pieces were being danced even before the seventh century, the practice of *padams* in dance seems to have begun in the sixteenth century in the courts of the Nayak kings. The annals of the courts of the Nayak kings, who were based in Tanjavur and Madurai, indicate the proliferation of the *Shringaraprabandam*. The *padams* were the clearest examples of *shringara* poetry. The period from the mid-sixteenth century to the mid-nineteenth century is popularly referred to as the golden age of South Indian music and dance, probably because it was a time of peace and the arts received ample patronage. The kings were responsible for patronage, and artists flocked to the courts. Since there was a great deal of output in dance musical forms, different kinds of dances also became prolific. Love poetry has been present in South Indian literary and oral traditions for a long time. The earliest mention of love lyrics is in the second century during the Sangam period, in writings such as the *Tolkappiyam* and the *Silappadikaram*. Later, writers such as Ksetrayya became famous for their love lyrics.

8. "It was an upsurge of devotionalism centered on a personal deity—Visnu or Siva—which originated among the Tamils and eventually spread to the entire Indian subcontinent," writes anthropologist George Kliger (1993). The translator, poet, and critic A. K. Ramanujam (1985) outlines some of the features of the movement. These include the devotion to God's personal presence in the world and his accessibility to the devotee, the urge to "dance and sing one's god" and to depict him in poetry, painting, and sculpture, and also feeling one's relation to God as of a human lover with all the connotations of human sexual passion where union with the lover is seen as union with God.

9. Ksetrayya was married to a woman named Rukmini but was in love with a *devadasi* named Mohanangi, and it was because she ultimately shunned him that he ended up writing about love and longing. But this was a love and longing not just for the *devadasi* herself but for the god Krishna in the form of Muvvagopala. See my master's thesis for more detail (P. Srinivasan 1997).

10. See Anusha Kedhar's excellent reading of this article in her award-winning conference paper, "The Specter of the Devadasi: Bharata Natyam and Indian Ethnicity in the U.S.," Society of Dance History Scholars, Stanford University, June 2009.

CHAPTER 7

1. *Mridangam* is a double-headed barrel drum, part of the music ensemble along with the vocalist and instrumentalist that composes the orchestra for dance. The *Alapana* is a melodic improvisation devoid of text, focused primarily on finding key phrases that highlight the raga, melodic scale. *Bowli* is one of many thousands of ragas.

2. Saris have a complex history of production. Some are handwoven, others are mass produced in textile mills and factories, while many others are created through a combination of handwoven and industrial technologies (Lynton 2002; Bhachu 2004).

3. Cultural citizenship, as Aihwa Ong (2004) defines it, is "a cultural process of 'subjectification,' in the Foucauldian sense of self-making and being-made by power relations that produce consent" (156). She develops Renato Rosaldo's (1993) argument that cultural citizenship is the right of the minority individual to be different from the dominant national community without compromising the right to belong. But she argues that this argument is overly utopian and instead suggests that cultural

practices ambivalently negotiate power but are never able to avoid its manipulation. Ong shows the complicated process by which a range of disciplinary forces come together to socialize variously classed and raced groups of citizens. In underscoring the force of disciplinary institutions, she suggests that adaptation, accommodation, and negotiation are the only options to cultural incorporation in the United States. I use this argument in this chapter to better understand the cultural practices of Indian Americans.

4. Although primarily young girls are pressured to learn classical Indian forms, in recent years, young boys are also beginning to learn classical Indian music.

5. Although I have developed the notion of the dancer as commodity throughout this book, I suggest in this chapter that the female dancer as laborer both uses objects that are commodities and functions herself as commodity in the global market. Usually the products of a dancer's labors are ephemeral, never quite separating from the laborer. However, when the dancer as laborer is viewed in whole terms as "use value," her function as commodity becomes more apparent. See, for example, Richard Sennett's *The Culture of the New Capitalism* (2006) for further insights into this concept.

6. I refer here to the standard Euro-American dance critics' responses to live performances. See June Vail in Gere et al. 1995 for more details. Usually in Bharata Natyam, these items are treated as fetish objects separate from the performance practice as a whole. The Bharata Natyam dancing body is thus overdetermined by its heavy layers of eye-catching and exotic paraphernalia that distract the dance critic or researcher from focusing on a "technique" that forever remains inaccessible. Such readings of the Bharata Natyam body place it in opposition to the modern or postmodern dancing body where the latter emphasizes a lack of costuming and thrives on the "natural," where indeed technique can be examined, analyzed, and dissected devoid of other distractions. This focus on the layers of clothing and the fabric that catches the eye contribute to an overdetermined nationalist, orientalist reading of the Bharata Natyam body.

7. I am informed by the work of third world feminist scholars, such as Chandra Mohanty, Ann Russo, and Lourdes Torres (1991); Margo Okazawa-Rey and Gwyn Kirk (2004); Piya Chatterjee (2001); and others, who argue there can be no feminist analysis without a critique of capital.

8. I refer to the works of Saskia Kersenboom (1987) and Amrit Srinivasan (1983), which have instigated debates and discussion on the *devadasi* question in dance circles in India and abroad.

9. There is an inherent binary at work here where Indian men wear Western clothes and Indian women are expected to wear traditional clothes. This in part exemplifies how the Indian nationalist movement works through the pressures of colonialism.

10. Usually the abstract and rhythmical dance element of *nritta* is performed to complementary abstracted formations in the music. However, in this piece, the vocalist was singing *sahityam*, a text-based piece that would normally be interpreted through dramatic expression, *natya* or *abhinaya*, and thus the dancer's interpretation through *nritta* was unusual.

11. Legend has it that Parvati, Siva's wife, was transformed into a peacock (*mayil*) and born on Earth. She waited at the site where the Kapaleeswarar Temple was built and was rejoined with Siva in her female human form after performing penance for

many years. The temple has a peacock gazing up from one of its turrets and is unique in this aspect. Hence, it can be identified in performance through the depiction of the peacock. It is also said that the neighborhood became known as the peacock town and was subsequently translated into English by the British as Mylapore.

12. My friend is a Bharata Natyam dance guru in Southern California and one of her teenage students was having her *arangetram* shortly. Apparently the girl needed a few extra things to complete her trousseau for the gala evening event. I offered to help complete this trousseau.

13. *Pochampally* saris are famous for their durability, vibrant colors, and comfortable cotton material. The name also refers to a small town in the state of Andhra Pradesh where the saris are woven. In general, sari names reflect the town in which they were traditionally woven.

14. My great-grandfather C. S. Srinivasachari (1939), a renowned Indian historian, has argued persuasively that the history of the Kapaleeswarar Temple in Chennai goes back to the Pallava Empire in the seventh century c.e. However, he argues that archaeological evidence suggests that the history of this temple is not what it seems, suggesting that Portugese traders destroyed the temple in the sixteenth century and built a cathedral over it in its original location by the seashore in Santhome (a suburb of Chennai). Although there are artifacts within the temple that date back to the seventh century, the present temple foundations were built as recently as three hundred years ago. It is believed that remnants from the temple were moved from its original location and rebuilt in Mylapore.

15. Saskia Kersenboom (1987), in her excellent anthropology of the *devadasi* practice in Thiruvaroor, has elaborated on their various temple rituals.

16. South Indian Hindu beliefs in the evil eye range from protecting human beings to temple deities from harm. While in the case of a human, a small lamp is used in a circular pattern three times clockwise and three times counterclockwise, for the deity, *devadasis* would wave large pot-lamps before the deity as the procession circumambulated the temple.

17. *Nayanmars* are the sixty-four men and women saints celebrated in South Indian Hindu history as great devotees of Lord Siva. These men and women sang and wrote praises of Siva, many of their texts remain inscribed on the walls of temples today.

18. Dancing women and in particular saris became important symbols in the struggle for national independence. According to Partha Chatterjee (1986), Indian nationalists attempted to resolve the stigma of colonization and the woman question by demarcating the public sphere as a male agenda and relegating women's practices to the private sphere. Women were therefore expected to maintain pure Indian culture by performing the agendas of a fixed notion of "tradition" that valued the icon of the "ideal woman," understood as Brahmin and upper class/upper caste. The sari became the symbol of "tradition" and therefore of the "inner" Indian sphere that had to be guarded, and thus functioned as a metaphor for womanhood and nation.

19. Kersenboom's (1987) monograph details the kinds of saris worn by *devadasis*. Additionally, photographs of *devadasis* from the late nineteenth and early twentieth centuries reveal that they wore saris that were from the local region where they were based. These saris were often cheaper than *Kanjeevaram* silks, which are the trend now among Bharata Natyam dancers.

20. This sari house began in the 1930s, when K. Thiruvengadam Chettiar opened shop. It grew in popularity along with nationalist independence struggles, but it began flourishing in 1959 when it opened a large modern showroom and created unique designs working with highly specialized weavers.

21. I am interested in examining more closely the technologies of the hand related to Bharata Natyam mudra formation. In Bharata Natyam practice the articulation of the hand and particular fingers are extremely important in laboring to create symbolic meaning. In this section, I explore the ways in which a reading of finger movement in sari display as performance can reveal alternate forms of labor that provide a materialist understanding of dance practice.

22. NRI is an acronym for nonresident Indian, often used as a derogatory comment to refer to Indians from the diaspora, particularly from the United States. What this scenario demonstrates is the outsourcing of labor that happens in the Bharata Natyam practice in diaspora. The objects that construct the Bharata Natyam performance cannot be easily obtained in the United States and so the journey to India has to be undertaken to buy the various "authentic" accoutrements including the sari, the dancing bell, the jewelry, and flowers. Recently, however, an online store has begun advertisements offering some of these products to dancers in the United States so that they do not need to travel to India for their objects.

23. By the mid-nineteenth century, the export, import, and manufacture of goods moved from the hands of independent Indian merchants to intermediaries hired by the British East India Company. Often this required force. Sepoys of the East India Company were sent to destroy the factories owned by Indian rivals. Independent weavers who refused to work for the pitiful wages that the East India Company offered had their thumbs cut off. In a matter of three decades, the East India Company achieved a virtual stranglehold on the economic and political life of Eastern India (Sinha 1956).

24. Kersenboom (1987) notes that *devadasi* performers had many kinds of dance items in their repertoire. Here I refer to the *kollam* dance where *devadasis* used their feet to manipulate different colored powders to create an artistic painting while dancing.

25. Three separate regions existed in the South of India around the fifth century c.e. The three regions, known as Chola, Chera, and Pandya, formed the Tamil Kingdom.

26. There is controversy surrounding the date of the literary text. The renowned Indian historian Nilakanta Sastri dates it to the ninth century while many others date it to the fifth and second centuries.

27. I discuss the presence and contribution of these early Indian dancers elsewhere in greater detail (Srinivasan 2003, 2007, 2009).

28. Grace Hong (2006) suggests that "the cultures of racialized and gendered labor are an expression of global capital's contradictions, excesses, and ruptures" (109).

EPILOGUE

1. *Superstars of Dance* was a reality TV show that aired on NBC in January 2009. The show featured dances from eight countries and was hosted by Michael Flatley (of Lord of the Dance fame) and cohosted by former Miss USA Susie Castillo. It was created by executive producers Nigel Lythgoe and Simon Fuller, who were coproducers of *So You Think You Can Dance?* and *American Idol*.

2. Amrapali was an undergraduate studying at UCLA when I was working toward my master's between 1995 and 1997. She went on to work with Cirque du Soleil and began appearing in cameo roles on TV shows such as *Heroes*, *Boston Legal*, and *E.R.* More recently, she has been featured in several Indo-American films. She continues to perform Kathak onstage in solo and ensemble work.

3. Initially, NBC recorded an above-average viewership for *Superstars of Dance*, even competing strongly with ABC's *Desperate Housewives*, which screened at the same time slot. See http://en.wikipedia.org/wiki/Superstars_of_dance.

4. Mythili was also a young girl when I first met her in her mother's garage dance studio in Los Angeles in 1995. I watched her mature into a fine dancer over the years. Nakul Dev Mahajan was a recent graduate of the Department of Dance at the University of California–Riverside, so I was quite familiar with him and his work.

5. See Arvind Sharma (1995) for more information on Adi Sankara's Advaita philosophy.

6. I am not suggesting that Indian philosophies are "pure" philosophies. They, too, are hybrid.

References

Abrahams, Ruth. 1974. "Appendix: Performance Chronology of Asian Dance in New York City, 1906–1976." In *Selected Papers from the 1974 CORD-SEM Conference*, 125–145. New York: CORD.

Abu-Lughod, Lila. 1998. *Remaking Women: Feminism and Modernity in the Middle East*. Princeton, NJ: Princeton University Press.

Aguilar-San Juan, Karin. 1993. "Landmarks in Literature by Asian American Lesbians." *Signs* 18 (4): 936–943.

Albright, Ann Cooper. 1997. *Choreographing Difference: The Body and Identity in Contemporary Dance*. Hanover, NH: Wesleyan University Press.

Anderson, Benedict. 1983. *Imagined Communities: Reflections on the Origin and Spread of Nationalism*. London: Verso.

Anzaldua, Gloria, and Ana Louise Keating, eds. 2002. *The Bridge We Call Home*. New York: Routledge.

Appadurai, Arjun. 1996. *Modernity at Large: Cultural Dimensions of Globalization*. Minneapolis: University of Minnesota Press.

Arondekar, Anjali. 2009. *For the Record: On Sexuality and the Colonial Archive in India*. Durham, NC: Duke University Press.

Assisi, Francis. 2007. "Indian Slaves in Colonial America: Evidence of 'East Indians' in Seventeenth- and Eighteenth-Century Virginia." *India Currents* (May 16), http://www.indiacurrents.com/news/view_article.html?article_id=e26c1cc3bcc0503da89fc4511af72bd5.

Bald, Vivek. 2006. "Overlapping Diasporas, Multiracial Lives: South Asian Muslims in U.S. Communities of Color, 1880–1950." *Souls: A Critical Journal of Black Politics, Culture, and Society* 8 (4): 3–18.

———. 2007. "'Lost' in the City." *South Asian Popular Culture* 5 (1): 59–76.

Banerjee, Sumanta. 2000. *Under the Raj: Prostitution in Colonial Bengal*. New York: New York University Press.

Banerji, Sures Chandra. 1990. *A Companion to Indian Music and Dance: Spanning a Period of over Three Thousand Years and Based Mainly on Sanskrit Sources.* Delhi: Sri Satguru Publications.

Basu, Dilip Kumar. 1975. "Asian Merchants and Western Trade: A Comparative Study of Calcutta and Canton, 1800–1840." Ph.D. diss., University of California–Berkeley.

Behar, Ruth. 2003. "Ethnography and the Book That Was Lost." *Ethnography* 4 (1): 15–39.

Berger, Raoul. 1989. *The Fourteenth Amendment and the Bill of Rights.* Norman: University of Oklahoma Press.

Bhabha, Homi. 1994. "Of Mimicry and Man: The Ambivalence of Colonial Discourse." In *The Location of Culture*, 85–92. New York: Routledge.

Bhachu, Parminder. 2004. *Dangerous Designs: Asian Women Fashion the Diaspora Economies.* New York: Routledge.

Bhattacharjee, Ananya. 1992. "The Habit of Ex-Nomination: Nation, Woman, and the Indian Immigrant Bourgeoisie." *Public Culture* 5 (1): 19–44.

———. 1997. "A Slippery Path: Organizing Resistance to Violence against Women." In *Dragon Ladies: Asian American Feminists Breathe Fire*, edited by Sonia Shah, 29–45. Boston: South End Press.

Bhoi, Sukhdeep. 1996. "The Indian Immigrant Outrage against Canadian Injustices, 1900–1918." M.A. thesis, Queens University, Canada.

Bose, Mandrakanta. 1995. *The Dance Vocabulary of Classical India.* Delhi: Sri Satguru Publications.

Bourdieu, Pierre. 1985. *Distinction: A Social Critique of the Judgement of Taste.* Cambridge, MA: Harvard University Press.

Breckenridge, Carol, and Peter van der Veer, eds. 1993. *Orientalism and the Postcolonial Predicament: Perspectives on South Asia.* Philadelphia: University of Pennsylvania Press.

Brooks, Daphne. 2006. *Bodies in Dissent: Spectacular Performances of Race and Freedom, 1850–1910.* Durham, NC: Duke University Press.

Burns, Lucy. 2008. "Splendid Dancing: Filipino Exceptionalism in Taxi Dance Halls." *Dance Research Journal* 40 (Winter): 8.

———. Forthcoming. *Puro Arte: On the Filipino Performing Body.* New York: New York University Press.

Burton, Antoinette, ed. 2006. *Archive Stories: Facts, Fictions, and the Writing of History.* Durham, NC: Duke University Press.

Butler, Judith. 1991. *Bodies That Matter: On the Discursive Limits of Sex.* New York: Routledge.

Ceylik, Zeyneb. 1996. "Colonialism, Orientalism, and the Canon." *Art Bulletin* 78 (2): 202–205.

Chakrabarty, Dipesh. 2002. *Habitations of Modernity: Essays in the Wake of Subaltern Studies.* Chicago: University of Chicago Press.

Chakravorty, Pallabi. 2000. "Choreographing Modernity: Kathak Dance, Public Culture, and Women's Identity in India." Ph.D. diss., Temple University.

———. 2008. *Bells of Change: Kathak Dance, Women and Modernity in India.* Delhi: Seagull.

Chan, Sucheng. 1991. *Asian Americans: An Interpretive History.* New York: Twayne.

Chatterjea, Ananya. 2004. *Butting Out: Reading Resistive Choreographies through the Work of Jawole Willa Jo Zollar and Chandralekha*. Middletown, CT: Wesleyan University Press.

Chatterjee, Partha. 1986. *Nationalist Thought and the Colonial World: A Derivative Discourse*. Minneapolis: University of Minnesota Press.

Chatterjee, Piya. 2001. *A Time for Tea: Women, Labor, and Post/Colonial Politics on an Indian Plantation*. Durham, NC: Duke University Press.

Clifford, James. 1994. *The Predicament of Culture: Twentieth-Century Ethnography, Literature, and Art*. Cambridge, MA: Harvard University Press.

Cohen, Selma Jeanne, ed. 1972. *Doris Humphrey: An Artist First*. Highstown, NJ: Princeton Book Company.

Comaroff, John, and Jean Comaroff. 1992. *Ethnography and the Historical Imagination*. Boulder, CO: Westview Press.

Conquergood, Dwight. 1991. "Rethinking Ethnography: Towards a Critical Cultural Politics." *Communication Monographs* 58: 179–194.

Coorlawala, Uttara. 1992. "Ruth St. Denis and India's Dance Renaissance." *Dance Chronicle* 15 (2): 123–152.

Crapanzano, Vincent. 1985. *Tuhami: Portrait of a Moroccan*. Chicago: University of Chicago Press.

Daly, Ann. 2002. *Critical Gestures: Writings on Dance and Culture*. Middletown, CT: Wesleyan University Press.

Daly, Joseph. 1917. *The Life of Augustin Daly*. New York: Macmillan.

Das Gupta, Monisha. 2006. *Unruly Immigrants: Rights, Activism, and Transnational South Asian Politics in the United States*. Durham, NC: Duke University Press.

Davis, Janet. 1993. Spectacles of South Asia at the American Circus, 1890–1940. *Visual Anthropology* 6: 121–128.

Davis, Tracy. 1991. *Actresses as Working Women: Their Social Identity in Victorian Culture*. New York: Routledge.

De Certeau, Michel. 2002. *The Practice of Everyday Life*. Berkeley: University of California Press.

DeFrantz, Thomas, ed. 2002. *Dancing Many Drums*. Madison: University of Wisconsin Press.

de Lauretis, Teresa. 1987. *Technologies of Gender: Essays on Theory, Film, and Fiction*. Bloomington: Indiana University Press.

De Mille, Agnes. 1956. *Martha: The Life and Work of Martha Graham*. New York: Random House.

Derrida, Jacques. 1998. *Of Grammatology*. Translated by Gayatri Chakravorty Spivak. Baltimore: Johns Hopkins University Press.

Derrida, Jacques, and Eric Prenowitz. 1995. "Archive Fever: A Freudian Impression." *Diacritics* 25 (2): 9–63.

Desmond, Jane. 1991. "Dancing Out the Difference: Cultural Imperialism and Ruth St. Denis' *Radha* of 1906." *Signs* 17 (Autumn): 28–49.

Dirks, Nicholas B. 2008. *The Hollow Crown: Ethnohistory of an Indian Kingdom*. Cambridge: Cambridge University Press.

Dixon Gottschild, Brenda. 1996. *Digging the Africanist Presence in Performance: Dance and Other Contexts*. Westport, CT: Greenwood Press.

Dolan, Jill. 1991. *The Feminist Spectator as Critic*. Ann Arbor: University of Michigan Press.

Eng, David. 2001. *Racial Castration: Managing Masculinity in Asian America*. Durham, NC: Duke University Press.

Enloe, Cynthia. 1990. *Bananas, Beaches, and Bases: Making Feminist Sense of International Politics*. Berkeley: University of California Press.

Erdman, Joan. 1996. "Dance Discourses: Rethinking the History of the 'Oriental Dance.'" In *Moving Words: Rewriting Dance*, edited by Gay Morris, 288–304. London: Routledge.

Espiritu, Yen Le. 1996. *Asian American Women and Men: Labor, Laws, and Love*. Thousand Oaks, CA: Sage.

Fabian, Johannes. 1983. *Time and the Other: How Anthropology Makes Its Object*. New York: Columbia University Press.

Felheim, Marvin. 1956. *The Theater of Augustin Daly: An Account of the Late-Nineteenth-Century Stage*. Cambridge, MA: Harvard University Press.

Feuerstein, Georg. 2006. "Tantrism and Neotantrism." *Moksha Journal*, no. 2, http://www.santosha.com/moksha/tantrism1.html.

Foster, Susan. 1988. *Reading Dancing: Bodies and Subjects in Contemporary American Dance*. Berkeley: University of California Press.

———.1995. "Introduction." In *Corporealities: Dancing Knowledge, Culture, and Power*, edited by Susan Foster, xi–xvii. New York: Routledge.

Foucault, Michel. 1980. *Power/Knowledge: Selected Interviews and Other Writings, 1972–1977*, edited by Colin Gordon. Brighton, UK: Harvester Press.

———. 1984. *The Foucault Reader*. New York: Pantheon.

Franko, Mark. 1995. *Dancing Modernism/Performing Politics*. Bloomington: Indiana University Press.

———. 2002. *The Work of Dance: Labor, Movement, and Identity in the 1930s*. Middletown, CT: Wesleyan University Press.

Gaston, Anne Marie. 1996. *Bharata Natyam: From Temple to Theatre*. New Delhi: Manohar.

Geertz, Clifford. 1973. *The Interpretation of Cultures: Selected Essays*. New York: Basic Books.

Gere, David, Lewis Segal, Patrice Clark Koelsch, and Elizabeth Zimmer, eds. 1995. *Looking Out: Perspectives on Dance and Criticism in a Multicultural World*. New York: Macmillan.

George, Nadine. 2000. *The Royalty of Negro Vaudeville: The Whitman Sisters and the Negotiation of Race, Gender, and Class in African American Theater, 1900–1940*. New York: Palgrave Macmillan.

Ghosh, Amitav. 1992. *In an Antique Land: History in the Guise of a Traveler's Tale*. New York: Vintage.

Gonzalves, Theodore. 2009. *The Day the Dancers Stayed: Performing in the Filipino/American Diaspora*. Philadelphia: Temple University Press.

Gopinath, Gayatri. 2005. *Impossible Desires: Queer Diasporas and South Asian Public Cultures*. Durham, NC: Duke University Press.

Gould, Harold A. 2006. *Sikhs, Swamis, Students, and Spies: The Indian Lobby in the United States, 1900–1946*. Thousand Oaks, CA: Sage.

Graff, Ellen. 1997. *Stepping Left: Dance and Politics in New York City, 1928–1942*. Durham, NC: Duke University Press.

Greenstein, M. A. 1998. "Bharata Natyam: Translation, Spectacle, and the Degeneration of Arangetram in Southern California Life." *Society of Dance History Scholars Conference Proceedings*, 127–134. Eugene: University of Oregon.

Grewal, Inderpal. 2005. *Transnational America: Feminisms, Diasporas, Neoliberalisms*. Durham, NC: Duke University Press.

Grewal, Inderpal, and Caren Kaplan, eds. 1994. *Scattered Hegemonies: Postmodernity and Transnational Feminist Practices*. Minneapolis: University of Minnesota Press.

Halberstam, Judith. 2001. "The Transgender Gaze in *Boys Don't Cry*." *Screen* 42 (3): 294–298.

Hall, Roger. 2001. *Performing the American Frontier, 1870–1906*. Cambridge: Cambridge University Press.

Hong, Grace K. 2006. *The Ruptures of American Capital: Women of Color Feminism and the Culture of Immigrant Labor*. Minneapolis: University of Minnesota Press.

hooks, bell. 1992. *Black Looks: Race and Representation*. Cambridge, MA: South End Press.

Hughes, Russell Meriweather (La Meri). 1933. *Dance as an Art Form*. New York: A. S. Barnes.

———. 1977. *Total Education in Ethnic Dance*. New York: Marcel Dekker.

Imada, Adria. 2004. "Hawaiians on Tour: Hula Circuits through the American Empire." *American Quarterly* 56 (March): 111–149.

Jensen, Joan M. 1988. *Passage from India: Asian Indian Immigrants in North America*. New Haven, CT: Yale University Press.

Joseph, May. 1999. *Nomadic Identities: The Performance of Citizenship*. Minneapolis: University of Minnesota Press.

Jowitt, Deborah. 1989. *Time and the Dancing Image*. Berkeley: University of California Press.

Kaeppler, Adrienne. 2000. "Dance Ethnology and the Anthropology of Dance." *Dance Research Journal* 32 (1): 116–125.

Kang, Laura. 2002. *Compositional Subjects: Enfiguring Asian/American Women*. Durham, NC: Duke University Press.

Kantha Das, Rajani. 1923. *Hindusthani Workers on the Pacific Coast*. Berlin: Walter De Gruyter.

Kedhar, Anusha. 2009. "The Specter of the Devadasi: Bharata Natyam and Indian Ethnicity." Paper presented at the annual international conference for the Society of Dance History Scholars, June 19–22, Palo Alto, CA.

———. 2011. "On the Move: Transnational South Asian Dancers and the 'Flexible' Dancing Body." Ph.D. diss., University of California–Riverside.

Kersenboom, Saskia. 1987. *Nityasumangali*. Delhi: Motilal Banarsidass.

Khandelwal, Madhulika. 2002. *Becoming American, Being Indian: An Immigrant Community in New York City*. Ithaca, NY: Cornell University Press.

Khokar, Mohan. 1961. "Western Interest and Its Impact on Indian Dance." *Bulletin of the Institute of Traditional Cultures Madras* 2: 203–217.

———. 1983. *His Dance, His Life: A Portrait of Uday Shankar*. New Delhi: Himalayan Books.

Kim, Claire. 1999. "The Racial Triangulation of Asian Americans." *Politics and Society* 27: 105–138.

Kishore, Anuradha. 1999. "Imagining Inheritance: Bharata Natyam in Los Angeles." M.A. thesis, University of California–Los Angeles.

Kliger, George, ed. 1993. *Bharata Natyam in Cultural Perspective.* New Delhi: South Asia Books.

Kondo, Dorinne K. 1997. *About Face: Performing Race in Fashion and Theater.* New York: Routledge.

Koritz, Amy. 1997. "Dancing the Orient for England: Maud Allan's *The Vision of Salome.*" In *Meaning in Motion,* edited by Jane Desmond, 133–152. Durham, NC: Duke University Press.

Kowal, Rebekah. 2009. "The World Dances through Manhattan: Parsing the Postwar Resurgence of 'Ethnologic' Dance." Paper presented at the annual international conference for the Society of Dance History Scholars, June 19–22, Palo Alto, CA.

Kraditor, Aileen. 1970. *Ideas of the Woman Suffrage Movement, 1890–1920.* New York: Anchor Books.

Kramer, Eric, ed. 2003. *The Emerging Monoculture: Assimilation and "Model Minority."* Westport, CT: Praeger.

Krasner, David. 1997. *Resistance, Parody, and Double Consciousness in African American Theatre, 1895–1910.* New York: St. Martin's Press.

Kraut, Anthea. 2008. *Choreographing the Folk: the Dance Stagings of Zora Neale Hurston.* Minneapolis: University of Minnesota Press.

Kristeva, Julia. 1982. *Powers of Horror: An Essay on Abjection.* New York: Columbia University Press.

Kwan, San San. 2011. "Performing a Geography of Asian America: The Chop Suey Circuit." *Theatre and Drama Review* 55, no. 1 (Spring): 120–136.

Lazzarini, John, and Roberta Lazzarini. 1980. *Pavlova: Repertoire of a Legend.* New York: Schirmer Books.

Lee, Esther Kim. 2006. *A History of Asian American Theatre.* New York: Cambridge University Press.

Lee, Josephine. 1998. *Performing Asian America.* Philadelphia: Temple University Press.

Lee, Robert. 1999. *Orientals: Asian Americans in Popular Culture.* Philadelphia: Temple University Press.

Lei, Daphne. 2006. *Operatic China: Staging Chinese Identity across the Pacific.* New York: Palgrave Macmillan.

Leonard, Karen. 1992. *Making Ethnic Choices: California's Punjabi Mexican Americans.* Philadelphia: Temple University Press.

Lewis, Reina. 2004. *Rethinking Orientalism: Women, Travel, and the Ottoman Harem.* New Brunswick, NJ: Rutgers.

Locke, Robinson. 1870–1920. *Robinson Locke Scrapbook Covering the Life and Career of Augustin Daly.* Billy Rose Theatre Division. New York Public Library of the Performing Arts, New York City.

Lott, Eric. 1993. *Love and Theft: Blackface Minstrelsy and the American Working Class.* New York: Oxford.

Lowe, Lisa. 1996. *Immigrant Acts: On Asian American Cultural Politics.* Durham, NC: Duke University Press.

Lynton, Linda. 2002. *The Sari.* London: Thames and Hudson.

Maira, Sunaina. 2002. *Desis in the House: Indian American Youth Culture in New York City*. Philadelphia: Temple University Press.

———. 2008. "Belly Dancing: Arab-Face, Orientalist Feminism, and U.S. Empire." *American Quarterly* 60 (2): 317–345.

Manning, Susan. 2006. *Modern Dance, Negro Dance: Race in Motion*. Minneapolis: University of Minnesota Press.

Martin, John. 1946. *The Dance: The Story of the Dance Told in Pictures and Text*. New York: Tudor.

Martin, Randy. 1998. *Critical Moves: Dance Studies in Theory and Politics*. Durham, NC: Duke University Press.

Meduri, Avanthi. 1996. "Nation, Woman Represented: The Sutured History of the Devadasi and Her Dance: 1856–1960". Ph.D. diss., New York University.

———. 2005. *Rukmini Devi Arundale (1904–1986): A Visionary Architect of Indian Culture and the Performing Arts*. Delhi: Motilal Banarsidass.

Meduri, Avanthi, and Jeffery L. Spear. 2004. "Knowing the Dancer: East Meets West." *Victorian Literature and Culture* 32 (2): 435–448.

Merleau-Ponty, Maurice. 2002. *Phenomenology of Perception*. New York: Routledge.

Metzger, Sean. 2004. "Charles Parsloe's Chinese Fetish: An Example of Yellowface Performance in Nineteenth-Century American Melodrama." *Theatre Journal* 56 (4): 627–665.

Mohanty, Chandra T., Ann Russo, and Lourdes Torres, eds. 1991. *Third World Women and the Politics of Feminism*. Bloomington: Indiana University Press.

Ness, Sally. 1992. *Body, Movement, and Culture: Kinesthetic and Visual Symbolism in a Philippine Community*. Philadelphia: University of Pennsylvania Press.

Odell, George C. D. 1939. *Annals of the New York Stage*. Vol. 11, *1879–1182*. New York: Columbia University Press.

Okazawa-Rey, Margo, and Gwyn Kirk, eds. 2004. *Women's Lives: Multicultural Perspectives*. 3rd ed. New York: McGraw Hill.

Okihiro, Gary. 2001. *On Common Ground: Reimagining American History*. Princeton, NJ: Princeton University Press.

Omi, Michael, and Howard Winant. 1994. *Racial Formation in the United States: From the 1960s to the 1990s*. New York: Routledge, 1994.

Ong, Aihwa. 1999. *Flexible Citizenship: The Cultural Logics of Transnationality*. Durham, NC: Duke University Press.

———. 2004. "Cultural Citizenship as Subject-Making: Immigrants Negotiate Cultural Boundaries in the United States." In *Life in America: Identity and Everyday Experience*, edited by Lee D. Baker, 156–178. Malden, MA: Blackwell.

O'Shea, Janet. 2001. "At Home in the World: Bharata Natyam's Transnational Traditions." Ph.D. diss., University of California–Riverside.

———. 2007. *At Home in the World: Bharata Natyam on the Global Stage*. Middletown, CT: Wesleyan University Press.

Palumbo-Liu, David. 1999. *Asian/American: Historical Crossings of a Racial Frontier*. Stanford, CA: Stanford University Press.

Phelan, Peggy. 1996. *Unmarked: The Politics of Performance*. London: Routledge.

Prakash, Gyan, and Douglas Haynes, eds. 1992. *Contesting Power: Resistance and Everyday Social Relations in South Asia*. Berkeley: University of California Press.

Prashad, Vijay. 2000. *The Karma of Brown Folk*. Minneapolis: University of Minnesota Press.

Purkayastha, Bandana. 2005 *Negotiating Ethnicity: Second-Generation South Asians Traverse a Transnational World*. New Brunswick, NJ: Rutgers University Press.

Rakesagupta. 1967. *Studies in Nayaka-nayika-beheda*. Aligarh, India: Granthayan.

Ramachandran, Nirmala. 1966. "Bharata Natyam: Culture and Dance of the Ancient Tamils." Paper presented at the First International Conference Seminar of Tamil Studies. Kuala Lumpur, Malaysia. Available at http://www.tamilnation.org/culture/dance/index.htm#Dance%20and%20Music%20in%20Cilapathikaram.

Ramanujan, A. K. 1985. *From Poems of Love and War: From Eight Anthologies and Ten Long Poems of Classical Tamil*. New York: Columbia University Press.

Rangaswamy, Padma. 2000. *Namasté America: Indian Immigrants in an American Metropolis*. University Park: Pennsylvania State University Press.

Rao, Ubhayakar, S. Krishna, and U. K. Chandrabhaga Devi. 1993. *A Panorama of Indian Dances*. Delhi: Sri Satguru.

Ratnam Raj, Anita. 1992. *Narthaki: A Directory of Classical Indian Dance*. New York: Lotus Fine Arts.

Rosaldo, Renato. 1993. *Culture and Truth: The Remaking of Social Analysis*. Boston: Beacon Press.

Rudrappa, Sharmila. 2004. *Ethnic Routes to Becoming American: Indian Immigrants and the Cultures of Citizenship*. New Brunswick, NJ: Rutgers University Press.

Said, Edward. 1979. *Orientalism*. New York: Random House.

———. 1985. "In the Shadow of the West." *Wedge* 7/8 (Winter/Spring): 4–11.

Sarada, S. 1985. *Kalakshetra: Rukmini Devi*. Madras, India: Kala Mandir Trust.

Sarma, Vimala. 1994. "Martha Graham: A Primal Force." *Sruti* (September): 37–39.

Sassen, Saskia. 1990. *The Mobility of Labor and Capital: A Study in International Investment and Labor Flow*. Cambridge: Cambridge University Press.

Savigliano, Marta. 1995. *Tango and the Political Economy of Passion*. Boulder, CO: Westview Press.

———. 2003. *Angora Matta: Fatal Acts of North-South Translation/Actos Fatales de Traducción Norte-Sur*. Middletown, CT: Wesleyan University Press.

Schlundt, Christena. 1962. *The Professional Appearances of Ruth St. Denis and Ted Shawn: A Chronology and an Index of Dances, 1906–1932*. New York: New York Public Library.

Sennett, Richard. 2006. *The Culture of the New Capitalism*. New Haven, CT: Yale University Press.

Shah, Nayan. 2005. "Between 'Oriental Depravity' and 'Natural Degenerates': Spatial Borderlands and the Making of Ordinary Americans." *American Quarterly* 57 (3): 703–725.

———. Forthcoming. *Stranger Intimacy: Contesting Race, Sexuality and the Law in the North American West*. Los Angeles: University of California Press.

Shah, Sonia, ed. 1997. *Dragon Ladies: Asian American Feminists Breathe Fire*. Boston: South End Press.

Shankar, Lavina, and Rajini Srikanth, eds. 1998. *A Part, Yet Apart: South Asians in Asian America*. Philadelphia: Temple University Press.

Shankar, Uday. 1932. "Shan-Kar's Dances." Souvenir Program Notes. Uday Shankar Collection. New York Public Library of the Performing Arts, New York.

Sharma, A. 1995. *The Philosophy of Religion and Advaita Vedanta: A Comparative Study in Religion and Reason*. Philadelphia: Pennsylvania State University Press.

Shawn, Ted. 1960. *One Thousand and One Night Stands*. New York: Doubleday.

Shea Murphy, Jacqueline. 2007. *The People Have Never Stopped Dancing: Native American Stage Dance and Modern Dance History*. Minneapolis: University of Minnesota Press.

Shelton, Suzanne. 1981. *Divine Dancer: A Biography of Ruth St. Denis*. New York: Doubleday.

Shimakawa, Karen. 2002. *National Abjection: The Asian American Body on Stage*. Durham, NC: Duke University Press.

Shukla, Sandhya. 2003. *India Abroad: Diasporic Cultures of Postwar America and England*. Princeton, NJ: Princeton University Press.

Sinha, Narendra K. 1956. *The Economic History of Bengal*. Calcutta: Firma K. L. Mukhopadyay.

Siu, Lok. 2001. "Diasporic Cultural Citizenship: Chineseness and Belonging in Central America." *Social Text* 69 19 (4): 7–28.

Sklar, Deirdre. 2001. *Dancing with the Virgin: Body and Faith in the Fiesta of Tortugas, New Mexico*. Berkeley: University of California Press.

Snow, Richard. 1984. *Coney Island: A Postcard Journey to the City of Fire*. New York: Brightwaters Press.

Spivak, Gayatri. 1985. "The Rani of Sirmur: An Essay in Reading the Archives." *History and Theory* 24 (3): 247–272.

———. 1988. "Can the Subaltern Speak?" In *Marxism and the Interpretation of Culture*, edited by Cary Nelson and Lawrence Grossberg, 217–315. Chicago: University of Illinois Press.

———. 1999. *A Critique of Postcolonial Reason*. Boston: Harvard University Press.

Srinivasachari, C. S. 1939. *The History of Madras*. Madras (Chennai), India: P. Varadachary.

Srinivasan, Amrit. 1983. "The Hindu Temple Dancer: Prostitute or Nun?" *Cambridge Anthropology* 8 (1): 73–99.

———. 1988. "Reform or Conformity? Temple 'Prostitution' and the Community in the Madras Presidency." In *State Community and Household in Modernizing Asia*, edited by Bina Agarwal, 175–198. Delhi: Kali for Women.

Srinivasan, Priya. 1997. "Kalanidhi Narayanan and Padam Revival." M.A. thesis, University of California–Los Angeles.

———. 2003. "Performing Indian Dance in America: Modernity, Tradition, and the Myth of Cultural Purity." Ph.D. diss., Northwestern University.

———. 2007. "The Bodies beneath the Smoke or What's behind the Cigarette Poster: Unearthing Kinesthetic Connections in American Dance History." *Discourses in Dance* 4 (1): 7–47.

———. 2009. "The Nautch Women Dancers of the 1880s: Corporeality, U.S. Orientalism, and Anti-Asian Immigration Laws." *Women and Performance: A Journal of Feminist Theory* 19 (1): 3–22.

Stacey, Judith. 1999. "Ethnography Confronts the Global Village: A New Home for a New Century?" *Journal of Contemporary Ethnography* 28 (6): 687–697.

Staiger, Janet. 2000. *Perverse Spectators: The Practices of Film Reception*. New York: New York University Press.

St. Denis, Ruth. 1926. Small Notebooks and Journals. Ruth St. Denis Collection. Charles E. Young Research Library, University of California–Los Angeles.

———. 1927. Diary. Ruth St. Denis Collection. Charles E. Young Research Library, University of California–Los Angeles.

———. 1939. *An Unfinished Life: An Autobiography*. New York: Harper.

Steedman, Carolyn. 2002. *Dust: The Archive and Cultural History*. New Brunswick, NJ: Rutgers University Press.

Steen, Shannon. 2010. *Racial Geometries: The Black Atlantic, the Asian/Pacific, and American Performance*. New York: Palgrave Macmillan.

Stoler, Ann Laura. 2010. *Along the Archival Grain: Epistemic Anxieties and Colonial Common Sense*. Princeton, NJ: Princeton University Press.

Sunder Mukhi, Sunita. 2000. *Doing the Desi Thing: Performing Indianness in New York City*. London: Routledge.

Takaki, Ronald. 1990. *Strangers from a Different Shore: A History of Asian Americans*. New York: Penguin.

Taylor, Diana. 2003. *The Archive and the Repertoire: Performing Cultural Memory in the Americas*. Durham, NC: Duke University Press.

Tchen, John K. 2001. *New York Before Chinatown: Orientalism and the Shaping of American Culture, 1776–1882*. Baltimore: Johns Hopkins University Press.

Tharu, S., and K. Lalita, eds. 1991. *Women Writing in India: 600 B.C. to the Present*. Vols. 1 and 2. New York: City University of New York.

Thomas, Helen. 1995. *Dance, Modernity, and Culture: Explorations in the Sociology of Dance*. New York: Routledge.

Tomko, Linda. 1999. *Dancing Class: Gender, Ethnicity, and Social Divides in American Dance, 1890–1920*. Bloomington: Indiana University Press.

———. 2004. "Considering Causation and Conditions of Possibility: Practitioners and Patrons of New Dance in Progressive-Era America." In *Rethinking Dance History*, edited by A. Carter, 80–93. New York: Routledge.

Tsing, Anna. 2004. *Friction: An Ethnography of Global Connection*. Princeton, NJ: Princeton University Press.

Vatsyayan, Kapila. 1968. *Classical Indian Dance in the Literature and the Arts*. New Delhi: Sangeet Natak Akademi.

Visweswaran, Kamala. 1994. *Fictions of Feminist Ethnography*. Minneapolis: University of Minnesota Press.

White, Hayden. 1987. *The Content of Form: Narrative Discourse and Historical Representation*. Baltimore: Johns Hopkins University Press.

Williams, Raymond. 1980. *Culture and Materialism: Selected Essays*. New York: Verso.

———. 1983. *Culture and Society, 1780–1950*. New York: Columbia University Press.

Wong, Diane Y., and Asian Women United of California. 1989. *Making Waves: An Anthology of Writings by and about Asian American Women*. Boston: Beacon Press.

Wong, Yutian. 2002. "Towards a New Asian American Dance Theory: Locating the Dancing Asian American Body." *Discourses in Dance* 1 (1): 69–90.

———. 2010. *Choreographing Asian America*. Middletown, CT: Wesleyan University Press.

Wood, J. G. 1885. "Dime Museums: From a Naturalist's Point of View." *Atlantic Monthly* 55: 758–65.

Yegenoglu, M. 1998. *Colonial Fantasies: Toward a Feminist Reading of Orientalism.* London: Cambridge University Press.

Yessayan, Maral. 2010. "Performing Jordan in an Era of Transformative Globalization: The Emergence of Alternative Labor Markets and the New Working Female Dancer." Ph.D. diss., University of California–Riverside.

Yoshihara, M. 2002. *Embracing the East: White Women and American Orientalism.* Oxford: Oxford University Press.

———. 2007. *Musicians from a Different Shore.* Philadelphia: Temple University Press.

Yuh, Ji-Yeon. 2002. *Beyond the Shadow of Camptown: Korean Military Brides in America.* New York: New York University Press.

Yung, Judy. 1995. *Unbound Feet: A Social History of Chinese Women in San Francisco.* Berkeley: University of California Press.

Index

Page numbers in *italics* refer to glossary pages.

Priya Srinivasan is an Associate Professor in Critical Dance Studies at the Department of Dance, University of California, Riverside. In 2008, she received the Gertrude Lippincott Award given by the Society of Dance History Scholars for the best English-language article published in dance studies.